THE END OF
GLOBALIZATION

Dr Alan M. Rugman is Thames Water Fellow in Strategic Management at Templeton College, University of Oxford. He is also Professor of International Business at the Kelley School of Business at Indiana University and was previously at the University of Toronto. He has been a consultant to many major private sector companies, international organizations, research institutes and government agencies. He has lectured widely throughout the world, and has also been a visiting professor at Harvard University, Columbia Business School, and the Sorbonne in Paris.

UNIVERSITY OF
GLOUCESTERSHIRE
at Cheltenham and Gloucester

THE END OF GLOBALIZATION

ALAN RUGMAN

RANDOM HOUSE

BUSINESS BOOKS

This edition published in 2001 by Random House Business books

First published in 2000 by Random House Business Books,
Random House, 20 Vauxhall Bridge Road, London SW1V 2SA

Random House Australia (Pty) Limited
20 Alfred Street, Milsons Point,
Sydney, New South Wales 2061, Australia

Random House New Zealand Limited
18 Poland Road, Glenfield,
Auckland 10, New Zealand

Random House (Pty) Limited
Endulini, 5a Jubilee Road, Parktown 2193, South Africa

The Random House Group Limited Reg. No. 954009

Papers used by Random House are natural, recyclable
products made from wood grown in sustainable forests.
The manufacturing processes conform to the environmental
regulations of the country of origin.

ISBN 0 7126 8495 6

Companies, institutions and other organizations wishing to make
bulk purchases of books published by Random House should
contact their local bookstore or Random House direct:

Special Sales Director
Random House, 20 Vauxhall Bridge Road, London SW1V 2SA
Tel 020 7840 8470   Fax 020 7828 6681

www.randomhouse.co.uk
businessbooks@randomhouse.co.uk

Typeset in Goudy and Gill by MATS, Southend-on-Sea, Essex
Printed and bound in Great Britain by
Biddles Ltd, Guildford and King's Lynn

LOAVES AND FISHES

This is not
the age of information.

This is *not*
the age of information.

Forget the news,
and the radio,
and the blurred screen.

This is the time
of loaves
and fishes.

People are hungry,
and one good word is bread
for a thousand.

Reproduced with permission of David Whyte.
The House of Belonging, Langley, Washington: Many Rivers Press, 1999 (p. 88).

CONTENTS

PART II:
THE ECONOMIC AND MANAGEMENT ACTORS AFFECTING GLOBALIZATION

Preface

I have written this book because I have been convinced by the evidence. Over a thirty year academic career I have conducted research into the economic activities, financial performance and business strategies of the world's 500 largest multinational enterprises. These are the institutions who drive 'globalization'. Yet, as globalization has been criticized, and frequently misunderstood in recent years, I have been surprised by the lightweight nature of the debate and saddened by the distorted criticisms levelled at multinational enterprises and their managers.

It is to help redress this highly relevant but potentially sterile debate that I have written this book. The material here is a popularization and up to date restatement of the research that I have conducted throughout my career, principally in Canada, at successively the University of Winnipeg, Dalhousie University and the University of Toronto, and now at Templeton College, University of Oxford.

I am keen to participate in a debate about globalization as it crystalizes my research work. My career as a professor of international economics, then international finance and now international business has been driven by a search for knowledge about the performance and behaviour of the world's large multinational enterprises. These dominant actors in international business are the focus of this book.

As an educator, I have participated on radio and TV current affairs shows, in Canada and the UK, when the subject relates to my research on trade and investment policy, the WTO, and other aspects of globalization. The media usually want a proponent and a critic of business on their shows. But entertainment value comes more from strong statements than a dispassionate analysis of the facts. I have been struck on these occasions by the strong opinions, but lack of facts, presented by critics of multinational enterprises. Again on the internet, a huge volume of material is available on the subject of globalization, but most of it is unscientific and insubstantial at best and downright wrong at worst.

We now need to move on and look at the evidence on the activities of multinational enterprises. This book is an attempt to redress the balance in the debate on globalization.

As this book was written during the second half of 1999 I received tremendous and dedicated assistance from Denise Edwards at Templeton College. Her professional competence has been matched by a cheery disposition in the face of a daunting workload. My writing for the book has been edited in the most professional manner by Helen Gough. Other invaluable editorial assistance and advice was provided by Helen Rugman. Finally, but most important, Cecilia Brain helped in the preparation of all the tables and data-related items in this book. Working from her base in Toronto and during a visit to Oxford, Cecilia helped the book tremendously.

A previous version of the second half of Chapter 5 was developed with Galith-Miriam Levy.

I am grateful to Professor Richard Hodgetts of Florida International University of his help in the development of many of the case studies in Chapters 9 and 10. I have learnt much from Richard, especially in the writing of our textbook of International Business, about the necessity for good writing. I have also received helpful advice and encouragement from Professor Regina Greenwood of Kettering University.

I have received comments, especially on several drafts of Chapter 1, from Jean Boddewyn, Baruch College, City University of New York.

I have also received very helpful advice and comments from several colleagues at Templeton College: Michael Gestrin; Rory Knight; Karl Moore; Robin Pedler; Marc Thompson.

Previous versions of Chapter 1 have been presented at the following professional academic conferences:

University of Paris, Sorbonne, June 1999

G7 Pre-Summit Conference, Bonn, June 1999

Australia-New Zealand International Business Academy, annual conference, Sydney, September 1999

Academy of International Business Annual Conference, Charleston, South Carolina, November 1999

European Academy of International Business, Manchester, December 1999

University of West Indies, Trinidad, December 1999

Previous versions of Chapters 2 and 5 have been presented at these research conferences:

G7 Pre-Birmingham Summit Conference, sponsored by Clifford Chance, London, May 1998

WTO Seminar for Norwegian Economics and Business Association, Oslo, April 1999

International Economics Study Group, University of Birmingham, September 1999

I am indebted to participants at these conferences for critical questions, helpful comments and, in general, for pushing forward the debate.

Finally, I have enjoyed the working atmosphere and challenging insights into management education and the practice of strategic management provided by my colleagues at Templeton College, the newest graduate college, and the only one specializing in management, at the University of Oxford. In particular, Dean Rory Knight has been supportive of my efforts to write for practising managers.

I am also indebted to my imaginative editors at Random House Business Books: to Simon Wilson for suggesting that we do the book in this form; to Thomas Wilson for help in production; to Clare Smith for very helpful advice on marketing and sales and to Simon King for his enthusiasm and promotion of the book.

Alan M. Rugman
Oxford, January 2000

List of Abbreviations

ABAC	APEC Business Advisory Council
ACP	Africa, Caribbean and Pacific
AD	Anti-dumping
APEC	Asia Pacific Economic Community
ASC	Automotive Standards Council
ASEAN	Association of South-East Asian Nations
CFIUS	Committee on Foreign Investment in the USA
CSA	Country specific advantage
CVD	Countervailing duty
DISC	US Domestic International Sales Corporation
EC	European Commission
ENGO	Environmental Non-Governmental Organization
EU	European Union
FAO	Food and Agriculture Organization
FDI	Foreign direct investment
F/T	Ratio of foreign to total operations
FSA	Firm specific advantage
FTA	Canada/US Free Trade Agreement
GATS	General Agreement on Trade in Services
GATT	General Agreement on Tariffs and Trade
IAP	Individual action plan
IJV	International joint venture
IPE	International political economy
ISP	Internet service provider
ITAC	International Trade Advisory Committee
ITO	International Trade Organisation
JV	Joint venture
M&A	Mergers and acquisitions
MAI	Multilateral agreement on investment
MAPA	Manila action plan for APEC
MFN	Most favoured nation
MNE	Multinational enterprise
NAAEC	North American Agreement on Environmental Co-operation
NAFTA	North American Free Trade Agreement
NGO	Non-governmental organisation
OECD	Organisation for Economic Co-operation and Development

ROA	Return on assets
ROFA	Return on foreign assets
SAGITS	Sectoral Advisory Group on International Trade
SME	Small to medium enterprise
SOE	Small open economy
TAFTA	Transatlantic Free Trade Agreement
TNC	Transnational corporation
TNO	Trade Negotiation Office
TQM	Total quality management
TRIMS	Trade-related investment measures
TRIPS	Agreement on Trade-Related Aspects of Intellectual Property Rights
UNCTAD	United Nations Conference on Trade and Development
WTO	World Trade Organisation

1

Introduction

The myth of globalization

I believe we are witnessing the end of globalization. Asian economic growth collapsed in 1997 and the worldwide recession of 1997/98 followed. The riots in Seattle in December 1999 have been interpreted as a defeat for free trade and globalization. But globalization is a myth; it never really occurred anyway. As the new analysis in this book shows, the vast majority of manufacturing and service activity is organized regionally, not globally. Multinational enterprises (MNEs) are the engines of international business – and they think regional and act local.

MNEs continue to play the leading roles on the stage of international business. They operate from the 'triad' home bases of the United States, EU, or Japan, at the hub of business networks in which clusters of value-added activities are organized. The process of globalization is a triad and management driven one. Politics, culture, law and related issues are indirectly affected by the fallout, but these are secondary effects and such indirect outcomes should not be confused with the drivers of international economic activities – the MNEs.

Globalization has recently developed a bad name, partly as a result of the Asian financial crisis and its effect on the rest of the world. The perceived failure of global market-based capitalism has led to calls for tighter financial regulation and capital controls. Yet globalization actually has very little to do with recent world financial turmoil, which has been caused by short-term investors in financial capital. Instead, the correct focus of globalization is on the activities of MNEs. Foreign direct investment (FDI) by MNEs is the engine that drives international business. FDI is defined as equity investment by a parent firm to control the operations of a subsidiary corporation in another country. MNEs also engage in non-equity foreign operations, through activities such as joint ventures, strategic alliances and licensing agreements. The international operations of MNEs have caused the world's standard of living to rise over the last 30 years. In the 1950s and 1960s, US FDI led the post-war recovery in Europe and, later, Japan. By the 1980s, Japanese FDI helped sustain growth in North America and Europe.

Today the world's 500 largest MNEs, based in the United States, the European Union, and Japan, account for more than 80% of the world's stock of FDI and over half of world trade. They are commonly perceived to be the causes of globalization. Yet more accurate analysis reveals that these MNEs are not really 'global'. Instead they operate on a triad-regional basis. Most FDI is intra-regional, rather than inter-regional. Data which follow in Chapters 7 and 8 will substantiate this point, at triad level, and at industry level.

For example, more than 85 per cent of all the automobiles produced in North America are built in North American factories owned by Japanese and European MNEs as well as by General Motors, Ford and Daimler-Chrysler. In Europe the story is the same, as it is in Japan.[1] In the speciality chemicals sector, over 90 per cent of all paint is made and used regionally by triad-based MNEs. The same goes for steel, heavy electrical equipment, and much of the rest of the manufacturing sector, including energy and construction. Only consumer electronics and high-value added goods with low transport costs can approach being global.

In the service sector, which now employs 70 per cent of people in North America, Western Europe and Japan, activities are essentially local or regional. MNEs operate in local clusters in their home-based economies. So we do not really have a global economy, but a triad-based regional one. I shall explore the implications for trade policy of local service activities, such as education, social services, health, public administration and culture in Chapters 4, 5 and 6. In particular, I shall show why these sectors are exempted from the national treatment provisions of trade and investment treaties, while manufacturing is included.

How does this analysis help explain the current problems of globalization? It helps us to see that there is a temporary disequilibrium. The Japanese/Asian side of the triad reflects poor corporate and poor financial markets performance. In contrast, US and European MNEs are performing better. Recent research on some 200 of the world's largest MNEs found that, between 1996 and 1998, Japanese MNEs had an average return on foreign assets of 2.22 per cent. This is dismal compared with a 6.39 per cent return for MNEs based in the United States and 5.71 per cent for European MNEs,

---

[1] The data to support such statements as these appear later in the book, principally in Chapters 7 and 8. For example, the statement about the concentration of automobile production by triad is demonstrated later in Table 8.9. There it shows that 93.5 per cent of all the cars registered in Japan are produced domestically; that 85.1 per cent of all the cars sold in the United States are produced in North America and that 91.2 per cent of all new motor vehicles sales in Canada are of cars assembled in North America.

including 7.34 per cent for British ones. These figures reflecting the slower pace of trade and investment liberalization in Japan compared with the other two parts of the triad are taken from the *Templeton Global Performance Index* 2000, shown in Table 1.1. As a result of liberalization and deregulation the North American and European-based MNEs have been more successful. This index is discussed further in Chapter 7.

Table 1.1: Average Returns on Foreign Assets (ROFA) by Triad Region

Region	Average ROFA 1998	No. of Companies Covered
United States	6.39	100
Europe	5.71	54
Japan	2.22	46

Source: Gestrin et al (2000)

The success of regional and bilateral agreements and the failure of multilateral agreements, such as the Organization for Economic Cooperation and Development's (OECD) multilateral agreement on investment (MAI) and the lack of progress at the World Trade Organization (WTO) in setting new agendas for trade and investment liberalization, are signals of the problems of globalization and the power of closed regional/triad blocs.

In this chapter I elaborate on these points and apply them to more general issues of globalization. I also define globalization and introduce the theme of the key role of MNEs as regionally-based producers. Finally, I relate the political and social aspects of globalization and governance issues to that of the reality of triad-based regional economic production.

Main themes of the book

Five themes are developed in this book:

- Global business is dominated by the 500 largest multinational enterprises from a total of some 30,000 MNEs. These 500 MNEs account for 90 per cent of all the world's FDI, and over half of its trade.

- Operating globally for an MNE really means operating regionally, i.e. in the triad markets of North America, the EU and Japan. For example, production and assembly in the motor vehicles industry are regional, and strategic perceptions should be regional but are often global.
- Most global trade and investment by MNEs is now intra-firm and is conducted within triad-based business networks or clusters, e.g. most vehicles/chemicals/pharmaceuticals etc.
- Managers of large MNEs often serve as leaders of 'flagships' in regional business networks; many other firms have roles as network partners, e.g. key suppliers, customers, etc. Small and medium sized businesses are partners in business networks led by the largest MNEs. Government can also be a partner in successful business networks (as in Japan), but by acting as a facilitator to help improve competitiveness, not as a regulator.
- Regional trade and investment blocs are being reinforced by four political developments:
  - the discriminatory protectionist application of trade remedy law
  - bilateral investment treaties with many exempted sectors
  - the biased administration of health, safety and environmental laws to benefit insiders at the expense of outsiders
  - related bloc-specific institutional measures such as internal subsidies for export promotion programmes and conditional national treatment.

Definitions of Globalization

The word 'globalization' is much abused, and presents a problem for scholars across the social sciences who define it from the viewpoint of their own discipline. For an economist and business school professor such as myself, globalization can be defined as 'the activities of multinational enterprises engaged in foreign direct investment and the development of business networks to create value across national borders'. Sociologists, such as Anthony Giddens and John Tomlinson, argue that such an economic definition of globalization is too narrow. They believe that it is multi-dimensional, best 'understood in terms of simultaneous, complex related processes in the realms of economy, politics, culture, technology and so forth . . .' (Tomlinson 1999, p.16). It is argued that globalization has created the modern social, cultural and political problems of the world, and that the power and influence of modern multinational enterprises operating their businesses within different countries are the perceived causes of global harmonization in areas such as culture.

John Tomlinson's book is based on the ideas of Anthony Giddens, currently Director of the London School of Economics. Gidden's argument is that, with globalization, social relations are no longer local but stretch across time and space. A common global capitalist culture is alleged to be spread by the power of multinational enterprises. A more sophisticated version of the broad school of globalization critics argues that 'deterritorialization' of culture is occurring due to the hybridization of cultures. This process is being speeded up by global mass media and communications technologies. The conclusion is that the global culture which is emerging is complex and deterritorialized rather than simplistic and monolithic. This complexity exists because culture is not linked to local nation states but is deterritorialized, which, in turn, links to a cultural process of enforced proximity and cosmopolitan politics (Tomlinson, 1999). The confused thinking, inherent in this broad sociological definition of globalization, is addressed in this book, especially in Chapters 3 and 4. I demonstrate that the correct, economic, definition of globalization leads to a clear and penetrating analysis of the nature of international business activity today, and the regional triad-based levels of production by MNEs.

Giddens defines globalization too broadly: 'Globalisation is political, technical and cultural, as well as economic.' (Giddens 1999, p.10) He states that globalization is 'new' and 'revolutionary' and is mainly due to the 'massive increase' in financial foreign exchange transactions. This has been facilitated by dramatic improvement in communications technology, especially electronic interchange facilitated by personal computers.

The trouble with this very broad perspective is that the key drivers of globalization, the multinational enterprises, are badly misrepresented. International trade and multinationals have existed for two millennia. Moore and Lewis (1999) find evidence of the existence of MNEs in the ancient world; in the Assyrian, Phoenician, Greek and Roman empires. This aspect of globalization is not recent, as alleged by its critics. MNEs are old news.

The Role of Multinational Enterprises

I shall use the standard definition of economic 'globalization' as the worldwide production and marketing of goods and services by multinational enterprises. An MNE is defined, in turn, as a firm with production and/or distribution facilities in two or more countries. This definition is based on economics and business strategy. With this type of globalization, MNEs can realize economies of scale and build dispersed production networks. They are able to produce and sell goods and products across national borders, often within their own internal networks of subsidiaries, or in close alliances with partner firms. I have used this definition repeatedly (Rugman, 1996). My key point is that the very same definition describes the activities of triad-based MNEs operating 'regionally'. The firm-level evidence from research on the activities of MNEs and the empirical data at industry level on MNE activities support this regional finding, as shown in Chapters 7 and 8. In addition, strategic management analysis, coupled with fieldwork and interviews with top managers of MNEs, also reveals the triad-based nature of their operations, as shown in Chapters 9 and 10.

Another reason for the myth of globalization is that MNEs are neither globally monolithic nor excessively powerful in political terms. They are not monolithic because the largest 500 are evenly based in the triad economies of the United States, the European Union and Japan. Across a wide variety of industrial sectors and traded services, these triad-based MNEs compete for global market shares and profits. Yet the process of regional competition itself erodes any possibility of sustainable long-term rents of these MNEs. Research shows that the world's largest 500 MNEs do not earn excess profits over time and that economic efficiency is enhanced by their activities (Rugman, 1981, 1996). In turn, the nature of triad-based competition faced by these MNEs limits their ability to pursue political goals, since they are forced to concentrate on their day to day operational efficiency and strategic planning in order to survive.

It is a common mistake to associate the very large economic size of MNEs with political power, as does Strange (1988, 1996, 1998). While many of the largest 500 MNEs have total revenues greater than the gross national products of many medium to small countries, they have been observed to act within the parameters of regulations and rules set by governments and international organizations. These enterprises are preoccupied with survival, profitability and growth and, in general, are far too busy to deal in any meaningful way with the social, cultural, and related non-economic areas of government activity. I will return to this theme in Chapters 3, 4 and 5.

Some of the work by political scientists criticising globalization and market forces is extremely naïve. Former Oxford don, John Gray, argues that MNEs operate in a system of global free trade policed by the WTO (Gray, 1998). In fact, the WTO has a small secretariat of around 200 professionals, mainly trade law lawyers, and its role is to be an appeal court for trade disputes between member countries. It is basically a reactive quasi-judicial body rather than a policy making and enforcement mechanism for free trade. Indeed, most of the disputes arise from the closing of markets by the misuse of trade remedy laws, rather than from market opening issues. The role and nature of the WTO is discussed in Chapter 2.

Where there is some conflict between MNEs and government is in the area of international political economy, which I interpret as the ability of MNEs to lobby and otherwise influence the policies of national (and sub-national) governments. This occurs in areas such as trade, investment, science and technology, and in the administration by bureaucracies of these policies. Yet, even here, the interests of MNEs are largely triad-based. For example, Japanese MNEs will mainly help to develop Japanese competitiveness in their home base, and only contribute peripherally to the public policies of the host countries in which they have subsidiaries. In summary, groups of MNEs can help to develop their home economies, but the nature of triad competition erodes any sustainable global market power of individual MNEs.

Triad-Based Production

Multinational enterprises dominate international production across major industries such as automobiles, consumer electronics, chemicals and petrochemicals, petroleum, pharmaceuticals, etc. In these sectors there is a very large amount of intra-industry, indeed intra-firm, trade and investment. Data to confirm this appear in Chapters 7 and 8.[2] For example, as Chapter 8 shows, the United Nations annual *World Investment Report* estimates that as much as 60 per cent of trade and investment in these sectors is intra-firm. Of that, well over 80 per cent of the world's stock of FDI and over half of its trade are conducted by the very largest MNEs listed in Table 1.2.

---

[2] The relevant data are reported in Chapter 7 and in the Appendix tables to Chapter 7. These demonstrate, unambiguously, that for example in 1997, 60.6 per cent of EU exports are intra-regional (Appendix, Table 7.1). It can also be demonstrated that all EU manufacturing sectors have a majority of trade that is intra-regional, with figures as high as 87.7 per cent for gas; 81.5 per cent for pulp and waste paper; 66 per cent for petroleum; 61 per cent for chemicals and so on, see Table 7.2.

Table 1.2: The World's 500 Largest MNEs

Country/Bloc	Number of MNEs in 1999
United States	179
European Union	148
Japan	107
Canada	12
South Korea	12
Switzerland	11
China	10
Australia	7
Brazil	3
Other	11
Total	**500**

Source: Adapted from *Fortune*, 'The Fortune Global 500', August 2, 1999.

Advances in technology intensify the concentration of economic power in the hands of MNEs. It is not so much in the creation of new knowledge (as here smaller, innovating firms can do well) but in the application to mass production that the MNE has an advantage. Most of the manu-facturing productivity advances in Japanese MNEs have occurred in incremental process improvements reflecting efficient organizational structures. Pure research, when needed, can be bought from abroad; as the Japanese MNEs have done through their activities in California's Silicon Valley and other US-based research centres. It is the proprietary internalization of technology that gives MNEs the edge in their worldwide production and marketing (Rugman, 1996).

A second mistake in globalization thinking is to equate the innovative production and intensive global marketing of MNEs with the development of a homogenized global culture. While the success of MNEs in producing goods and services increases worldwide consumption (or materialism) there is little evidence that the end result of triad-based MNEs is a global culture. Rather, we observe an increase in standards of living offering consumers greater choice, as MNEs respond to the growth of divergent tastes with niche products and services.

Research by Professors Yves Doz (at INSEAD), Chris Bartlett (at Harvard Business School) and Sumantra Ghoshal (London Business School) demonstrates that many MNEs are 'nationally responsive' and/or are both scale economy driven and nationally responsive at the same time (Bartlett and Ghoshal, 1989, 1998). In other words, MNEs do not all pursue global low cost or differentiation strategies, which could, perhaps, lead to homogenization of culture. Some are in a strategic space where they need to adapt their products and services to the different political, cultural and religious systems all too pervasive in the world today. I will discuss the strategies of 20 MNEs, using this approach, in Chapter 10.

If there is anything to the homogenization argument it is that there may be strong regional effects, i.e. each of the triads may be spreading its influences regionally rather than globally. In North America, the US influence is apparent in Canada and Mexico (although the language difference in Quebec and Mexico is a strongly mitigating factor). In Asia, Japanese economic (but not cultural) influence is widespread. In Europe there is relatively little cultural homogenization, as strong national differences persist despite the success of the Brussels bureaucracy in developing EU-wide economic policies with common legal standards and practices.

Regional Production and Marketing

The MNEs listed back in Table 1.2 are the vehicles for increasing global interdependence, yet are also strongly based in the triad of North America, the EU, and Japan – 441 of the 500 come from these regions.[3] These triad blocs are in some danger of becoming even more protectionist, since they all adopt non-tariff barriers to trade and investment to limit access to their internal markets and/or give preferential access to certain partners in return for reciprocal advantages. Examples of non-tariff barriers include rules of

---

[3] These data on the triad-based disposition of the world's 500 largest MNEs are not all well understood by the critics of globalization. For example, Anthony Giddens, in his Reith Lectures states that 'many of the most visible cultural expressions of globalisation are American – Coca-Cola, McDonalds, CNN' and that 'most of the giant multinational companies are based in the US too'. Giddens (1999, p.15) Yet only 185 of the world's largest 500 MNEs are American, while 256 are either European or Japanese-based. Basically, the facts disagree with Giddens. His misunderstanding of these most basic data makes one wonder about the value of his other statements.

origin, discriminatory health and safety codes used to keep out agricultural products, new environmental regulations in the EU and NAFTA, exempted sectors from the principle of national treatment (such as culture, education, health etc.), poorly administered anti-dumping and countervailing duty laws, and so on.

The extent of non-tariff barriers in the triad serves to limit access to their home base markets. Many US restrictions are aimed at Japanese and European competitors, and vice versa. Three strong regional trading and investment blocs have developed. The world automobile industry is not really globalized. As I have argued, and will show in Chapters 8 and 9, well over 85 per cent of production and sales take place in each of the three separate triad markets, using intra-bloc networks of suppliers and distributors. Agreements like the North American Free Trade Agreement (NAFTA) build on over 35 years of US-Canadian automobile managed trade. The regional nature of the auto industry is replicated in chemicals, petrochemicals, steel and other major industrial sectors. The name of the game is market access on a regional, rather than a global, basis. While this is good news for triad-based MNEs, it makes life difficult for MNEs from non-triad economies, since they need access to a triad market even to start a global strategy. This leads to a re-interpretation of the wave of mergers and acquisitions going on. The M&A are largely intra-triad with some inter-triad ones for market access reasons. This is discussed in Chapter 8.

This point is reconfirmed in Table 1.3, which reports the 20 most 'transnational' MNEs, MNEs with over two thirds of their activities outside their home base. These are the true MNEs. The index of transnationality is a simple mean of the ratio of foreign to total activities for three indexes; sales, assets and employees. To some extent Table 1.3 is the inverse of the strong home base triad argument of Table 1.1. In this new table, the MNEs are usually from smaller, non-triad countries such as Switzerland or Canada, and they need foreign sales to obtain global status. For example, Canada has a small market, only one tenth the economic size of the United States and EU and so Seagram, Alcan and Thompson will realize the great majority of their sales outside their home country. Even the EU MNEs in Table 1.3 are from countries such as the UK, Holland and Sweden, so they are MNEs whose home country market is small, relative to the larger integrated market of the EU. For these MNEs from smaller economies, access to the triad market is central to their success and they have all developed such regional market access strategies, sometimes in accord with regional trade and investment agreements like the EU and NAFTA.

Table 1.3:
World's Leading Transnational Enterprises, 1997

Rank	Company Name	Home Country	Index of Transnationality
1	Seagram Co.	Canada	97.6
2	Asea Brown Boveri	Switzerland	95.7
3	Thomson Corporation	Canada	95.1
4	Nestlé SA	Switzerland	93.2
5	Unilever N.V.	Netherlands	92.4
6	Solvay	Belgium	92.3
7	Electrolux AB	Sweden	89.4
8	Philips Electronics N.V.	Netherlands	86.4
9	Bayer AG	Germany	82.7
10	Roche Holding AG	Switzerland	82.2
11	Holderbank Financiere Glarus AG	Switzerland	80.8
12	Akzo Nobel N.V.	Netherlands	79.5
13	BTR	United Kingdom	78.2
14	Glaxo Wellcome Plc	United Kingdom	78.2
15	L'Air Liquide Group	France	78.1
16	Hoechst AG	Germany	76.5
17	Imperial Chemical Industries	United Kingdom	75.0
18	Cable and Wireless Plc	United Kingdom	74.7
19	Novartis	Switzerland	74.4
20	Total SA	France	73.2

Source: Adapted from United Nations, *World Investment Report*, (Geneva, UN Publications, 1999)

Regionalization and business networks

To summarize, my theme is that a paradox of globalization is that it has never really occurred anyway; it is a myth. Instead, the vast majority of MNE manufacturing and service activity is (and has always been) organized regionally, not globally. While MNEs are the engines of international business, their strategies are regional. Political factors and institutional organizations reinforce business at a regional level rather than at the multilateral level required for full globalization. As already stated, world manufacturing is dominated by a set of 500 very large MNEs operating in regional business networks. They operate in each others' home triad markets, giving a regional set of activities which is commonly confused with globalization. Ford, General Motors, IBM, GE and Du Pont all have hundreds of thousands of employees in dozens of country subsidiaries across the triad. Toyota, Matsushita, Sony and NEC have outsourced much of their component production to South East Asia and employ thousands of Americans and Europeans. European firms like Unilever, Shell, Nestlé, ABB, and Phillips are even more decentralized across the triad with a large degree of autonomy for subsidiary managers (Bartlett and Ghoshal, 1989).

Also, as I mentioned earlier, large MNEs often serve as 'flagships' in regional business networks; many other firms have roles as network partners, as key suppliers, key customers, and so on (Rugman and D'Cruz 1997, 2000). Small and medium sized businesses are partners in business networks led by the largest MNEs. Government can also be a partner in successful business networks (as in Japan), but by acting as a facilitator to help improve competitiveness, not as a regulator.

As a result of what they call globalization, various writers have argued that there is an emerging homogenization of world products and services, for example Ohmae (1990). The collapse of communism and the triumph of market-based democracies has reinforced this viewpoint that western (including Japanese) based consumerism is the dominant force behind the success of the MNEs. This is 'the end of history', discussed by Fukuyama (1992).

While in some sectors (such as consumer electronics) this view of globalization is correct, in many others it is not supported by the evidence. For example, in both automobiles and chemicals, over 90 per cent of products produced in each of the triad regions are sold within that region. There is no global car. Instead, there are US, European and Japanese bases for automobile production, supported by the paints and plastics business of the chemicals sector and regional triad-based steel producers. Indeed, most manufacturing activity is regional, not global. Data indicate that in terms of output (goods and services produced and sold) and input (number of employees and financing) well over 90 per cent of MNE manufacturing is intra-regional rather than global (Rugman and Hodgetts, 1995).

In the service sectors the lack of pure globalization is even more apparent. Except for professional service providers (such as consultants, film stars and business school professors) well over 95 per cent of all employees in this sector are local, not global. For example, virtually all health care workers are local, being 'location-bound' by either national or regional professional regulatory and accreditation bodies. Regions have cultural attributes and political borders which are stronger than the economic forces of globalization. There are no global drugs. Instead, MNEs have to engage in FDI and satisfy national state regulations in order to sell locally; centralized production and worldwide distribution are not possible for pharmaceutical MNEs. Managers of MNEs are likely to make major mistakes if they believe their business is global when it is regional. The managerial consequences of the lack of pure globalization has led to the need for regional, triad-based strategies by MNEs.

The influential home country 'diamond' model of international competitiveness (Porter, 1990), is fully consistent with the triad/regional theme presented here. An MNE will build upon the strong home base diamond characteristics of the United States, EU or Japan and use the appropriate triad market as a staging ground for activities in other markets. But the great majority of the MNE's production and sales will be concentrated in its home triad. This is especially true for US and Japanese MNEs, and perhaps less so for British ones, although most European, for example German, MNEs sell mainly within the EU. Smaller firms, such as the German Mittelstand, make virtually all their sales within the EU.

In terms of my two country, 'double diamond' model, again, the role of the triad is dominant. Smaller economies can develop MNEs only if these firms have access to a neighbouring triad market (Rugman, 1996). For example, Canadian MNEs such as Northern Telecom, Alcan and Bombardier have developed double diamond relationships with the United States. Korean chaebols sell both to Japan and the United States, using two double diamonds. Mexico is developing MNEs within NAFTA, using a Mexico-US double diamond approach. The double and single diamond theories do not support pure globalization strategies of MNEs, rather they help explain the reality of regional/triad production and sales.

The work of international institutions such as the General Agreement on Tariffs and Trade (GATT)/WTO reinforces regional production, as most tariff cuts and investment liberalization are agreed upon bilaterally and not 'across the board' and thus originate regionally, rather than in a generic multilateral manner. The voluntary 'club' membership of the GATT/WTO leads to mutual accommodations by trade partners, rather than agreement to sweeping new free market principles (Ostry, 1997). The failure of the OECD's multilateral agreement on investment is the latest sign that the trade and investment liberalization required for globalization are slowing down and even going into reverse, promoting regionalization.

The imperfect nature of global markets has been reinforced by political developments and new institutional structures. The emergence of NAFTA is a mixed blessing. While tariffs are eliminated and the national treatment principle is applied to foreign direct investment, these benefits of liberalization are offset by the erection of new non-tariff barriers to trade. These include restrictive rules of origin affecting automobile and textile production in Mexico, which effectively deny entry to the US market, Rugman (1994). In addition, many service sectors, including health, social services, education, transportation and financial services, are exempted from national treatment, leading to the institutionalization of discriminatory investment measures. The domestic laws protecting Canada's medicare system are listed in the NAFTA Annexes as exemptions from the principle of national treatment, thereby retaining national sovereignty in the administration of health care. Using this analysis, NAFTA has emerged as a relatively closed regional bloc, though not as closed as the EU. In particular, the local service sector (including health care) is now protected regionally as well as nationally against the forces of globalization and free markets.

The EU single market measures of 1992 and the single currency of 1999 signal an increase in intra-regional trade and investment in Europe, rather than a movement towards globalization. The continued use of anti-dumping trade remedy law by the EU, examined by Ostry (1997), plus protectionist trade measures in the form of, for example, newsprint quotes against Canada, and the discriminatory application of health and environmental regulations against 'outsiders', are further evidence of the closing of the EU bloc due to the political lobbying of 'insider' firms and organizations. Indeed, the use of environmental regulations and health codes as a trade-related barrier to entry is one of the major anchors of regional (EU, NAFTA) policy (Rugman, Kirton and Soloway, 1999).

The Asian financial crisis has slowed down the emergence of an Asian triad bloc led by Japan and put the Association of South East Asian Nations (ASEAN) off the rails. This started as a political security group but has moved steadily towards an economic bloc. The biggest problem is the lack of progress in the Asian Pacific Economic Cooperation (APEC) Forum. The failed meeting in Malaysia in 1998 and the largely technical one in New Zealand in September 1999 indicate a lack of commitment to free trade and investment liberalization. Only if APEC moves ahead will globalization prosper; without it, regional blocs will persist. The implication of this is that governance issues are regional, not global. I shall build on this in the remainder of the book.

Support for my regionalization thesis comes from the modern political scientists. 'New' regionalism is defined by Hettne et al (1999) 'as a multidimensional form of integration which includes economic, political, social and cultural aspects . . .' It goes beyond the 'old' regionalism of 25 years ago which was concerned only with the economics of free trade regimes and customs unions or the politics of security alliances. However, the new regionalism is a complement to globalization, not a substitute for it. It complements the mostly economic aspects of globalization by adopting a broader, multidimensional challenge to the Westphalian nation state. In new regionalism there are multiple stakeholders and a multipolar global order.

The EU is the only core region with a formal political organization, since North America (with NAFTA) and the Asian-Pacific (with APEC) lack a regional political order, although they are pursuing increased economic integration. Intermediate regions are being drawn into these three core regions, a process which has the appearance of globalization but is actually quite different. In some cases (US-Canada in NAFTA) new regionalism is replacing bilateralism; in others (South Asia) it is not. Hettne (1999) argues that new regionalism is supposed to contribute to the three preferred outcomes of peace, development and ecological sustainability, and that new regionalism can support a new multilateralism. New regionalism is a big tent. It can accommodate these more moderate liberal views with the extremist rhetoric of Samir Amin (who defines globalization as the five monopolies over technology, finance, resources, media and weapons of mass destruction) and Richard Falk's long list of aspects of 'negative globalism'.

Multinational Enterprises as 'Flagship Firms'

The leading role of multinational enterprises in regional triad development is even greater when we note that the very large MNEs in Table 1.2 usually serve as 'flagship' firms. By a flagship firm I mean an MNE operating at the hub of an extensive business network, or cluster. Usually the flagship has long term relational contracts with a set of four other partners; key suppliers, key customers, key competitors and the non-business infrastructure. This provides us with the 'five partners' model, where the flagship firm is the core or hub of a business network with the other four partners.

The non-business infrastructure includes network partners in research and educational institutes and it can also include efficiency-related aspects of government (rather than the regulatory and redistributional function of government). An example of a network relationship with a university business school would be a customized executive course developed with an external organization in which the business school faculty creates new and specialized materials to improve the skills and/or strategic thinking of the organization's managers. An example of a non-network relationship is the MBA programme, which is general and not customized.

In recent years, my colleague Joseph D'Cruz of the University of Toronto and I have found that flagship relationships exist, to some degree, across the major triad-based industrial sectors such as automobiles, chemicals, telecommunications, the agri-food business, and in some of the service sectors such as banking. In these sectors we can identify the 500 large MNEs as flagship firms, competing globally. They now have strong linkages to independent key supplier firms (who, in turn, are sometimes MNEs). For example, Du Pont is a key supplier of paint to General Motors, while Nortel is a key supplier to Bell Canada/Stentor, as is Alcatel to France Telecom (Rugman and D'Cruz, 1997, 2000).

Large MNEs also have similar long term relationships with key customers and distributors. These organizations usually have skills in dealing with final consumers in foreign markets. With a successful key customer relationship the MNE need not internalize the sales and distribution functions and can forego the costly development of skills in learning about foreign cultures and languages. Other MNEs are a fourth partner of MNEs today, driven into key competitor relationships by the high costs of research and development, and the difficulty of securing access to new markets. These strategic alliances are more unstable than the key supplier/key customer linkages.

The key supplier relationship is built on performance and trust. The key suppliers in the automobile sector are those that have been the quickest to adopt the quality standards of the automobile MNEs. The set of key suppliers (with a large part of the value added in the component market) is much smaller than the large number of other suppliers who still interact with automobile assemblers on a more variable and strictly price-driven basis. The key suppliers and flagship MNEs are mutually dependent and exhibit more trust in their long-term managerial relationships than would be normal between suppliers and MNEs.

The fifth and final set of partners is in the non-business infrastructure, usually service organizations. Today over 70 per cent of people in the Western economies work in the service sector, compared to 30 per cent in manufacturing. The productivity of these service sector organizations (which include health, social services, education, cultural industries as well as transportation and financial services) can be a major influence on competitiveness. The MNE serves as a vehicle to build bridges to the service sector, including government. The logic of the flagship/five partners framework of international competitiveness is that various units of government (such as research groups, industry and agriculture specialists, etc.) can have efficiency-related linkages to the business sector, and, by interacting with MNEs, gain a regional triad perspective, with better competitive benchmarks.

The implication is that MNEs provide the triad-based strategic perspective for the five partners and that each true partner does not need a separate international strategy except to be a 'key' partner of the MNE. This is, of course, difficult for governments to accept, but it clarifies their role as a facilitator (but not a determinant) of competitiveness. The western flagship/five partner system is, of course, similar in many respects to the Japanese keiretsu and, to a smaller extent, the Korean chaebols. Even the Chinese family/clan system which is a much looser 'network' has strong elements of the tacit trust relationships at the heart of the flagship/five partners system. In all four types of business systems the MNE adopts a flagship role and has strong partners, including a more active role by governments and banks in the Asian networks.

Key Managerial Implications

The multinational enterprise is the key actor on the stage of international business. It is the organization which leads globalization and operates as the flagship firm for sets of regionally-based business networks and clusters. The MNE interacts with governments but is not powerful enough to pursue a separate agenda of world economic domination. Instead, the reality of regional triad power is that MNEs need to compete for market share and profits. The energies of their top managers are fully devoted to operational efficiency and the successful implementation of strategy decisions, and not to global political issues.

The literature advocating globalization is far too simplistic. While there are some economic drivers of globalization there are extremely strong cultural and political barriers preventing the development of a single world market. Only in a few sectors, such as consumer electronics, is there a successful firm-level strategy of globalization, with homogeneous products being sold on price and quality. For most other manufacturing sectors, and all service sectors, regionalization is much more relevant than globalization. The triad regions are characterized by heterogeneity more than homogeneity.

Managers need to change their thinking as the end of globalization is here. They must 'think regional and act local', to paraphrase the work of Doz, Bartlett and Ghoshal. They should:

a) design strategies to take account of regional trade and investment agreements (such as NAFTA, the single market of the EU, Mercosur) rather than multilateral agreements (such as the GATT/WTO, MAI)

b) design organizational structures which develop triad-based internal know-how capabilities and organizational competencies, rather than use international divisions or unworkable global organizational structures

c) develop new thinking and knowledge about regional business networks and triad-based clusters, and assess the similar attributes of ⁻ triad competitors, rather than develop so-called global strategies

d) develop analytical methods to assess regional drivers of success, rather than globalization drivers

e) think regional, act local; forget global.

2

The World Trade Organization: The Politics of Trade and Investment Agreements

The Crisis at the WTO

THE World Trade Organization is in a crisis. Portrayed by many of the left-wing critics of globalization as the driver of free trade, in reality it is an understaffed and overworked technical bureaucracy with no political clout at all. The WTO is the secretariat to the General Agreement on Tariffs and Trade, which has succeeded in its 51 years of existence in serving as a facilitator for national governments to cut tariffs, mainly on manufactured goods (but not much on agricultural products and textiles). The history of the GATT/WTO is that of a well-intentioned but small technocratic group acting, often opportunistically, to broker concessions by national governments in the broader interests of free trade.

But the WTO is not politically powerful. All of its successful eight 'rounds' of tariff cuts had to be negotiated, and then implemented by sovereign governments. The WTO has no army to enforce its will. It only has a staff of 200 professionals, mostly trade lawyers and economists. It is little more than a conference organizer for governments, with an appellate body tacked on to monitor the rules. The rules themselves are not much more than gentlemen's agreements, based on the assumption that governments treat each other respectfully, like members of an exclusive (or, at least, expensive) London Club. The WTO is similar to the club executive secretary, sending out reminders when dues are not paid and suspending access to the restaurant or swimming pool when rules have been broken.

The basic way to infringe the WTO's rules is to fail to accept the discipline of most-favoured nation, non-discriminatory treatment. If the United States allows one of its exporters to 'dump' a product in Europe, then the EU can have the European Commission bring an 'anti-dumping' action, and if successful, impose a tariff duty on the dumped imports. If Britain subsidises an export to the United States, and a US firm complains to the US International Trade Commission, then it may recommend that a 'countervailing' duty be imposed to offput the margin of subsidy. Both the anti-dumping and countervailing duty actions are consistent with the WTO and the GATT's Uruguay Round Agreement of 1994.

The WTO-consistent 'retaliation' that a country can take, always in response to an infringement of its negotiated rights, is to re-impose tariffs or duties against the offending party's home country. Thus all the action is between governments. The WTO acts as a traffic cop, directing what are really domestic legal actions involving international players. Its only direct role is to hear appeals about failures to observe due process in the application of these trade laws. Here it can render a judgement, according to the timing of Table 2.1.

Table 2.1: Dispute Settlement at the World Trade Organization

Time	WTO Activity
60 days	WTO Report (for consultation)
9 months	WTO Panel
60 days	WTO Appellate Body
15 months	Implementation by Countries
After 15 months	WTO Sanctional Retaliation

Source: Adapted by author from WTO Website

The end of the WTO

The WTO is in trouble and may even fail for three reasons:

- First, it is a technical body, lacking in political power and even political understanding. It was successful for 51 years in dealing with a technical series of tariff cuts, but it is not equipped to deal with the new agenda of international trade and investment liberalization. Tariff cuts have allowed 'shallow' integration across many manufacturing sectors (but not in agriculture and textiles). Today's agenda, set by multinational enterprises engaging in foreign direct investment, is one of 'deep' integration. Here the issue is how to make domestic markets internationally contestable. This involves negotiating the role of government in society – a hopeless task for the WTO secretariat with its small staff of professionals in Geneva. The WTO is not designed to deal with non trade and investment issues such as environmental regulations, labour standards and human rights. These only come onto its agenda as indirect, technical matters in trade disputes. These 'big issues' are better handled in different international fora, eg human rights at the United Nations, labour standards at the International Labour Organization and environmental regulations at a new world environmental agency. But these issues are well beyond the capacity of the WTO to address, let alone resolve.

- Second, the WTO could fail because its acute lack of political skill led it to make the dreadful mistake of giving standing to non-governmental organizations at the abortive Seattle Millennium Round of December 1999. For the WTO to succeed it must only work with governments, as it was designed to do. This is what the GATT did. The members of the GATT/WTO are nations, not firms, nor NGOs. Each country government negotiates on behalf of its businesses and NGOs. Throughout its existence the GATT has refused even to hear representations from business groups, MNEs or individuals. Now the WTO has given the NGOs a platform. So the NGOs can have two bites of the cherry; first they can lobby their home governments, then they can lobby the WTO (which is representing their governments again).

  Multilateralism is dead. The agent of multilateralism, the WTO, has always been a small, weak technocratic body. If it talks directly to NGOs, it cannot begin to function as a facilitator for governments to consider issues of deep integration. NGOs must be banished from such multilateral forums. They should be briefed by their home governments, just as is business. Neither business groups, nor other NGOs should be present at future meetings of the WTO. They should lobby their home governments and live with the results of government to government bargaining at the WTO.

- Third, the catalyst for the probable failure of the WTO may, somewhat paradoxically, be a technical decision. The United States has lost a case to the EU involving export subsidies paid for many years by the US Domestic International Sales Corporation (DISC). The potential scale of retaliation by the EU against the United States runs into several billions of US dollars. In contrast, the 'wins' by the United

States against the EU on the bananas and beef hormones cases (discussed in detail below) were both under US$ 200 million. The vast scale of potential EU retaliation could cause a firestorm of protest in the US Congress and, I predict, even lead to the withdrawal of the United States from the WTO. This could be achieved by a simple majority vote in the US Senate, based on the Dole Amendment of 1994. At that time, Senator Dole, as leader of the Senate majority Republican Party, convinced the Senate to pass and implement the GATT Marrakesh agreement, subject to the ability of the Congress to revisit it in the future. One trigger for revisiting the Marrakesh Agreement (which established the WTO) is the loss of three US appeals at the WTO. This threshold has already been reached.

In the presidential election year of 2000, with major congressional elections also taking place in November 2000, the United States is poised to turn its back on multilateralism and embrace economic isolation again. A trade war with the EU, over DISC sanctions, coupled with the ongoing US current account deficit with Japan (the other triad power) will open the doors for US protectionism to emerge. The US advocacy of free trade, and its advancement of national treatment for foreign investment, has always been fragile, with the executive branch office at odds with the more protectionist Congress. The approval of NAFTA in October 1993 by the first Clinton administration was the last case of 'first-track' authority and, in retrospect, the end of US leadership in trade liberalization. The MAI failed at the OECD in Paris partly because of a lack of US commitment.

As the United States retreats from the global stage, the NGOs take its place. Many of these NGOs, especially the environmental ones, are US based and funded. Most of the others are from Canada and Western Europe. They represent sectional interests in the rich countries. As I will show, especially in Chapters 3, 4, and 6, the NGOs' anti-business activities are fundamentally opposed to the economic interests of poorer countries. NGOs, by reversing the benefits of multilateralism and free trade, are hindering the economic development of poorer Asian, African and emerging countries. Their anti-business activities are profoundly illogical.

NGO activities, the probable withdrawal of the United States from the WTO, its lack of commitment to free trade, and the dissolution of the post war consensus about the virtues of free trade will lead to the end of globalization. But globalization was a myth anyway. Economic and business activities have been organized in the triad/regions, as is demonstrated empirically in Chapters 6, 7 and 8.

How the WTO really works

The World Trade Organization, established on 1 January 1995, is the umbrella organization which governs the international trading system. It oversees international trade arrangements and provides the secretariat for the General Agreement on Tariffs and Trade based in Geneva since its inception in 1948. The GATT has undertaken eight 'rounds' of multilateral trade negotiations which have been successful in achieving major cuts in tariffs and, since the 1970s, some reductions in related non-tariff barriers to trade. The latest GATT round, the Uruguay Round, took seven years as its agenda had broadened to include trade in services and intellectual property, and a revised system of dispute settlement mechanisms.

Contrary to popular belief, the WTO did not replace the GATT. An amended GATT remains as one of the legal pillars of the world's trade and, to a lesser extent, investment systems. The other pillars, set up in the Uruguay Round's Marrakesh agreement of 1994, include the General Agreement on Trade in Services (GATS) and the Agreement on Trade-Related Aspects of Intellectual Property Rights (TRIPS).

The members of the WTO now account for well over 90 per cent of the world's trade and virtually all of its investment; by 1998 the organization's membership had increased to 132, from the 76 founding members of 1995. Nearly all the developed, and most of the developing countries, have joined; a notable exception is the People's Republic of China, the entry of which was blocked by the United States throughout 1998 and 1999 on the grounds that its economy is not open enough and that intellectual property rights are not sufficiently protected.

The WTO's origins can be traced back to the Atlantic Charter of 1941, developed by then US President Franklin Roosevelt and British Prime Minister Winston Churchill. In order to counter US isolation, the principle of the Atlantic Charter was for an international trading system with equal access to trade for all nations. This was seen as a complement to an effective world political forum, the United Nations, established in 1946 with its permanent headquarters in New York City. The United States organized an international conference on trade and employment which resulted in the Havana Charter of 1948, in which it was proposed to establish the International Trade Organization (ITO). Twenty three countries agreed to a set of tariff cuts and these were ratified by the GATT, which was set up as a transitory arrangement to be subsumed under the ITO. However, the ITO was never ratified and the GATT continued for 47 years, until the WTO finally emerged in the last stages of the Uruguay Round to take on the role originally designed for the

ITO. The WTO now stands with the World Bank and the International Monetary Fund as the third leg of the global economic system.

A successful institution such as the WTO has many parents. The first public call for a world trade organization to be established was a proposal by the Canadian Government in early 1990, which was itself strongly influenced by Dr Sylvia Ostry, Chair of the Centre for International Studies at the University of Toronto. The Canadian proposal built on the work of Professor John Jackson and others at an informal meeting in Geneva in 1989. It was then incorporated into the 'Dunkel Text' of 1991, which eventually became the final text of the Uruguay Round adopted at Marrakesh in April 1994. In approving the Uruguay Round on its 'fast track' system, the United States insisted on the name World Trade Organization, rather than the European Community's preference for Multinational Trade Organization. So the Canadian proposal literally gave the WTO its name.

Principles of the WTO

The WTO continues the key GATT principle of non-discrimination; i.e. any barrier to trade should be applied equally to all member countries. It also keeps the 'most favoured nation' (MFN) principle; i.e. any liberalization measures, with some exceptions, should be granted to all members. To understand these principles, it helps to think of the WTO as a club with membership rules which require that all members receive the same treatment. If one member rescinds a trade concession, then other affected members can retaliate by withdrawing their reciprocal concessions, or receive compensation to equivalent commercial effect. If trade disputes arise, they can be settled by the WTO's unified dispute settlement mechanism, which can ensure timely compliance, in contrast to the basically voluntary procedures of the GATT. Decisions made by a WTO dispute panel cannot be blocked by the disputant party, as was possible under the GATT. Panel findings can be subject to review by an Appelate Body of the WTO. In addition, the publication of trade policy reviews and the activities of the Trade Policy Review Body (which regularly monitors the trade policies of member countries) complement the WTO's dispute settlement activities by significantly enhancing transparency.

There are four important exceptions to the key GATT principle of non-discrimination:

- Developed countries can give tariff preference to developing countries.

- Countries entering into regional free trade agreements do not need to extend the preferences negotiated in this context on an MFN basis.
- A country can invoke temporary 'safeguard' protection to one of its industries suffering serious injury due to a surge of imports.
- Temporary quantitative restrictions can be invoked by a country with serious balance of payment problems.

In the latter two cases, these measures are temporary exceptions to the member's commitment to the GATT, and a public investigation has to be undertaken to allow for limited relief from GATT obligations.

Another important principle of the WTO, which significantly improves on the GATT, is the 'single undertaking'. WTO members must accept all of the obligations of the GATT, GATS, TRIPS and any other corollary agreements. This ends the 'free ride' of some developing countries which under the old GATT could receive the benefits of some trade concessions without having to join in and undertake their full obligations. Most developed countries in North America and Western Europe were already making the single undertaking and the WTO meant few new obligations.

Unresolved issues at the WTO

The major tensions in the WTO relate to the issues of agriculture, trade in services and trade-related investment measures. None of these issues was included in the GATT's original mandate, which dealt with trade in goods. There are committees looking at these issues and their reports were the basis for the proposed Seattle Round of the WTO.

Agriculture is a sector which most governments subsidize, and it was badly neglected in the GATT. One technical advance (undertaken largely at the OECD) which helps to increase the transparency of subsidies is the calculation of producers' subsidy equivalents. As a result, in the Uruguay Round some progress was made towards the future reduction of the most egregious agricultural subsidies through a process of 'tariffication', i.e. the translation of existing subsidies and other barriers to trade into tariff equivalents. Thus regulations and codes to keep agriculture prices artificially high, such as marketing boards in Canada, had to be replaced by tariffs. Some of the milk tariffs in Canada were put at over 200 per cent. Much work remains to be done in future rounds to liberalize agricultural trade.

Today, services account for 70 per cent of employment and value added in advanced industrialized countries, and also for at least half the world's trade and investment. The Uruguay Round started to address issues of trade in services with the establishment of GATS. Trade-Related Investment Measures (TRIMS) were also considered, and a substantive agreement prohibiting a number of investment requirements affecting cross-border trade in goods was reached. For example, the TRIMS agreement restricted the imposition of export requirements on foreign investors. Future negotiations at the WTO (following the last Uruguay Round of the GATT) will need to develop a deeper and more comprehensive set of rules for multinational investment than the TRIMS agreement. These may well be based upon the model of NAFTA, using the national treatment principle as the basic logic. National treatment states that foreign investors should not be discriminated against, but receive the same treatment as domestic firms in the application of domestic laws.

The WTO Seattle Round could have built upon a multilateral agreement on investment which was partially negotiated by the Paris-based OECD over the 1995-1998 period. Investment issues are still being discussed at the WTO, in the context of the Working Group on the Relationship between Trade and Investment which was established and given a two-year mandate at the 1996 ministerial meeting in Singapore. Another important working group established during the same meeting is still examining the interaction between trade and competition policy.

The GATT has moved forward over the last 51 years to the extent that today's new constitution for international trade, as embodied in the WTO, includes an even fuller agenda of policy issues than was envisaged by its pioneering founders. These issues include:

- further reduction of tariffs
- a set of rules for multinational investment and competition policy
- the development of increased linkages between trade and issues of social policy, such as the environment and labour policy.

The hurdles in the way of achieving these three sets of objectives are lower for tariff cuts, higher for investment and highest of all for environmental and other social issues.

The Millennium Round Agenda of the WTO

While the left-wing anarchy and violence in Seattle in December 1999 has delayed the formal launch of a new Round of the WTO, background research and preparation continues. The agenda is pretty much agreed and has been for several years. For example, former leading US trade policy bureaucrat, Gaza Feketekuty, organized a conference in October 1996 at his Monterey Institute of International Studies to help develop the new agenda for US trade policy. This led to a set of 18 essays which covered all the topics for the Seattle round of the WTO in December 1999. The Council on Foreign Relations sponsored and published Feketekuty and Stokes (1998), and it deserves credit for pushing the agenda beyond parochial American concerns towards the underlying analytical and policy issues confronting the WTO.

The general theme of virtually all the papers is support for a multilateral rules-based system at the WTO rather than a triad/regional power-based system. The current 'multitrack' strategy of the United States seeks to use bilateral, regional and multilateral trade negotiations simultaneously. Within this, much more attention is given to Japan and China, and even to NAFTA, than to US-Europe trade relations. To redress this balance, Preeg and Stokes, among others, advocate a Transatlantic Free Trade Agreement (TFTA).

A discordant note in this book is struck by Washington trade lawyer Thomas Howell in his chapter on US trade remedy law. He criticises the Canadian members of the five person bi-national panel on softwood lumber as being 'biased panelists . . .' with '. . . an apparent lack of competence . . . to interpret the laws of another country . . .' (p.315). This is rich; Howell's law firm lost the Softwood lumber case. His law partner, Alan Wolff, repeats the criticism of the lumber case and how it 'violated' US law (p.376). Such advocacy introduces an unwelcome subjective note into what is claimed to be an objective book. This 'practitioner' influence in the US trade policy community somewhat devalues the thoughtful research of the more independent academic contributors to this book such as Richardson, Frost, Whitman, Hufbauer, Schott, Graham, Hart and Lawrence.

Robert Lawrence is representative in arguing, at a new round of the WTO, for strong US support for a multilateral rules-based system, extending into the new areas of competition policy, investment and perhaps environment and labour standards. Yet in the last four years Congress has persisted in denying 'fast track' negotiating authority to the President for any trade deals, including a new WTO Round, while aggressive US bilateral policy with Japan, China and other countries appears to be the new norm. If books like this can turn the tide in Congress back towards support for the United States as a leader in multilateral trade and investment liberalization, then the world will benefit.

Most less developed countries are also in favour of a new WTO Round.

The trade ministers of four Caribbean economies endorsed the Seattle Round. Yet some academics still criticize the GATT/WTO. For example, Khan (1999) has published a set of technical economic papers dealing with aspects of structural adjustment in Pakistan. The ten papers are linked together by two rather thin introductory and concluding sections which talk critically about World Bank and IMF policies from the perspective of economic development in Pakistan. The author, a macroeconomist, attempts to analyze the distinction between 'neo-liberalism' and 'alternative critiques' with little appreciation of political science considerations such as complex institutional responsiveness and its links to the business decisions behind inbound foreign direct investment. Instead of narrow economic-based research it would be more useful for development economists to get out of their offices and actually talk to some managers. Then they would find out that the real barriers to FDI in countries like Pakistan are domestic, political and bureaucratic problems, not a perceived failure of neo-liberalism. Framing the conditions for inward FDI is a precondition for consideration of the distributional aspects of structural adjustment, including impacts on the poor, gender, health, the environment and food security. Pakistan continues to experience huge development problems, not due to World Bank failures, but due to poor internal government policies which have increased political risk and reduced the incentive for inward FDI.

The EU and United States Trade Wars

Bananas: The strategic issues

The authority of the WTO and its dispute settlement body was threatened in 1999 by the banana war between the United States and the EC. Such trade law cases are brought to the WTO by the European Commission which is the executive body of the EU. Chiquita Brands (formerly the United Fruit Company) and Dole successfully lobbied the US government to take the EC's banana regime to the courts of the WTO. Bananas produced by US companies in Central and South America can be up to 60 per cent cheaper than those produced in the Caribbean, but have faced tariffs, quotas and distribution barriers in Europe. The EC's banana regime gives preferential treatment to bananas originating from ex-colonies belonging to the Lomé Convention and to EU producers. Caribbean producers are guaranteed a market for their products at a much higher price than would be the case in an open market. The WTO has ruled against the EC twice but the EC has been reluctant to comply fully, choosing instead to modify its regulations and let the WTO re-examine the case (WTO, 1997, 1998, 1999).

The dispute is about free access to the EC banana market. Restrictions on US imports practically guarantee a market for Caribbean bananas. However, the US fruit MNEs, together with Del Monte, form an oligopoly that controls 66 per cent of the world's supply of bananas. Moreover, US domestic production of bananas accounts for less than 0.02 per cent of the world total. Mostly produced in Hawaii and Puerto Rico, US grown bananas are destined for domestic consumption. The United States is clearly fighting the battle for US based MNEs whose productions sites are located in South and Central America.

Chiquita Brands has a long and controversial history in Latin America and has experienced problems drawing the lines of its involvement with national governance. When countries like Honduras and Guatemala faced civil unrest, the US government sent its navy to protect the company's interests. Similarly, in 1954, The United Fruit Company was involved in the United States' decision to overthrow the left-wing government of Guatemala. (Economist, Dec. 20, 1997; Adams, 1999.) More recently, Chiquita Brands, through its chairman, contributed more than $1 million to the Democratic Party. It also contributed heavily to the Republican Party, assuring itself allies in the US government.

Bananas: The legal issues

The EC's banana regime had created trade tensions for decades before it was disputed under GATT and eventually the WTO/GATT proceedings resulted in the First and Second Banana Panels. These rulings and diplomatic tensions pressured the EC to change the banana regime, but never to the extent that it could satisfy all the parties involved. The United States could not act until the Marrakesh Agreement of 1994 was agreed, as this established the General Agreement on Trade and Services (GATS), which opened an appeal to the WTO on bananas.

On February 5, 1996, the United States and four Latin American countries requested consultations with the EC. It was the beginning of a long dispute resolution process under the WTO, involving 40 member countries. The complainants argued that the EC's preferential treatment regime towards African, Caribbean and Pacific (ACP) countries was inconsistent with the GATT 1994, the Agreement on Import Licensing

Procedures, the Agreement on Agriculture, the GATS and the TRIMS Agreement.

In 1993, as a result of the single market measures, the EC had adopted Council Regulation 404/93 to replace a previous system in which all countries, with the exception of ACP countries, faced a 20 per cent ad valorem. The new regulation imposed tariffs and quotas for non ACP importers. This preferential system dated back to 1975 when the First Lomé Convention (previously called Yaoundé Convention) was signed. The convention is a trade and aid agreement and constitutes one of the largest development programmes of the EC. In 1989, the EC and 68 ACP countries signed the Fourth Lomé Convention, which, like its predecessors, contained a Banana Protocol. The Banana Protocol stated that 'no ACP State shall be placed, as regards access to its traditional markets and its advantages on those markets, in a less favourable situation than in the past or at present'. In December 1994, a waiver was granted allowing the EC to forego its obligations under GATT 'as required by the relevant provisions of the Fourth Lomé Convention' until February 29, 2000.

The United States and its Latin American partners disputed the legality of the new regulation and the interpretation of the Lomé waiver. Additionally, the distribution system allocated licensed rights to import and effectively guaranteed these rights to a handful of domestic distributors, such as Fyffes from Britain.

Europe is acting to protect one of its most important international development programmes but is also protecting the interests of domestic distributors through its licensing system. The system provides income to EC farmers and keeps quota rents in the EC. However, the net effect of the licensing system in the EC is uncertain and possibly negative. Not only are consumers faced with high prices, their administrative governments are burdened with a costly bureaucratic process.

The EC amended its banana regime as a result of the first and second panel findings but never fully complied. This prompted the United States to impose sanctions of $191.4m on nine products: lithographs (UK), batteries (UK), bath preparations (UK), handbags (France and Italy) and coffee and tea makers (Germany). At one stage Britain was targeted (as a key interest in the EU) and the Scottish cashmere industry was threatened. When Prime Minister Blair supported President Clinton in the Kosovo conflict with Serbia in spring 1999, the cashmere industry was promptly dropped from the US list.

Beef: The strategic issues

A dispute between the United States and the European Union over hormone-treated beef turned into a trade war when the EC failed to comply with the findings of the WTO's dispute settlement body. In 1996, the EC consolidated a series of regulations that prohibited the use of six hormones for growth promotion purposes, claiming that these were hazardous to human health. Two panels found against the EC. But, to date, no changes have been made to its regulations. EU citizens support the European Parliament in what appears to be a health and safety regulation.

Six hormones are under dispute: three natural (oestradiol-17ß, testosterone and progesterone) and three synthetic (zeranol, trenbolone and MGA); these mimic the natural hormones. They can be used to influence growth and gestation of cattle. Scientists agree that very large intakes of these hormones are carcinogenic, however, there is no conclusive proof that the small levels administered under WHO/FAO international standards pose any serious threat to human health. Scientists disagree on the effects of prolonged exposure to small doses. The lack of information available at this time and the level of scientific uncertainty allows the EC to defend its policy under the precautionary principle.

Whether the EC is motivated by health and safety concerns or is attempting to disguise a trade barrier is not clear. The EC common agricultural policy is a well known subsidy to farmers but it has not been challenged on a trade barrier; this makes other agricultural practices more vulnerable to actions. Prior to the EC beef regulation, there was a beef surplus in the EU that was discussed during proceedings to ban hormones beginning in the early 1980s. Yet there has been no significant change in total imports of beef products to the EU since the 1970s. Instead, imports shifted from hormone-treated beef to hormone-free beef. A large decline in US exports to the EU is mainly attributed to the country's reliance on growth promoting substances. Ninety per cent of US beef is hormone treated (FAO, 1999).

Beef: The legal issues

Proceedings under the WTO were subject to controversy. The first panel found that the EC had not followed a proper risk assessment and that it must change its regulations and allow imports of hormone treated beef. While the first and second panels found for the United States, the integrity of the first panel was called into question by the second panel. The good faith of the panel was questioned because testimony by scientists was purposely misquoted and misinterpreted by the panel. The second panel also overturned the finding that human error and negligence should not be considered when assessing risk. It allowed the EC a grace period to investigate further the effects of beef hormones on human health.

The EC produced a study of beef products that showed that US regulations on the use of hormones were frequently ignored by cattle ranchers. It also commented on the easy availability of these hormones. The EC did not change its regulations and the United States threatened to retaliate with US$202 million in tariffs. The EC argued that the United States was inflating the damage caused by the ban. In July 1999, arbitration by the WTO set the amount of damage to the US cattle industry at US$116.8 million.

Foreign Sales Corporations

The United States has appealed against a 1999 decision by the WTO that its foreign sales corporations tax scheme is an illegal export subsidy. Foreign sales corporations are offshore subsidiaries of large US corporation, mostly located in tax havens such as the US Virgin Islands, and in the former British colony of Barbados. They carry out export transactions of behalf of their parent corporation. Fifteen per cent of a foreign sales corporation's profits are exempted from corporate income tax by the United States, adding up to US$2 billion in tax relief. The EC challenged this on the grounds that the tax scheme was directly tied to exports and was therefore an export subsidy that provided an unfair advantage to US corporations.

Boeing, General Motors, Eastman Kodak, Microsoft and Caterpillar are just a few US corporations to benefit from the scheme. US affiliates of foreign corporations, such as Daimler-Chrysler, can also claim tax relief. They set up a skeleton company in a tax haven to fill the requirements for a foreign sales corporation. There are 3,600 corporations located in the US Virgin Islands and in Barbados with only a few dozen employees processing invoices.

Originally, for a foreign sales corporation to be able to claim tax exemptions on its profits, the goods had to be 50 per cent manufactured in the United States. This is still the case, but under a new clause in the Taxpayer Relief Act of 1997, software makers can ship master tapes overseas, make copies, and use their foreign sales corporations to receive a tax subsidy (Barlett and Steele, 1998). Movie makers already enjoyed these benefits. Ultimately, this clause creates jobs in overseas countries while increasing the net profit of US corporations.

Manufacturing industries are the largest sector benefiting from foreign sales corporations. Non-electrical machinery, chemicals, electrical machinery and transportation equipment accounted for a large part of total foreign sales corporations relief. Most industries, including manufacturing, must prove that goods funnelled through a foreign sales corporation have 50 per cent domestic content. Theoretically, this should increase the export performance and thus the international competitiveness of US made goods. Domestic content should increase, at least to some degree, the amount of manufacturing in the US economy.

Critics of the scheme in the United States call it a corporate welfare system paid at the expense of tax payers. Large MNEs reap most of the benefits. These are already well established exporters who would export anyway. It is argued that the tax relief puts US based corporations, who have the largest stake in foreign sales corporations, on a better footing than international competitors. It targets particular industries and is therefore vulnerable to GATT/WTO sanctions which can affect subsidies not generally available to all industries.

Whether or not exports increase as a direct result of tax relief, Boeing is several million dollars better off every year than it would be without a foreign sales corporation. This money can be used to expand R&D, marketing or to undertake large capital investments. US companies are thereby better prepared to fight in the international arena, and to protect their own market from exports. The foreign sales corporations also provides an incentive for foreign companies to set up affiliates in the United States by decreasing the amount of corporate taxes that they would have had to pay otherwise.

The Legal Issues

In 1997 the EC held consultations with the United States regarding foreign sales corporations. Mutual agreement was not reached and the EC requested a WTO panel. In 1999, the panel decided that foreign sales corporations were an export subsidy directly related to export performance. Foreign sales corporations were found to be inconsistent with the obligations of the United States to the WTO, and the GATT's agreement on agriculture. The panel recommended that the United States withdraw the foreign sales corporations subsidies by October 1 2000 (WTO, 1999).

The United States will appeal. If it loses the appeal, one alternative would be to withdraw the alleged subsidies from its key industries. Another option would be to keep the DISC scheme and accept EU retaliation, which could aggregate to as much as US$6 billion. This case will test the authority of the WTO and the consequences will be far reaching; the end of globalization and a new regionalism.

3

The new social actors are slowing globalization

The Role of NGOs

GLOBALIZATION is at an end. MNEs do not rule the world – despite their size and power, there is no uniform integrated world market. Instead, there are strong 'triad' blocks in which nation states still make the rules, imposing regulations such as environmental and health codes. The non-governmental organisations have challenged the MNEs; as witnessed by the defeat of the MAI. The new agenda of NGOs and governments is explained in the first half of this chapter. In the second, environmental protection is related to corporate strategy.

Internet Anarchy

Even before the Seattle WTO riots of December 1999, a widely reported example of the organizational capabilities of NGOs occurred on Friday 18 June 1999, when a mass demonstration disrupted the City of London. It was organized via an Internet site, J18, which co-ordinated the separate activities of groups of NGOs. The more radical of these received most of the media attention as the peaceful demonstration planned to coincide with the G7 Summit in Cologne turned into a full scale riot. The major targets were two McDonald's restaurants, which were trashed, and the London International Financial Futures (and Options) Exchange (LIFFE), which was invaded.

According to press reports, a handful of young radical extremists organized much of the demonstration, which attracted more than 2,000 people. A group called Reclaim the Streets (RTS) and a Cambridge chapter of People's Global Action (PGA) were prominent. These groups were able to promote the demonstration by using Internet sites to publish maps and details of London's financial institutions. On the day they provided leaders to incite groups to attack property and the police.

Radical groups such as these do not appear to differ in any marked manner from the student activist groups of the late 1960s, who organized sit-ins and demonstrations at leading universities from Berkeley to Columbia to LSE. If anything, the number of core activists appears to be far fewer. But today they can use Internet sites to gain worldwide attention. Previous generations of anarchists spread their ideas via the underground press and small circulation magazines and broadsheets; the current generation can tap into a potentially broader stream of support by using new technology.

One of the disadvantages of fast global communications via the Internet is that small activist groups can disseminate propaganda quickly and easily. The Internet has no quality control mechanism; junk sites and politically networked ones count equally with commercial and academic sites. There is no screening mechanism such as is provided by the mainstream media, where extremist views would find little space or airtime. The Internet taxes knowledge to subsidise anarchy. The anti-capitalist agenda is the same; only the communication medium has changed.

The Power of NGOs

The NGOs are new and powerful actors on the stage of international business. From 1997 to 1998, they assumed a more effective role than before, which led to the defeat of the OECD's multilateral agreement on investment. Canada's self-promoting Council of Canadians, chaired by economic nationalist Maude Barlow, was prominent in orchestrating the NGOs. In a clever campaign of misinformation and half truths, exhibited in the Clarke and Barlow propaganda booklet on the MAI (Clarke and Barlow, 1997), the Council filled the web sites of NGOs with anti-MAI hysteria which then influenced the media.

With the US and Canadian governments treating the MAI on a technical rather than political level, and ministers being poorly briefed by second-rate trade bureaucrats, there was little political will to counter the gross distortion offered by unelected and unaccountable NGOs. Business leaders were unwilling to speak out on the MAI's advantages, leaving its defence to a handful of industry association spokespeople. Finally, the academic world – with a few exceptions – had not researched the issue (this being especially true of economists who have no parallel theory of free trade to apply to liberalization of investment). Consequently, almost none were available or willing to debate the substantive issues of the MAI in public, while engaged in their full-time professional duties. The absence of informed government, business and academic commentary left the media open to the distorted propaganda of unrepresentative NGOs.

The NGOs' success in defeating the MAI built upon their less spectacular but consistent progress in capturing the environmental agenda of international organizations. The first notable success of environmental NGOs (entirely US and Canadian) occurred in the North American Free Trade Agreement when the first Clinton administration in 1993 made the mistake of inserting two side agreements, after NAFTA had been successfully negotiated over the 1990-1992 period by the Bush administration. These side agreements set up an environmental body, the Commission on Environmental Cooperation (CEC) (in Montreal) and a labour standards body (in Dallas).[1]

The UNCED Rio Earth Summit of 1993 was a jamboree for environmental NGOs, leading to an unbalanced agreement with sets of commitments which the governments concerned were unable to meet. Despite these lessons, the Kyoto Summit in December 1997 resulted in standards for reduction of greenhouse gas emissions that, again, most countries will not meet. Ratification of the Kyoto protocol is unlikely, since the United States, Canada, Japan and many other countries are unlikely to sign it – only the EU appears to have the political will. In Canada's case, this is due to its federal nature; the provinces have the power to control natural resources. So Alberta, the largest energy-producing province, will need to agree to implement Kyoto in order for the government of Canada to recognise the treaty.

Analysis of the NGOs' Role in the MAI

This brief description of recent events portrays a gulf between the environmental and self-serving agendas of NGOs and the economic reality of global business. What analysis can be used to explain this dichotomy? Two theories will be considered. First, there is a traditional division between the redistributional/equity concerns of NGOs and the economic/efficiency drivers of business. Political parties in the West have taken these dual concerns into account when formulating policies, allowing voters to decide which direction to follow. Recently, this has not worked, since NGOs are operating outside democratic political representation.

---

[1] For discussion of the political process in the United States at the time of approval of NAFTA see Susan Liebler in Rugman (1994).

For example, since failing to influence the Liberal Party of Canada (now the Canadian government), Maude Barlow has chaired the Council of Canadians which performs as a stand-alone political unit. In the 1993 federal election the Council supported the Economic Nationalist Party, led by Edmonton publisher Mel Hurtig. In that election, despite fielding a national slate of candidates, Hurtig's party secured less than one per cent of the total popular vote. Yet this complete rejection of the Economic Nationalist platform (including its opposition to NAFTA) was ignored by Maude Barlow's Council of Canadians, which has continued with a nationalist agenda, even though it is divorced from the party platforms of all Canada's major political parties. Most US and European NGOs have behaved in a similarly unrepresentative and politically unacceptable way. Whereas the labour movement and business groups are linked directly to political parties and so have their agendas voted upon in elections, most NGOs are scared to face the voters. Yet their unrepresentative views have a vastly disproportionate influence on the media.

Complementary to the undemocratic nature of NGOs, especially in their biased understanding of international trade and investment, is an intellectual failure of academic theory. The twin basic paradigms of economics and politics are found wanting as explanations of today's global economy and the nature of foreign direct investment. In economics, the traditional efficiency-based neoclassical paradigm (with its associated theory of comparative advantages and the overall country gains from free trade) is unsuitable as an explanation of FDI. Despite the efforts of international business writers over the last 30 years to develop a modern theory of the multinational enterprise, most economists are unable to take on board this explanation of the reasons for FDI (Rugman, 1996). Consequently, the GATT and WTO. have developed institutional frameworks to deal with the 'shallow' integration of tariff cuts, but have failed to deal with the 'deep' integration of FDI.

The political science focus on the nation state is related to the out-of-date economics paradigm of free trade. Despite minor modifications to nation state paradigms, such as incorporating subnational units in decision making, there is limited buy-in to the alternative International Political Economy (IPE) viewpoint first popularized by Susan Strange (1988). Indeed, there is another unfortunate parallel between economics and political science, in that both sets of work on the role and power of the MNE have failed to change the out-of-date thinking of the majority of academics. This is despite abundant evidence of the relevance of MNEs to today's global economic and political systems. The NGOs have slipped into this vacuum with their simplistic view of MNEs as big, bad and ugly. Based on prejudice rather than evidence, NGO thinking is now more influential with governments in North America and Europe than the more scientific (and thereby more qualified) work of serious academic scholars working on MNEs (Ostry, 1997).

The issue here is one of process. There is an 'administrative heritage' of ideas. Today's journalists and other communicators are poorly trained in economics, politics and international business. Those few who have any training are usually victims of the paradigms of traditional economics and political science, which cannot explain FDI and the MNEs. Business school MBAs, who are now exposed to the new thinking on MNEs, are in business rather than the media. Professional intermediaries, such as management consultants, focus on their business or government clients rather than the media and their skills of confidential advice and in-house retraining make them poor advocates compared with the pessimistic and opinionated NGOs. Finally, the civil service is totally useless in dealing publicly with NGOs, since the role of bureaucrats is to support and influence ministers, not enter the public forum. This institutional failure of academics, consultants and bureaucrats to prepare a credible case for the MAI and debate it publicly leaves the field open to NGOs.

Although the NGOs can be credited with the defeat of the MAI, the real reason for its delay lies elsewhere. Even given the high profile activities of NGOs in 1997 and 1998, the MAI would still probably have been concluded at the OECD if one country had got its act together. That country was, of course, the United States. The real explanation for the delay of the MAI is the right of the US Congress to pass trade laws and the corresponding lack of presidential power to negotiate international trade and investment treaties. The President's failure to obtain 'fast track' negotiating authority from Congress in autumn 1997 (for a free trade area of the Americas, but also for a future round of the WTO, and for an MAI) was the single most important reason for the MAI's failure. The NGOs then stepped into the vacuum and stole the agenda.

Trade and investment agreements have little hope of success, without the full commitment of the United States to champion them. This is demonstrated by the MAI process. All countries are lobbied by various producer groups to exempt certain sectors from national treatment (e.g. cultural industries for Canada and France). The full participation of the United States is vital to broker an international agreement, as it is still the only country powerful enough to pull along other countries rife with internal dissent and sectioned interests. Yet although President Clinton pushed through NAFTA in 1993, he has since been unable to assemble a coalition to follow any free trade and investment liberalization initiatives.

Local Lobbies: The Power of NGOs

The end of globalization was reinforced in the second half of the 1990s by the emergence of very effective non-governmental organizations. All these grew up locally and most remain nationally based. A few have become 'global' in the sense that they opened branch offices in major foreign cities, but the vast majority are embedded in the local cultures which sponsored them.

Canadian NGOs

I am most familiar with the NGOs based in Canada.[2] Their common characteristic is a vocal adherence to Canadian economic nationalism, which peaked in 1987-1988 when a large coalition of NGOs formed under the umbrella leadership of the Council of Canadians to oppose the Canada-US Free Trade Agreement, negotiated between the Reagan and Mulroney governments during 1986-1987. The NGO anti-free trade coalition was extremely effective in the federal election of November 1988. It influenced the policies of the two opposition parties, the Liberals (led by John Turner) and the New Democratic Party (led by Ed Broadbent). Although these two parties won 60 per cent of the vote, the Mulroney government was re-elected for a second term since the opposition vote was split.

In the week after this defeat the Council of Canadians launched a new attack on free trade, blaming the closure of the US Gillette Company's factory in Toronto on the passage of the Free Trade Agreement. It subsequently published a long list of job losses in Canada allegedly caused by the FTA (Barlow, 1990, Hurtig, 1991). While the list was basically

---

[2] For an analysis of the development of national environmental pressure groups in Britain since the mid 1980s see Peter Rawcliffe (1998). He studies the interaction between ENGOs and established political interest groups, using political and social theory. His interviews were conducted between 1992 and 1997 and include analysis of Greenpeace, Friends of the Earth, the World Wide Fund for Nature and Green Alliance. In a related work on the political context of ENGOs, Jordan and Maloney (1997) examine the internal organization of Friends of the Earth and Amnesty International. The focus of both books, as in this chapter, is on these types of campaigning groups rather than on the political platform of the Green Party, which is extremely influential in Europe and indeed a co-partner in the current German government. However, its role as a mainstream political party, by definition, takes it beyond our analysis of NGOs.

nonsense – it included jobs listed in sectors literally exempted from the provisions of the FTA (such as most service sectors including broadcasting, financial services, transportation) – it became a rallying point for NGOs to oppose globalization.

To a Canadian, global business means American business. Eighty per cent of Canada's trade is with the United States and over 40 per cent of Canadian manufacturing is US-owned. Throughout the 1990s the Council of Canadians, and its fellow travellers, engaged in a vicious and totally misinformed attack on 'globalization' and the FTA. These were blamed for the recession of 1989-1993 and all job losses, for the rise of the federal and provincial governments' deficits and for a perceived loss of Canadian sovereignty. Even the Quebec separatist movement was alleged to have been given a push by globalization, since its support for the FTA gave the Québécois a ready market in the United States, instead of with the rest of Canada. (A similar argument, that Blairite devolution is a slippery slope which could lead to the continental EU replacing England as Scotland's major economic partner, is put forward in Scotland.)

NGOs opposed globalization in other countries besides Canada. Environmental NGOs, in particular, became influential in setting a green agenda for the EC in the early 1990s, at the Rio Summit of 1993 and the Kyoto Summit of 1997 on global warming. Most of the environmental NGOs were North American-based, with strong sector groups in the UK, Scandinavia and Germany, but with little spread of environmental thinking to Asia, Africa, Eastern Europe and South America. In other words, environmentalism is a rich man's game. Canada as a rich country has a large array of NGOs and environmental NGOs. Their most significant triumph came in 1998 with the defeat of the Multilateral Agreement on Investment. (For more details of the MAI debate see Chapter 5 on 'The Political Economy of the MAI'.)

This Canadian-led defeat of the MAI was the first defeat of the business agenda of globalization by the social agenda of NGOs. The MAI would have set multilateral rules for foreign direct investment, albeit with most service sectors exempted from the key instrument of national treatment. The defeat of the MAI spells trouble for multilateralism and it helps to reinforce triad/regional blocs. Without the MAI the EU becomes more insular, with 'outsiders' from Asia and North America lacking basic rights of national treatment. Similarly, NAFTA locks in Canada and Mexico more tightly with the United States. Finally, Japan is left high and dry as the economic leader of Asia but with no legal rights of access for its FDI in other Asian countries.

The implications of this are bad news for NGOs. Their leaders tend to have an anti-business agenda, but they have misunderstood the true nature of international business. In reality, globalization is not the enemy. Multinational enterprises do not operate in global free markets, but in tightly regulated regional/triad markets. The NGOs have fallen into the trap of supporting regional protectionist movements. This really will cause job losses, as inefficient business will carry on with shelter and the economic benefits of the most efficient FDI for the local economy will be lost.

Kanter's Local NGOs

Support for this global/local dichotomy comes from basically any serious writer on international business issues. For example, the major business-local community project reported by Rosabeth Moss Kanter in 1995 demonstrated in great detail the tremendous economic advantages to the United States of inward FDI. Despite the xenophobic attitude towards FDI (especially Japanese, but usually not European or Canadian) in such books as Tolchin and Tolchin (1988), Kanter's data reveal that FDI can reinvigorate local US communities. She found that Cleveland (Ohio), Miami, Seattle, the Boston area, and parts of South Carolina had created jobs and raised incomes because of strong partnerships between local community leaders and business – including foreign business. Local US jurisdictions still set the rules for business – they can either scare it away, or attract it.

According to Kanter (1995) the cities that can bring the benefits of the global economy to the local community have one of three attributes:

a) concepts, leading to knowledge-based services, led by 'thinkers', as in Boston and Route 128
b) competence, leading to manufacturing-based skills, often with foreign-owned 'markets', as in South Carolina
c) connections, leading to international service centres, led by 'traders', as in Miami.

These classifications have a degree of superficiality but can help to explain certain other triad-based activities and locations. Examples are:

- Austin (Texas) and Oxford (England) as concept-thinkers' centres
- Hong Kong (China), Newcastle-upon-Tyne (England) and Italian villages near Turin as competence-based makers

- the City of London and Singapore as connections networks of financial traders.

In all the cases cited, the role of foreign triad-based investors is critical. These are all 'world class' cities where discrimination in favour of the home team is not feasible. However, triad neighbours find it easier to be insiders than do rival triad firms.

Throughout the first half of the 1990s most US cities followed the worldwide trend of throwing open the doors to FDI. By 1990 over 40 states had trade and investment offices in Tokyo, all trying to attract Japanese FDI to their local area. Partnerships between local communities and new businesses (often foreign) have blossomed throughout the triad regions of North America and Europe. In Asia, the national governments are less supportive and, as in the case of Malaysia in 1998, sometimes hostile to FDI. Even the Japanese government has been slow to update regulations which restrict foreign business, especially in local distribution. China is a special case, where access has to be negotiated project by project.

The Role of Oxfam

The role of charities in promoting world income redistribution to help alleviate poverty in developing nations has led to another set of NGOs becoming involved in the international political economy of the agenda of international institutions. For example, in a representative book, Michael Edwards (1999) presents an argument for a stronger government role in development policy. Edwards has worked for Oxfam, Save the Children and the World Bank. Based on his experience in international development efforts, he has rediscovered the need for a middle way in economic development – 'between heavy-handed intervention and complete laissez-faire' (p.vi). He is quite critical of today's global 'system', which fails to distribute growth and incomes on an egalitarian basis, especially in African and Asian countries. He states that globalization has costs as well as benefits. He advocates measures to 'humanise capitalism', but is not in favour of government planning. His solution is more effective international co-operation, based on a stakeholder model of capitalism. Agencies like Oxfam should 'spearhead a global movement for change' (p.231). This will provide, suggests Edwards, quicker and better responses to humanitarian emergencies and global poverty by the 'great powers' (p. 225).

I am not sure that Edwards' views are as balanced as he thinks. For example, he is critical of 'irresponsible lending' and states that 'the point of global governance is not to organize world affairs for the benefit of speculators, but to promote reforms that are in the common interest, and despite the claims of economists there is no guarantee that markets will do this better than governments' (p.170). This is followed by criticism of a multilateral agreement on investment, which has excluded poor countries, and the trade liberalizing efforts of the GATT and WTO, whose appellate procedures are criticized as mechanisms which 'accelerate the international transmission of inequality' (p.173). These are not middle of the road views, but the sadly misinformed views of left-of-centre community activists.

The significance of this to our theme of the end of globalization is simple. To flourish, globalization needs world free trade and no restrictions on foreign direct investment. In practice, these conditions have never been met, except within the major economic blocs of NAFTA, EU and Japan. The growing importance and political clout of NGOs has stopped the movement towards trade and investment liberalization dead in its tracks. The 1998 defeat of the MAI signals the end of globalization. A new round of the WTO is unlikely to succeed in developing sound rules for FDI. Political momentum has swung to the left, with quasi-socialist governments in Britain and Germany. Business leaders are keeping a low profile and working on 'stakeholder' capitalism alongside NGOs. The NGOs have seized the agenda, which has changed from an economic-business driven one to a social-redistributive-green one. The regional blocs are closing their doors. Multilateralism is dead. Local politics have become regional. This is the end of globalization.

Free Trade and Environmental Protection

As discussed in Rugman, Kirton and Soloway (1999), NGOs have been particularly successful in linking environmental regulations to trade issues. Such environmental regulations are complex, and changing. They prevent the open access to foreign markets that companies need to be competitive. Such regulations are particularly costly when set up to benefit powerful coalitions of competing protectionist industries, often allied with politically influential environmental groups.

Over the past decade the number of trade disputes arising from such environmental regulations and coalitions has increased sharply. The major reduction in national border barriers to trade due to NAFTA, the EU and the Uruguay Round of the GATT has increased the visibility, importance and protectionist impact of regulatory standards at the local, national and international level. At the same time, the increasing severity of, and public concern about, environmental degradation has led to many new and innovative regulations.

Recent environmental disputes: lessons from NAFTA

Conflict between trade and the environment is growing steadily throughout the world across a wide range of industries. The EU has denied market access to genetically modified maize produced in North America, a move that has jeopardized overall EU-US trade relations. It has also refused to accept hormone-treated beef from the United States and Canada since 1989, prompting acute controversy and disputes at the World Trade Organisation.

The US ban on Mexican tuna caught using a 'dolphin-unfriendly' process led to years of acrimony between Mexico and the United States. It was the subject of two GATT dispute settlement panels. Similarly, the US ban on shrimps caught using a 'turtle-unfriendly' process has been the subject of a dispute involving Malaysia, Thailand, Pakistan and India. The WTO has ruled against the ban. Disputes over discriminatory eco-labelling schemes imposed by Europe and North America on timber products from less developed nations have been so severe as to warrant separate international treaty negotiations.

Disputes have occurred at all levels of regulation (subnational, national and international) and affected many domestic and multinational companies. In the early 1990s, a dispute arose in the pulp and paper sector over a Californian regulation that imposed a minimum 50 per cent recycled fibre content on all newsprint. This had an adverse impact on newsprint producers in British Columbia, who depended heavily on California as an export market but were unable to obtain the requisite amount of recycled newsprint locally. They eventually overcame the regulatory barrier through changes in strategy.

In another dispute, in 1992, the province of Ontario imposed a CAN$0.10 per can recycling tax on all aluminium beer cans – 90 per cent of which came from the United States. This issue, part of a larger dispute between the United States and Canada over beer distribution, was eventually solved through bilateral negotiations.

It is clear from these cases – and many similar ones throughout the world – that environmental regulation can have a serious impact on business competitiveness.

Corporate responses

Companies facing such regulatory obstacles have traditionally had a limited number of corporate and political strategies at their disposal. At the corporate level they have had the option of adapting their products and production methods to meet the regulations, or of establishing overseas subsidiaries that can conform more readily. Politically, the options are to mobilize one's home government to help with litigation in a foreign trade law system, to hire lobbyists, or to form coalitions with foreign suppliers and customers to surmount the barrier.

Such strategies tend to be time-consuming and costly, and are often unsuccessful. This is especially the case for companies from smaller countries whose corporate fortunes depend upon sales in the triad markets of the United States, EU and Japan.

In recent years, however, managers have had the opportunity to pursue a new kind of political process. This has been made possible by the emergence of conditions of complex institutional responsiveness centred around strong international regimes for trade and environment. Companies can activate relatively neutral, rules-based mechanisms to challenge regulations that threaten legally guaranteed access to markets abroad. Managers can thereby resolve and even prevent disputes without expensive and lengthy litigation. Companies can participate in a process of harmonizing national regulations in ways that open the wider international market to everyone within a free trade area. They can form coalitions with other companies, environmental groups and government agencies to constrain the discriminatory impact of regulations or to create favourable regulatory regimes at a multilateral level.

Essentially, new trade and environment regimes open new strategic avenues to companies faced with the threat of environmental regulatory protectionism. Companies can mobilize international institutions in new and complex ways to achieve market access that would otherwise be denied. Such an approach can complement the basic corporate and simplistic political strategies of the past.

The process of complex institutional responsiveness is flourishing within North America. Large and medium-sized enterprises from Mexico, the United States and Canada are seeking access to the entire NAFTA marketplace. Their aim, in part, is to equip themselves for intensified global competition.

NAFTA came into force in January 1994. It is the world's most advanced international regime for balancing and integrating rules and procedures for trade liberalization and environmental protection. The core NAFTA trade agreement has created three innovative trilateral dispute settlement mechanisms to cover anti-dumping and countervailing duty disputes, general disputes and direct foreign investment disputes. Its accompanying North American Agreement on Environmental Co-operation (NAAEC) has created three surveillance and enforcement mechanisms to constrain national environmental regulatory activity that affects trade.

The 50 regional institutions created or empowered by these agreements are managing and preventing disputes. As a result, national environmental regulations are converging in ways that can redirect international trade. The regional institutions have created a process of complex institutional responsiveness in which companies can join with agencies at home and abroad to influence dispute settlement and management, regulatory convergence and environmental co-operation. Ultimately they can also influence national politics and market dynamics.

Managers must consider four practical issues:

- How should they respond to this complex array of international institutional arrangements to enhance market access? They need to use the NAFTA trade and environment institutions and participate in the process of making them work.
- When should they mobilise the regional NAFTA institutions, rather than market-based, national governmental or broader multilateral processes? Generally they need to use NAFTA-based institutions together with ongoing attempts to broaden their use in the multilateral setting of the WTO.
- When, how and in what combination should managers rely on NAFTA's mechanisms for dispute settlement, regulatory convergence, or regional co-operation and coalition-building? Only when other institutional mechanisms do not work should managers use their legal advisors to take advantage of NAFTA's investor-state dispute settlement mechanisms.
- How can their national governments best assist them in this process and accordingly shape the trade-environment regimes of the future? Managers need to help bureaucrats and politicians to develop a deeper understanding of corporate strategy.

Mechanisms for settling disputes

NAFTA has created an innovative system of legal and political mechanisms for managing environment-related trade disputes in ways that advance trade liberalization while respecting environmental values. At its heart are the Chapter 19 provisions for settling disputes over the national determination of anti-dumping and countervailing duties, and the Chapter 20 provisions to cover general disputes. Under Chapter 11, NAFTA has also established a novel set of rules and mechanisms for investment, a set that in many ways has served as a model in efforts to construct a multilateral agreement on investment. These establish the principle of national treatment, for foreign direct investment, but with certain sectors exempted, such as transportation, energy, telecommunications and the health, social and educational services.

NAFTA has also created 50 intergovernmental institutions that provide a permanent political system for dealing in advance with disputes, avoiding the need for formal litigation. One of these is the Automotive Standards Council (ASC) which has greatly improved voluntary industry environmental standards across the three countries. Others deal with agriculture and food issues, such as movement towards regulatory convergence in pesticides or with health, safety and product standards.

Alongside NAFTA came NAAEC. Its 'roving spotlight' provisions in Article 13 provide for secretariat-initiated investigation into matters of environmental concern throughout North America. Articles 14 and 15 additionally offer a process by which interested parties – companies, citizens and environmental groups – can petition directly for an investigation into a country's alleged non-enforcement of its environmental laws. And in Part 5, NAAEC gives the United States and Mexico the right to impose trade sanctions on each other, to punish systematic non-enforcement of government environmental regulations.

The NAFTA system for managing environment-related trade disputes is a marked improvement on the mechanisms available during the previous 15 years. Previously the domestic legal regimes of the three countries did not address these trade and environment issues. Since NAFTA began on 1 January 1994, it has diminished the number and severity of disputes, notwithstanding the newly opened borders and a new regulatory system in Mexico. It has enabled the companies and governments of North America to avoid the cumbersome and antagonistic process of the GATT/WTO and to find superior solutions for themselves. It has also adequately addressed not only the familiar environment-related trade disputes but also the new generation of associated conflicts arising from trans-border investment.

Canadian and Mexican firms are the major beneficiaries of NAFTA, as they have improved, more secure, access to the large US market. NAFTA's trade and environmental regulations help to reduce political uncertainty and make long-term investment decisions to operate across national borders less risky.

New environmental strategies

Companies are now doing business under conditions of complex institutional responsiveness. In this world, environmental regulations are urged on and adopted by governments, companies are becoming more international and integrated in their production, and international institutions – notably those of NAFTA – are emerging to manage the interaction between regulation and international business.

These new conditions have made life more challenging for even the largest organizations seeking to do business across international boundaries. Environmental regulatory protection is more frequent, widespread, entrenched, complex and costly than ever. But at the same time, these new conditions of complex institutional responsiveness offer strategies for companies wishing to improve competitiveness by reducing the costs created by shelter-seeking competitors, environmental groups and governments.

Before and after the advent of NAFTA, companies in general have followed their basic generic strategies of cost minimization, differentiation or nicheing. They have enjoyed only limited success with such traditional strategies as exemptionalism, 'pay and expand' and altered production. But now some companies are moving to produce to the standards of the major export market and, under the guarantees of NAFTA's Chapter 11, switching from exporting to foreign direct investment. They are also moving, in tandem with NAFTA's dispute settlement processes, to use an alternative strategy of private sector market sharing.

Companies are also employing a wide range of political strategies in response to environmental regulation. The use of traditional instruments has increased. These include:

- litigation in the home country or the regulating foreign country
- lobbying in both countries
- creating broad coalitions
- bilateral diplomatic intervention by the home government
- subsidy by the home government
- reciprocal retaliation
- above all, convergent national adjustment. However, by far the most striking development has been the use of NAFTA's dispute settlement mechanisms and institutions.

A recent review of 83 cases of environmental regulatory protection revealed a sharp increase in the use of international institutions, especially those at the regional level and those created or catalysed by NAFTA. To date, of the total of 59 NAFTA environmentally related trade cases resolved, 24 involve agricultural inspection; ten involve automobile emissions and fuels; ten involve farm and forestry conservation; four cover recycling; five cover dangerous goods transportation; four are environmental waste with the remaining two being for asbestos and trucking.

The innovative Chapter 11 dispute settlement mechanism for investment has been heavily used, and dispute management and prevention through other NAFTA institutions have risen sharply. Their operation during the agreement's first five years has led to regulatory convergence through negotiated, rules-governed mutual adjustment, the formation of transnational coalitions, the creation of regional coalitions for multilateral standards-setting, and private sector standardization. Selective use of the most appropriate political and corporate strategies, new and old, has benefited all companies – domestic producers competing with imports, home-based exporters, home-based multinationals, and transnational enterprises.

Public benefits

While the United States is the largest beneficiary of NAFTA, Canada and Mexico prevail to a greater degree than their relative size would suggest. And in many dispute settlement cases, all three countries benefit. Canada and Mexico tend to succeed in sectors where they have relatively large industries, such as forestry and agriculture respectively. The United States' automotive sector seems to have done particularly well out of NAFTA, reflecting its market dominance and scientific capability, but consumers have gained through trade liberalization and environmental improvement. NAFTA has set in progress a system to transfer the benefits of the 'California-effect' of tight automobile emission controls and high standards across the other countries, thereby helping consumers and the environment.

In cases of internationally initiated environmental protection, the ecological vulnerability of the United States to its North American neighbours and the presence of a robust regional institution – the Commission for Environmental Co-operation – have led to an almost perfect equality of outcome. The Canadians and Mexicans have won twice as many cases as the Americans, despite the relatively greater size of the

United States economy. Taken together, the NAFTA institutions and rules are creating a new North American community in which companies and other stakeholders have direct access to international regulatory institutions in such a way that their interests and identities are merging.

Notwithstanding this impressive achievement, there are several ways in which North American companies and governments can continue to build their community. Managers can use their NAFTA instruments to develop further, through cross-border alliances and other means, the fully integrated production platforms they need to succeed in the global marketplace. They can also shape the global rules to reward the distinctive interests and values that flourish in North America. The pathbreaking trade and environmental mechanisms of NAFTA were used as a successful model for the November 1999 Seattle round of the WTO.

Policymakers can further strengthen NAFTA's trade institutions and the processes of trilateralism by creating trilateral institutional capacity in rapidly changing sectors such as energy. They can enhance the scientific capabilities, industry involvement and financial capacity of NAFTA's institutions. Finally, policymakers can broaden NAFTA by including the other free trade partners of the United States, Canada and Mexico.

Conclusions

Trade and environment disputes are a global problem but are resolved regionally, as in NAFTA, which offers general lessons, applicable well beyond North America. Smaller countries around the world are increasingly dependent on access to the large, rich triad markets in order to sustain global competitiveness.

The challenge of overcoming environmental regulatory protectionism has long been a defining feature of business in North America. Canada has depended on access to the US market – which is ten times larger – for its prosperity. This dynamic has intensified with the advent of regional free trade agreements, such as NAFTA, which embrace smaller partners such as Mexico.

Challenges like this appear in regional free trade agreements throughout the world. Within the EU, even large, export-orientated countries, such as the UK and Germany, have come to rely on access to the whole European marketplace to build the global scale they require. Rapidly developing countries, such as Greece and Spain, have also realized that this is essential to growth. In Asia, access to the Japanese market has long been critical to the success of the export-orientated 'tiger' economies, while Japan's own prosperity is coming to depend on access to the full North American and Asian market. Even the United States, with a largely closed domestic economy and one-third of its trade with North American partners, is increasingly dependent on access to Europe and Asia.

Pronounced trade liberalization and proliferating environmental regulation in an era of rampant globalization have rendered even the largest firms from the largest economies relatively vulnerable. They must now identify innovative strategies to deal with the regulations that keep them from the foreign markets they need. And a good place to start looking would be among the many companies that have flourished under NAFTA.

4

Politics, Healthcare and Ethics

The Regional Economies

THIS chapter's central theme is the decline of the nation state as the relevant unit of analysis for managerial decision making. Even until the early 1990s the nation state dominated the regulatory focus facing MNEs. But, today, the managers of the MNEs operate in regionally-based city states. As Ohmae (1996) has argued, these regional states are more closely linked to each other than to their home or host nations. Today MNEs are not centrally controlled, nor are they fully decentralized. Instead, they are complex mixtures of organizational structures in which pressures of economic globalization are consistently offset by the need for national responsiveness on a regional basis.

The dominant sub-national economic regions are in areas like the Boston-New York-Philadelphia-Washington DC corridor, or in Silicon Valley, while international clusters occur in the Detroit-Windsor-Toronto horseshoe (where the border does not matter for the automobile industry, and has not since the auto-pact of 1965). In Japan, the Tokyo-Osaka-Keio region is the focus of most economic activity, as are the Hong Kong-Ghondong and other coastal city areas of China.

Within states there is a lack of uniform development. In the UK, the South East (around London), has been the hub of growth for the last 20 years, as supported by all economic indications from real estate prices to average personal incomes.

Service Sector Jobs

As the service sector increases its dominance of economic activity the borders of the nation state become less rigid. The information technology revolution and the growing commercial use of the Internet make it difficult for national booksellers and publishers in Canada to restrict entry of published books by Amazon.com. Financial capital and international stock markets make financing available more widely to small and emerging businesses. Industrial consumers can use faster and cheaper transportation to move around the world to their favoured city states. Academics owe more allegiance to their professional guild than to the institutions which pay and tenure them. Research for conference papers and publications in international journals brings more prestige and greater rewards than commentary in the local media, or in teaching. Most MBA students look for jobs in investment banking and consulting rather than positions in the old machine bureaucracies of the private and public sectors.

Both the academics and the MBAs are highly mobile internationally, limited only by language, local pay and family obligations. In contrast, unqualified and untrained workers are highly immobile and are generally in lower paid positions on the periphery of the fast growing regional service economies.

Service sector professionals like academics, bankers, consultants and lawyers are the new aristocracy of business. They are the group of 'symbolic analysts' in the phrase of Robert Reich (1991), able to use their personal computers to assemble and analyze relevant data to solve problems. Their intelligence and skill is highly rewarded and is not location bound.

In contrast, untrained workers are immobile, stuck in dead-end service support 'McJobs', or in clerical positions, or in poorly paid public sector jobs as social workers, union leaders and teachers.

Highly skilled engineers and computer specialists are like the symbolic analysts – mobile and sought after. But unskilled factory workers are being replaced by robots on the assembly line and by computers in the service sector.

The farmer is often a prisoner of nation state subsidies and protectionism, such as the EU Common Agriculture Policy. The farmer no longer runs a farm but a subsidized franchise awarded by the local agricultural bureaucracy. Most farmers make no profits and only exist due to subsidies. They are a dying breed.

Britain today, for example, is a service economy. The City of London is the engine of the British economy. Young MBAs in banks have replaced miners, weavers and farmers. They are part of a trend which serves to replace the nation state with the triad region as the unit of analysis. There is no pure globalization, as triad barriers to trade and investment liberalization restrict full worldwide economic integration.

Globalization and Global Governance: Strange Views

A central tenet of globalization's left-wing critics (such as Susan Strange, 1986, 1998) is that the international financial markets are unregulated.

This, they believe, leads to a form of 'casino capitalism'; Strange (1998) argues that world financial markets have gone 'mad' as they are a casino beyond governmental control. Unregulated world financial markets are highly volatile; she argues that this influences the creation of new regulations and/or the replacement of out-of-date ones. Innovations in financial markets can also lead to the creation of new regulations. Strange concludes that the lack of a world regulatory body means the collapse of global financial capitalism is imminent. She states that the emerging strategy of the central banker's bank, the Bank of International Settlements (BIS) is to provide technical advice and let the bankers regulate themselves. The International Monetary Fund (IMF) places more emphasis on arranging intergovernmental cooperation. If the BIS and IMF are not effective regulatory bodies (and neither are the World Bank, WTO or any other international institution dealing with various aspects of trade and investment policy), then there is no realistic international institutional response to the perceived problems of volatility and deregulation of the world's financial system. Strange has identified a problem which is apparently insoluble.

Yet this type of work gives us only a partial view. For example, Strange (1998) equates financial market-based casino capitalism with globalization. Yet virtually all economic and management writers state that globalization is due to the activities of multinational enterprises undertaking foreign direct investment, in which equity control is exercised over the operations of foreign-owned subsidiaries. The data show that FDI is extremely stable and the major fuel for world economic development. Above all, it is not subject to speculation by hedge funds and is subject to the performance-based competitive discipline of MNEs. In contrast, financial capital is much more volatile, subject to speculation, and unregulated. To have managed to confuse FDI with financial capital shows a remarkable misreading by Strange of the literature of economics and management. If it is accepted that globalization is actually a result of FDI by MNEs, and that the data indicate that FDI is much more stable than financial capital flows, her basic argument is flawed.

Leaving this aside, I do agree with Strange that there is no effective world government or 'regime'. Instead, I would note that there are strong regional 'regimes'. My central theme is that globalization is really the triad-based activity of MNEs. In turn, strong regional governance is available. Susan Strange agrees with part of my regional thesis but her lack of understanding of the triad-based nature of FDI misleads her into a false conclusion about the lack of governance structures. These do exist, but at the regional rather than global level. Strange argues that both Japan and the United States 'are more international and engaged in their respective regional relations . . . than they are in global governance' (1998, p.54). She states that global governance is impossible since 'these days, no single hegemonic leader is strong enough or rich enough to fill the role unaided' (1998, p.55). My triad focus shows that the United States, Japan and the European Union are all preoccupied with a regional rather than a multilateral political agenda. Such regional regulatory agendas spell the end of globalization.

The United States saw its best success in a 1993 trade and investment treaty when President Clinton got Congress to approve NAFTA on the 'fast track' (i.e. with no amendments to the negotiated treaty). Since then, Congress has not authorized fast track authority for the President, so multilateral agreements, as in a new round for the WTO, have not proceeded. When the peso crisis of 1994 hit, the United States did respond quickly on a regional basis, as should Japan for an Asian crisis, or Germany for a European one. One of the problems with sovereign debt is that a country (like Mexico in 1982 and 1994) cannot be declared bankrupt by any credible multilateral or regional regime. Thus creditor nations (principally the United States) need to arrange bailouts. In 1982 the banks suffered; in 1994 the insurance and pension funds were at risk but were saved by the Clinton package of US$42 billion. Strange (1998) says that NAFTA was at risk but, in reality, it dealt with FDI and tariffs and its structure was unaffected by the Mexican financial crisis of 1994.

In Japan, the 1990s recession and underlying economic problems associated with potential insolvency of the banking system have turned political attention inwards. The outward Japanese FDI of the 1980s has been replaced by retrenchment and a continued movement of production and assembly to cheaper South East Asian neighbours. The result has been a depreciation of the yen (especially against the US dollar and European currencies) in the mid-1990s. Japan has been forced to pull in its horns.

In the EU the Brussels bureaucracy has been preoccupied by the launch of the single market for the euro in January 1999 and the move towards the common currency. In essence, the euro is an extension of French-German economic diplomacy and it will take until 2003 to make it work. Until then expect a lot of volatility and speculation.

In all three regions, the key political problems are domestic/regional rather than global/multilateral. In all three, inward-looking protectionist forces are becoming more powerful, further reducing the chance of global free markets and investment liberalization. In the language of political scientists there is no global hegemony. Between 1830 and 1930 Britain served as a hegemony, promoting world financial stability by being a lender of last resort. In the 1950-1980 period the United States provided hegemonic stability (Kindleberger, 1970). Japan might have taken on the role in the 1980s but failed, so today there is no single leader. Perhaps a coalition of these three countries could, at times of grave financial crisis (such as the Mexican peso devaluation of 1994 or the Asian crisis of 1997/98), form a temporary coalition to react to problems. The G7 has achieved some success, but it is a reactive group, not an effective institution. It seems very unlikely that a coalition could be formed to promote globalization.

The power of domestic politics and regulations to set an international agenda was earlier noticed in the development of the Eurocurrency market. Building on Dufey and Giddy's (1978) pioneering analysis of the Eurocurrency market, Chapter 5 of Rugman (1981) argued that the rapid growth and expansion of this market in the 1970s was due primarily to excessive regulations in the domestic US financial markets. Regulation Q, for example, limited interest payments on US deposits, whereas the same currency deposits in the City of London could earn higher interest rates. The 'spread' was also narrower in the unregulated Euromarkets as they operated more efficiently than the regulated domestic US markets. These US regulations led to the growth of offshore financial markets. Presumably, their removal is a better alternative than attempts at global governance of the world financial markets.

So it seems that all the elements of Susan Strange's thesis are incorrect:

- FDI matters, not financial flows
- FDI is not as volatile as financial flows
- globalization is regional not global
- there is no world government, but there are effective regional 'regimes'.

Giddens (1999), like Strange (1998), states that the driver behind globalization is the vast amount of financial capital flows in the foreign exchange markets. Yet the huge daily volume of financial transactions is today not significantly different (in relative terms) from the heyday of the Eurocurrency markets a quarter of a century ago. There has not been a 'massive increase from only the late 1980s', as Giddens argues. Dufey and Giddy (1978), using data for the 1970s, found that the value of transactions on foreign exchange markets was in the trillions of US dollars, on a daily basis, just as Giddens and Strange argue is the case today.

Table 4.1:
The top 100 Economies and MNEs, 1998

Rank	Country/Company	US$ billions	Rank	Country/Company	US$ billions
1	United States	7,921.3	51	Venezuela	81.3
2	Japan	4,089.9	52	Malaysia	79.8
3	Germany	2,122.7	53	Egypt	79.2
4	France	1,466.2	54	Philippines	78.9
5	United Kingdom	1,263.8	55	**AXA**	**78.7**
6	Italy	1,166.2	56	**Citigroup**	**76.4**
7	China	928.9	57	**Volkswagen**	**76.3**
8	Brazil	758.0	58	**Nippon Telegraph & Telephone**	**76.1**
9	Canada	612.2	59	**Nippon Life Insurance**	**76.1**
10	Spain	553.7	60	Chile	71.3
11	India	421.3	61	**BP Amoco**	**68.3**
12	Netherlands	388.7	62	**Nissho Iwai**	**67.7**
13	Mexico	380.9	63	Ireland	67.5
14	Australia	380.6	64	**Siemens**	**66.0**
15	Korea, Rep. of	369.9	65	**Allianz**	**64.8**
16	Russia	337.9	66	Pakistan	63.2
17	Argentina	324.1	67	**Hitachi**	**62.4**
18	Switzerland	284.8	68	Peru	61.1
19	Belgium	259.0	69	**U.S. Postal Service**	**60.1**
20	Sweden	226.9	70	**Matsushita Electric Industrial**	**59.8**
21	Austria	217.2	71	**Nestlé**	**59.5**
22	Turkey	200.5	72	**Credit Suisse**	**59.1**
23	Denmark	176.4	73	**Philip Morris**	**57.8**
24	**General Motors**	**161.3**	74	**ING Group**	**56.5**
25	Hong Kong	158.3	75	**Boeing**	**56.2**
26	DaimlerChrysler	154.6	76	New Zealand	55.8
27	Norway	152.1	77	**AT&T**	**53.6**
28	Poland	150.8	78	**Sony**	**53.2**
29	**Ford Motor**	**144.4**	79	**Metro**	**52.1**
30	**Wal-Mart Stores**	**139.2**	80	Czech Republic	51.8
31	Indonesia	138.5	81	**Nissan Motor**	**51.5**
32	Thailand	134.4	82	**Bank of America Corp**	**51.5**
33	Finland	124.3	83	**Fiat**	**51.0**
34	Greece	122.9	84	**Honda Motor**	**48.7**
35	South Africa	119.0	85	**Assicurazioni Generali**	**48.4**
36	Iran	109.6	86	**Mobil**	**47.7**
37	**Mitsui**	**109.4**	87	**Hewlett Packard**	**47.1**
38	**Itochu**	**108.7**	88	Algeria	46.5
39	**Mitsubishi**	**107.2**	89	Hungary	45.6
40	Portugal	106.4	90	**Deutsche Bank**	**45.2**
41	Colombia	106.1	91	**Unilever**	**44.9**
42	**Exxon**	**100.7**	92	**State Farm Insurance**	**44.6**
43	**General Electric**	**100.5**	93	**Dai-Ichi Mutual Life Insurance**	**44.5**
44	**Toyota Motor**	**99.7**	94	Bangladesh	44.0
45	Israel	95.2	95	**Veba Group**	**43.5**
46	Singapore	95.1	96	**HSBC Holdings**	**43.3**
47	**Royal Dutch/Shell Group**	**93.7**	97	Ukraine	42.7
48	**Marubeni**	**93.6**	98	**Toshiba**	**41.5**
49	**Sumitomo**	**89.0**	99	**Renault**	**41.4**
50	**Int. Business Machines**	**81.7**	100	**Sears Roebuck**	**41.3**

Sources: Adapted from World Bank, *World Development Report*, 1999/2000 (New York: Oxford University Press, 1999) and Fortune, 'The Fortune Global 500' August 2, 1999.

The data that Giddens and Strange use on financial market integration are correct, but this is not a new development. If, on their own terms, vast financial flows have been around for 25 years, why has the nation state has not already collapsed? Why will its power now, in their so called new era of globalization, suddenly be eroded?

In reality, the world financial markets are not the cause of globalization. As stated in Chapter 1 of this book, and demonstrated empirically in Chapters 7 and 8, it is the extent of trade and FDI by triad-based MNE which lies behind regional/triad integration. Financial transactions have been, on a daily basis, greater than the foreign exchange reserves at central banks for at least the last 25 years. There have been financial crisis before the 1998 Asian one, and the world economy has always recovered, partly because triad-based governments have been able to organize loans and other forms of financial redistribution. The lesson of the Asian financial crisis is not that globalization caused it, but that triad-led governments (principally the United States) saved the region from collapse.

The size of MNEs

A conventional indicator of the enormous size, economic power and implied political influence of MNEs is to rank the world's largest MNEs alongside the world's largest countries. This is reported in Table 4.1.

The ranking of countries is done in decreasing order of size of gross national product, with the US economy being the world's largest and a total of 23 countries being ranked ahead of the world's largest MNE, General Motors, which is ranked by size of sales. It is then apparent that there are nine MNEs with sales of over US$ 100 billion.

Yet, a more sober assessment of this table does not support the presumption that MNEs are powerful. The largest one, General Motors, has sales of US$ 161 billion, which is only a very small percentage of the size of the US economy at US$ 7,921 billion and Japan at US$ 4,090 billion. Also note that the EU is now even larger than the United States but that the table still reports the individual members of the EU. Even so, 11 of the 15 member countries of the EU are larger than General Motors. In turn, General Motors is over twice as large as the fifty-fifth ranked entry, insurance company AXA, which has sales of US$ 79 billion. Only 11 MNEs appear in the top 50 of the list. There are 39 MNEs in the lower 50 of the list.

Thus this table serves to reinforce the main theme of this book, namely the overwhelming economic power of the triad. The triad economies are gigantic compared to even the very largest MNEs. In turn, all of the 50 MNEs in the table are from the triad. Therefore, the table really shows the power of the northern triad and the lack of power of economies and firms from the 'south'. I shall discuss the issue of economic development and the role of MNEs later in this chapter.

A Framework for Analysis of Globalization and Sovereignty

In order to reinforce the main theme of this book, namely that manufacturing and international production are mainly triad-based (not global), it is useful to consider service sectors. Virtually all service sectors are now more regionally (or nationally) based than manufacturing. Basically, the delivery of education, social sciences, public administration, healthcare and culture is almost entirely local. Even the 'global' service sectors, such as airlines, telecom and banking are strongly regulated by national governments, thereby erecting barriers to globalization. As an example of a highly regulated, protected and locally-delivered service sector, let us consider healthcare.

One way of analysing globalization and health issues is to consider the dynamic interaction of two key sets of factors. The first is labelled 'globalization' and the second 'sovereignty'. This produces a 2 x 2 matrix as in Figure 4.1.

The globalization factors would include efficiency-based issues of the economies of scale in worldwide production and sourcing, the ability to use brand names and patents across national borders (as in pharmaceutical MNEs), and the managerial skills of finding new market niches for products and services. The issue of regional/triad governance will be ignored for now by assuming that MNEs operate regionally in the same manner as they would globally.

The sovereignty factors would include equity/distribution issues, where the main political instrument is regulation of health care by national authorities. In some federal systems, such as Canada, regulatory implementation is at subnational level (the provinces of Canada), although national Acts of Parliament establish programmes such as Medicare.

The matrix of globalization and sovereignty issues yields four possibilities:

FIGURE 4.1:

A FRAMEWORK FOR GLOBALIZATION AND SOVEREIGNTY

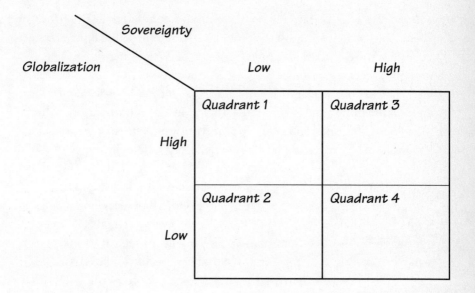

1 High globalization and low sovereignty: a situation where global market forces predominate and privatization of health care may be desirable
2 Low globalization and low sovereignty: a situation which ignores the realities of today's interdependent economic system and probably assumes health care to be entirely local
3 High globalization and high sovereignty; this is today's complex situation
4. Low globalization and high sovereignty: the historical situation in the UK where regulations (in the form of the National Health Service) have operated in the past independently of any global economic forces.

What does globalization mean?

Another area of confusion in the debate about globalization occurs in terms of the vertical axis of Figure 4.1 Some people do not see the merit of defining globalization in terms of the behaviour of firms (which is what occurs in Figure 4.1) instead of the behaviour of markets or, for that matter, of governments.

The following is a set of comments from one of my executive students, as a reaction to the matrix. This is followed by my reply.

'Globalization is a relatively new word to describe a process that has been going on for centuries: the process is the relentless breaking down of geographic boundaries or limits to markets. What's new is the word, not the process. The process arises, not because of the behaviour of firms per se, but because of other factors such as improvements in communications and transport, the flow of information, the movement of people, and changes to institutions defined or created by governments (particularly legal and regulatory systems).

To illustrate this point, consider the market for capital, (ie savings). The global capital market has existed for hundreds of years, and indeed existed long before firms as we know them today, or banks or even central banks. It has become a more global market over the years, and a much more efficient market at that, and firms have played a more important role in facilitating the flow of savings across the globe in recent years. But firms didn't create the global market. Firms have responded to changes in the market.

Globalization is a very important phenomenon. But, if our interest is in understanding what the strategic issues are for firms competing in global markets, then in my opinion the vertical axis in the matrix should refer to conditions in markets, and in particular should be capturing those changes which are either breaking down the geographic limits to markets, or are imposing geographic limits. Firms are not exogenous to the model. These changes are what create the opportunities or the threats for firms operating in global markets or seeking to enter global markets.

I suggest that sector three is not stable. It cannot possibly be stable because the dimensions of the matrix are interdependent, not independent. There is a complex interaction between the forces encouraging globalization and the political responses to those forces. Even under your definition of globalization this is so. As a consequence the matrix is inherently unstable.

Again, the market for capital illustrates this point. In 1983 the prospect of a change of government in Australia led to an unprecedented outflow of capital in just three days. The newly elected government immediately devalued the currency and the funds returned. Over the next eight months the government sought to manage a flexible peg exchange rate regime but the flow of capital in and out of the country became increasingly volatile. Eventually the government abandoned its exchange rate policy because in reality it had lost the capacity to set an exchange rate. In terms of your matrix, changes in the x-axis dimension (an upward move) led to changes in the y-axis dimension (a move to the left), which in turn prompted further moves in the x-axis dimension (an upward movement), which was followed by further changes in government policy (further moves to the left). That decision to move to a floating exchange rate precipitated an unprecedented wave of deregulation and facilitated further integration of Australian markets into wider global markets, providing both opportunities and threats to firms in these arenas. Wherever the market may have been in March 1983, it ended up much closer to segment one than it had ever been before, and it has continued to evolve in this direction ever since.

If the matrix is unstable, what is the point of asking which management structure suits sector three? The trend in the markets (are you moving towards sector one or sector four?) is a much more critical issue, as is the rate of change (how quickly are markets moving in that direction?). Whether or not the trend is likely to be reversed is also a relevant question (has there been any example where the trend has not been to move towards sector one?). When you understand these issues you can ask other questions such as whether your current management structure suits the evolving market, whether it can be adapted if it does not, what should the new structure be and what is the cost of not adapting? These are all important strategic management issues for firms in global markets.'

This is my response:

1 The vertical axis is clearly defined as 'economic integration'. This is fostered by MNEs. There is a vast literature in the field of international business to support this, plus data.
2 There is no global goods market; rather there are segmented markets. Government policy segments markets; firms react to these exogenous barriers to business. Again, a vast literature on internalization theory

supports this. Thus we have the horizontal axis of political sovereignty as exogenous to MNEs.

3 The matrix is robust: vertical axis is economics-driven and endogenous to MNEs; horizontal axis is exogenous to MNEs but determined by governments. This is a 'model' based on these premises. To refute it you need to present overwhelming evidence that the drivers of the axis are reversed, e.g. that governments determine economic globalization and that firms segment national borders – a position with which neither of us would agree.

4 Your example of the capital market is interesting but does not refute the model; rather it is nicely explained by it. The capital market you show is basically in Quadrant 1. It is there as government policy is responsive to capital flight, not a cause of it, and as Australia has a high degree of economic integration with the rest of the world.

5 On an industry/sector/firm basis the matrix is robust. It helps analyze the strategies and structure of MNEs, and why Quadrant 3 looks appealing from a strategic management perspective, but is difficult to achieve.

Globalization and healthcare

Most of the literature on the globalization of health, as summarized by Kelley Lee (1998, 1999) makes the correct point that there is movement up the vertical axis of Figure 4.1. Yet even the discussion of the faster spread of diseases due to increased travel and mobility, or the faster dissemination of health education through global communications, is not just about the vertical axis. In both these cases the horizontal axis has strong regulatory effects. For example, the transport sector is certainly not global but subject to intense domestic regulation, as is the telecommunication sector. In fact, both these sectors were exempted from the principle of national treatment in NAFTA (Rugman, 1994), and the draft OECD multilateral agreement on investment (Rugman, 1999). These issues, even as they apply to health, are in Quadrant 3 rather than Quadrant 1.

Fourteen MNEs in the pharmaceutical sector are listed in the Fortune 500, as shown in Table 4.2. These giant MNEs compete with each other for world market shares, spending huge amounts on R&D in order to develop new winning drugs. These winners are then protected by patents, but the value of the patents is eroded by legislation which allows manufacture by generic drug producers after a number of years. The host country's generic drug producers usually pressurize their governments to open up successful drugs more quickly. This domestic producer interest is often tied into the

Table 4.2: World's largest pharmaceutical companies as ranked by revenues (1999) (millions of dollars)

1999 rank	Firm	Revenues	Profits	Rank by profits	Share of foreign in total assets (%)	Country
100	Merck	32,714.90	5,890.50	15	24	United States
126	Johnson & Johnson	27,471.00	4,167.00	29	34	United States
192	Novartis	21,608.90	4,432.30	26	40	Switzerland
206	Bristol-Myers Squibb	20,222.00	4,167.00	29	46	United States
237	Astrazeneca	18,445.00	1,143.00	163	75	Britain
239	Roche Group	18,348.80	3,836.60	36	90	Switzerland
285	Pfizer	16,204.00	3,179.00	49	49	United States
349	Glaxo Wellcome	13,738.00	2,930.40	56	43	Britain
356	SmithKline Beecham	13,561.60	1,703.90	110	65	Britain
358	American Home Products	13,550.20	(1,227.10)	490	32	United States
362	Aventis	13,438.00	(1,034.70)	489	79	France
372	Abbott Laboratories	13,177.60	2,445.80	75	15	United States
381	Warner-Lambert	12,928.90	1,733.20	108	45	United States
485	Eli Lilly	10,002.90	2,721.00	62	26	United States

Source: Fortune Global 500, *Fortune Magazine*, 3 August 1998

Note: Hoechst Marion Roussel does not appear in the table although it is a wholly owned subsidiary of Hoechst that specializes in pharmaceuticals. It was formed in 1995 and became a wholly owned subsidiary of Hoechst in 1997. Hoechst is not counted as a pharmaceutical company because HMR only has $7.7 billion in revenues while Hoechst itself has $30 billion in revenues (i.e. only 26% of Hoechst's business is in pharmaceuticals).

interests of local consumers in levying lower prices for pharmaceuticals. National health authorities naturally favour home grown generic drug producers over MNEs. Indeed, the MNEs are subject to a large amount of regulation and, in general, have a strategy of compliance, since the licence to sell drugs in segmented national markets can potentially generate large rents. In principle, there is no significant difference in the strategic behaviour of MNEs listed in Table 4.2, in the face of powerful host nation governments.

The multinational pharmaceutical firms are in Quadrant 3 of Figure 4.2, where they need to operate strategies of both globalization and national responsiveness. This is a difficult task which requires a great deal of executive effort and expenditure on internal management training and development. The nature of international and regional trade agreements, such as NAFTA and the EU, is to reinforce this constraint on pure globalization. The MNEs need to develop skills in dealing with government regulation to the same degree that they have developed economic skills in branding and scale economies. If there were no such health-based regulations in a global free market, MNEs could be in Quadrant 1. In practice, regulations and discriminatory practices (such as the exemptions from national treatment for FDI in NAFTA) put pharmaceutical sector MNEs into Quadrant 3. The MNEs in North America and the EU need to be nationally responsive to country-specific health regulations. For example, they must invest in local R&D and otherwise satisfy host government requirements for approval for local sales and distribution. While the simplistic view of globalization, with homogenous products and no regulation does exist (in Quadrant 1), the reality for pharmaceutical firms is formulating strategies and structures for Quadrant 3.

While several of the trends towards globalization can simplify the strategies of MNE pharmaceutical companies, it is a mistake to assume Quadrant 1 applies, rather than the more complex Quadrant 3. Consider the following three issues:

i)   more scientific practice of medicine across the triad
ii) convergence of diets (but, perhaps, not lifestyles) across the triad and more similar patterns of health and disease
iii) sharing of information on the efficiency and safety of drugs by regulatory bodies such as the US FDA and the European Medicines Evaluation.

All these factors push up the globalization axis, but no simple strategy is available. Instead, pharmaceutical firms must develop a strategy for internationalization, and this may take the form of extensive expenditure to build up a network of overseas subsidiaries. In one test of the international expansion process, it was found that the US Upjohn Company followed a sequential process of entry to foreign markets (Fina and Rugman, 1995). Upjohn initially preferred to export, but was forced to switch to FDI in the face of barriers to trade and also to reduce information costs in dealing with host country regulatory forces. In addition, Upjohn had to use strategic alliances, particularly in the tightly regulated markets of Europe and Asia.

In 1995 Upjohn merged with the Swedish company Pharmacia AB, to form Pharmacia and Upjohn. Such mergers reflect the high risks (principally due to massive R&D expenditure) in attempting to come up with new blockbuster drugs. The financial markets value pharmaceutical MNEs on the basis of their R&D portfolio (vertical axis) but also on the basis of the success or failure of clinical trials and other regulatory entry issues (horizontal axis). When a major country tightens regulatory control, or changes its tax policy, then the markets react by devaluing the shares of MNE pharmaceutical firms, as happened in Canada in the 1980s due to frequent changes in policy towards generic drug producers (Rugman, 1996).

A document prepared by the World Trade Organization (1998) testifies to the lack of harmonization in health care services. This report notes the power of national health systems to regulate their markets and impose differential treatment and conditions of service. A huge negotiating agenda lies ahead to move towards even the acceptance of 'national treatment' let alone the 'mutual recognition' and 'reciprocity' assumed by proponents of globalization. All three of these measures are consistent with WTO procedures, but the first cannot, by definition, provide harmonization. Indeed, the WTO report contains this statement:

> Health services are normally provided in an environment significantly different from the textbook ideal of a market economy. A host of imperfections, distortions and information problems may prevent consumers and producers from contracting on an equal basis, in full knowledge of, and financial responsibility for, the ensuing results. For example, since there is not normally a direct relationship between the cost of medical treatment and an individual's contribution – reflecting basic equity considerations – supply tends to fall short of demand.
> Source: WTO (1998) item 28 on p.7.

Even in the EU the WTO (1998) report finds only slow progress towards an internal market for the health care system. The organization of the hospital sector in member states 'reflects national regulatory environments and national heritage' (p.14). Government is in the hospital beds. Cultural and language differences inhibit movement of health care professionals, such as nurses, even though there are significant shortages in some countries. Despite the mutual recognition of professional qualifications in EU law, there is little migration of health care workers. National health insurance schemes have not yet been harmonized within the EU. For example, purchases of medical goods such as spectacles and the provision of dental treatment have been subject to ambiguous rulings by the European Court of Justice. In both cases, denial of insurance cover for treatment outside the home system was found to be a barrier to the freedom to provide services, yet the Court also held that it is for the individual member states to determine membership and entitlement to benefits of their own health and social security systems. So, even in the most extreme case of political integration in the single market of the EU, significant differences still prevail, pushing health care into Quadrant 3. In the rest of the world, not even this legally-based movement towards harmonization exists, reinforcing the health care's place in Quadrant 3 rather than Quadrant 1.

Another advantage of Quadrant 3 thinking is that it can help avoid the polar extremes of policies based on Quadrants 1 and 4. If one holds the pure globalization view of Quadrant 1 and believes that there is some evidence around to the effect that MNEs operate in an unregulated world free market system, then the usual policy recommendation is for global governance. If MNEs are too big and powerful why not counter this by erecting a strong and effective system of global governance? In terms of health issues, advocates of this position believe that Quadrant 1 puts MNE interests above those of people and also that foreign multinational enterprises control public health systems. To fix this perceived problem, they argue that a managed global market for health is needed. This analysis accepts the potential for global governance in Quadrant 1, but not in the other quadrants – and especially not in Quadrant 3. Furthermore, there is no practical possibility of world institutions being developed to provide global governance in Quadrant 1, or elsewhere, in the area of health. The WTO is not effective at dealing with service sectors like health. Regulations at nation state level are likely to remain effective for the foreseeable future, making even a move towards 'national treatment' for health in multilateral agreements highly unlikely.

In contrast, Quadrant 4 thinking is also on the way out. Here old time social policy activists believe in very strong nation state regulations. This thinking was effective in the past in building up Britain's national health system, Canada's federal medicare system and other related state-supported health care systems. All of these are now in severe financial difficulties and national authorities are withdrawing as fast as possible from the excessive obligations inherent in such state-subsidized health care systems. In Quadrant 4 today there are non-price responses of queues, lower quality, and passing the costs on to other levels of government (as the federal government of Canada has done by reducing transfers to the provinces responsible for health care delivery). In short, Quadrant 4 does not work. Neither does Quadrant 1. We are left with today's reality of Quadrant 3 of Figure 4.1.

Public Policy and healthcare

The literature reviewed by Kelley Lee (1998, 1999) on globalization is only relevant to Quadrant 1 of Figure 4.1. While there are some economic drivers of globalization, extremely strong cultural and political barriers prevent the development of a single world market. Political regulations and cultural factors are barriers to globalization; they do not promote it. Only in a few industrial sectors, such as consumer electronics, is there a successful firm-level strategy of pure globalization, with homogeneous products being sold on price and quality, as in Quadrant 1 of Figure 4.1. For most other manufacturing sectors (especially pharmaceuticals) and all service sectors, including health, regionalization is much more relevant than globalization. The triad regions are characterized by heterogeneity rather than homogeneity. Consequently pharmaceutical MNEs and national health systems operate in Quadrant 3 of Figure 4.1.

Managers do not act as if the pure globalization of Quadrant 1 exists. Managers 'think regional and act local', to paraphrase the work of Bartlett and Ghoshal, (1989, 1998). They are reactive to the regulations of national and (potentially) regional governments in areas such as health codes and standards. This managerial strategy of 'national responsiveness' is a basic management skill to seek market access and grow the product line by compliance with sets of external host country regulations. In other words, MNEs do a Quadrant 3 of Figure 4.1 strategy.

The public policy implications of this analysis are relatively simple. The managerially-driven imperative of globalization is that MNEs cannot afford to lose world market share by assuming that the demand for their products is the same everywhere. Instead, they operate on the premise that national markets are segmented. In the health sector this national segmentation is maintained by strong government regulations. There is no realistic chance that a multilateral system, based on the WTO for example, will develop to reduce such segmentation. As a result, MNEs will operate regionally–based or country-specific strategies of 'national responsiveness'. They will be very responsive to health care regulations, attempt to secure country by country patents and related legally enforceable proprietary rights, and act always as good corporate citizens, since their activities are transparent and accountable to strong national governments. Public policy needs to recognize the true nature of triad/regional MNE business activity rather than be formulated on the basis of a misunderstanding of the drivers of globalization.

Public policy for health should focus on the first-order effects of globalization, rather than being diverted towards peripheral second-order effects. This analysis suggests that the causes and impacts of globalization are economic. It is not helpful to broaden the basic focus of globalization to include indirect impacts on other spheres. Indeed, the political, cultural, technological and environmental spheres are more often associated with high degrees of regulation than the alleged world 'free market' assumption of pure globalization. In a similar vein, the inclusion of 'temporal' and 'cognitive' dimensions does not help in the analysis of globalization, as such dimensions have indirect effects and often reflect shifting portfolios of opinions and values rather than any basic scientific premise.

Multinationals from the South

For many years developing countries have complained about the role of multinational enterprises. These firms, involved in private foreign direct investment, are thought to engage in practices solely geared towards their own economic efficiency, neglecting wider issues of social justice, income redistribution, technology transfer and growth; all of which are of course, of prime importance to developing nations. Whether this is true or not is a complex matter, but now the debate has a new element. In the last fifteen years several Third World nations have generated their own multinationals. Professor Wells, of the Harvard Business School, completed a remarkable study of these multinationals, based on many years of detailed field work and personal involvement in developing nations (Wells, 1983).

The theoretical framework used by Wells to analyse the Third World multinationals is interesting since he attempts to take on board part of the concept of internalization, namely the notion of firm-specific advantages. The firm-specific advantages (or competitive advantages) of Third World multinationals are:

- advantages due to small-scale manufacturing
- advantages due to local procurement and special products
- advantages due to access to markets
- miscellaneous advantages, including defence of export markets, low-cost production, ethnic ties, and diversification.

The focus on firm-specific advantages in marketing complements the traditional emphasis upon technological and cheap labour advantages. Third World multinationals tend to have advantages in labour-intensive adapted process technology, as well as in low-price, standardized products.

Wells also finds that tariffs and non-tariff barriers are important reasons for shifting from exporting to FDI, while the desire to control proprietary knowledge often precludes licensing.

He estimates that by 1980 the stock of FDI from Third World nations was between $5-10 billion. While this is only a small fraction of the total world stock of FDI, estimated by Stopford and Dunning (1980) to be about $600 billion for 1980, it is still an important and growing source of international activity. The basis for the generalizations about the nature of Third World FDI made by Wells is his 'data bank', consisting of 963 parent MNEs and their total of 1,964 overseas subsidiaries in 125 host nations. It is apparent that most of these Third World 'multinationals' must be fairly small firms, and they are likely to 'have much more in common with the smaller firms from the advanced countries than they do with the big multinationals' (Wells, p.48).

One of Wells' most significant findings is that virtually all of the Third World FDI is into other Third World nations. This instance of South-South investment linkages is one of the few successful examples of such cooperation in a world where trade and investment flows are still mainly North-South. It may seem somewhat paradoxical to some readers that this South-South transfer of technology by the process of FDI is being undertaken by a group of capitalist-type institutions, the multinationals. Perhaps MNEs are not necessarily the unmitigated villains of popular *dependencia* theory after all.

Further evidence of the attractiveness of Third World FDI is that 90 per cent of the 938 manufacturing subsidiaries identified were of the joint venture variety, rather than wholly-owned subsidiaries. In contrast, US-owned multinationals, on a world basis, have about 40 per cent of their subsidiaries as joint ventures, according to Wells, although this figure is much higher than in estimates for British multinationals made by Buckley and Davies. In any case it would appear that Wells has identified an interesting set of Third World international investment activity, most of which is not normally defined as multinational activity, i.e. wholly owned subsidiaries engaged in international production.

A further source of unnecessary confusion is the book's lack of a table listing, by name, the world's largest Third World multinationals. Although some of the firms are identified in the text itself, given the unusual nature of Well's definition of multinationals, I found this to be a particularly annoying oversight. Of course, from the annual *Fortune* magazine listings of the world's largest international (non-US) corporations it is possible to put together such a table. This I have done, and, for 1979 it reveals that eight of the largest 24 Third World multinationals were petroleum firms, viz. Petróleos de Venezuela, Petrobràs of Brazil, Pemex of Mexico, YPF of Argentinia, Kuwait National Petroleum, Indian Oil, Chinese Petroleum (Taiwan), and Korea Oil. Therefore, another fact emerges; most of the very largest Third World multinationals are state-owned. In fact, 14 of the largest 24 are state-owned, the seven from South Korea being privately held (Rugman, Lecraw and Booth, 1985). Another four of the largest 24 are mining multinationals from Chile, Zambia, Zaire and Brazil, and most of the remainder are in metal refining or textiles.

Table 4.3 updates this from 1999 data. Today the largest Third World MNE is Sinopec, the Chinese petroleum company, with sales in 1998 of US\$ 42 billion. There are 7 other Chinese MNEs in the list of the 25 largest Developing and Emerging Market MNEs.

The number of Developing and Emerging Market MNEs, by country is:-

South Korea	9
China	8
Brazil	3
Others	5

Most of these Developing and Emerging Market MNEs are resource based:-

8 in petroleum refining, oil, gas and mining
5 in trading companies
9 in banking, financial services, and telecoms
3 in manufacturing

The fact that there are a set of third world MNEs, as listed in Table 4.3, again calls into doubt some of the statements of Anthony Giddens. He argues that the giant MNEs 'all come from the rich countries, not the poorer

Table 4.3: The 20 Largest Third World MNEs, 1998

Rank	Firm	Country	Revenues Industry	US$ millions
1	Sinopec	China	Petroleum Refining	41,883.1
2	State Power Corporation	China	Utilities: Gas & Electric	36,076.1
3	PVDSA	Venezuela	Petroleum Refining	32,648.0
4	SK	South Korea	Petroleum Refining	31,997.3
5	Hyundai	South Korea	Trading	31,669.4
6	Samsung	South Korea	Trading	29,715.2
7	Samsung Electronics	South Korea	Electronics, Electrical Equip.	26,991.5
8	Pemex	Mexico	Mining, Crude-oil production	25,783.1
9	Hyundai Motor	South Korea	Motor vehicles and Parts	20,566.3
10	Industrial & Commercial Bank	China	Banks: Commercial & Savings	20,130.4
11	Indian Oil	India	Petroleum Refining	18,728.6
12	Daewoo Corp.	South Korea	Trading	18,618.7
13	China Telecommunications	China	Telecommunications	18,484.6
14	Banco Do Brasil	Brazil	Banks: Commercial & Savings	17,981.9
15	Bank of China	China	Banks: Commercial & Savings	17,623.8
16	Samsung Life Insurance	South Korea	Insurance: Life, Health (stock)	17,574.6
17	Petrobras	Brazil	Petroleum Refining	16,351.0
18	LG International	South Korea	Trading	15,177.6
19	Banco Bradesco	Brazil	Banks: Commercial & Savings	15,164.3
20	Sinochem	China	Trading	15,063.8
21	LG Electronics	South Korea	Electronics, Electrical Equip.	15,021.1
22	Petronas	Malaysia	Petroleum Refining	14,943.9
23	Old Mutual	South Africa	Insurance: Life, Health (stock)	14,550.4
24	Agricultural Bank of China	China	Banks: Commercial & Savings	14,127.8
25	China Construction Bank	China	Banks: Commercial & Savings	13,392.3

Source: Adapted from *Fortune*, 'The Fortune Global 500,' 24 July 2000.

areas of the world', Giddens (1999, p.15). This is an unwarranted exaggeration, as formerly third world countries like South Korea, Taiwan, Singapore and Hong Kong have all experienced tremendous economic growth over the last 25 years, and have maintained their increase in living standards, despite the temporary slowdown of the Asian financial crisis in 1998.

Conclusions

The key message of this chapter is that before policy recommendations for health issues are made, globalization must be properly understood. Economic integration by MNEs is increasing, but in the triad rather than globally. MNEs are helping to raise living standards in poorer countries and are also transferring to them technology, new production processes, and better health, safety and environmental standards. We must not forget, nor undermine, existing types of governance structures in the form of strong political sovereignty and national regulation, eg. in the health sector. The two simultaneous interactions of regional/triad economic integration and strong national/regional political governance structures in the health sector will continue in the future.

5

The Multilateral Agreement on Investment[1]

The Political Economy of the MAI

ONE of the remaining economic (and political) issues for the Millennium Round of the World Trade Organization is the liberalization of investment. As discussed in earlier chapters, multinational enterprises dominate world trade and investment. Over half of the world's trade and over 80 per cent of foreign direct investment is undertaken by MNEs based in the G7 countries, namely the United States, Japan and the large countries of Western Europe (Rugman, 1996, United Nations, 1998). While tariffs and many non-tariff barriers to trade have been negotiated away in seven successive rounds of the General Agreement on Tariffs and Trade, the issue of investment liberalization has been largely ignored on a multilateral basis. Only in the regional North American Free Trade Agreement was investment a central part of a trade agreement. As a result, it has been argued that the investment provision of NAFTA is a model for a multilateral agreement on investment.[2]

Unfortunately, the discussions to approve an MAI at the Paris-based Organization for Economic Co-operation and Development over the 1995-1998 period ended in failure. Yet the design and adoption of a clear set of multilateral investment rules should be a priority for the WTO. In the first half of this chapter, I present a framework for an MAI at the WTO. The nature and content of the MAI are outlined. The difference between shallow and deep integration, and the role of multinational enterprises are

---

[1] Previous versions of this chapter have been presented in papers in London, May 1998 and Oslo, April 1999.

[2] For further discussion of the relationship between NAFTA and the MAI and the argument that the MAI could be based on the investment provisions of NAFTA, see Gestrin and Rugman (1996), Rugman and Gestrin (1996a or b) and Rugman (1997). For discussion of the investment process of NAFTA see Rugman (1994).

explained. The Canadian experience with the MAI is used to illustrate the potential negative side of non-governmental organizations in the MAI process. Canada is a representative small, open, economy (SOE), whose experience is highly relevant for Latin American, Asian, Scandinavian and other SOEs. Following this, I shall discuss the strategies of ten MNEs after an MAI.

The Political Nature of the MAI

The life of the MAI at the OECD can be benchmarked between the Halifax G7 Summit of 1995 and the Birmingham G7 Summit of 1998.[3] At Halifax, in June 1995, the final communiqué endorsed the negotiation of a set of multilateral rules for investment (the MAI) at the OECD. Almost concurrently, ministers and delegates at the OECD launched technical and substantive discussions, hoping to conclude the MAI within two years, in April 1997.[4] Failure to conclude the agenda at that date led to a one year extension, but by April 1998, it was clear that final agreement on the MAI was still a long way off, so a six month pause in negotiations was accepted. Without a deadline to force agreement such a pause (which can lead into an indefinite period) signalled the political failure of the MAI.[5]

The substantive issues of the MAI were to be taken up at the World Trade Organisation, as part of the new Seattle Round of multilateral trade negotiations, which attempted to set an agenda in December 1999. The last, Uruguay Round, of the General Agreement on Tariffs and Trade took seven years to complete, so the immediate prospects for an MAI at the WTO are not great. It will be even more difficult to generate a consensus, as the WTO has 132 members, while the OECD only has 29. About 90 per cent of all the world's stock of foreign direct investment is undertaken by

---

[3] At a pre-summit conference in Halifax in May 1995, several academic papers expressed the need for an MAI. Some of these were subsequently published by Rugman and D'Cruz (1997a or b) and by Winham and Grant (1997). Other important contributions at that time include Brewer & Young (1995) and Smith (1995).

[4] In mid 1994 the OECD organised a conference on trade, investment, competition and technology policies to develop a 'New Trade Agenda' with more of a focus on the issues of 'deep integration' (i.e. investment related) rather than the traditional 'shallow integration' of tariff cuts. Following this, the OECD organised a series of Trade Committee sessions at which several important papers were prepared which laid out a policy for the MAI. The most important of these were subsequently published by Gestrin & Rugman (1996) Lawrence (1996) and Graham (1996).

[5] This can be recognized by other commentators, such as Daniel Schwanen (1998).

the 29 OECD members, (rich developed countries from Western Europe, North America and Asia). The economic logic of the OECD as the forum for discussion of rules for FDI remains strong, even if the political logic of formal involvement of all parties (including developing countries) through the WTO is of increasing relevance. However, it has become obvious that the real reason for the defeat of the MAI is the negative influence of non-governmental organizations as critics of international trade agreements (as indicated later and in Chapter 3) and has little to do with whether the OECD or WTO is the better forum.

A Framework for the MAI

The idea of economic efficiency and globalization as made operational by the activities of MNEs can be shown on the vertical axis of Figure 5.1. This is similar, conceptually, to Figure 4.1. A movement up the axis results in a greater degree of economic integration by international business activities, such as by MNEs. This yields a useful dichotomy between low and high economic integration. With low integration there is local small and medium-sized business. With high integration there are MNEs.

The concept of sovereignty and the independence of the nation state can be illustrated in the horizontal axis. Toward the right of the axis there is,

FIGURE 5.1

THE ECONOMIC INTEGRATION AND POLITICAL SOVEREIGNTY ANALYSIS OF INVESTMENT REGIMES

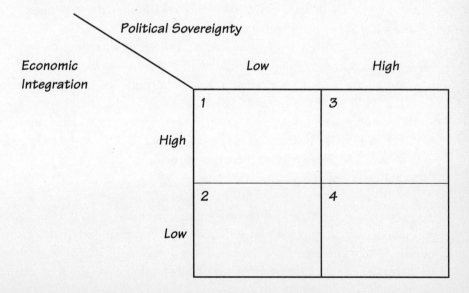

conceptually, a high degree of sovereignty, where the regime passes its own laws and regulations and has enforcement ability. To the left there is low sovereignty, meaning, in this context, that the regime has given up some of its power to others (either to firms or to other states in a multinational system). The matrix is a variant of Bartlett and Ghoshal (1989) and has been explored previously in Rugman (1996, 1997). The matrix yields four cases:

- *Quadrant 1*: Where triad-based MNEs would prefer to operate today, without regulation (an economics-based quadrant of pure economic integration). Here an MAI would yield transparent and liberal rules for MNEs, with special rights in areas such as intellectual property and rules for dispute settlement.
- *Quadrant 2*: Where small and medium-sized enterprises (SMEs) operate, mainly domestic non-traded issues arise and there is little need for an MAI. However, a strong MAI could have efficiency-enhanced effects, even for SMEs, when they are involved in trade and investment networks.
- *Quadrant 3*: The ideal quadrant for the MAI – it allows MNEs to be efficient yet affords key aspects of sovereignty (by way of sectoral exemptions from the national treatment principle and other non-conforming measures). It is also where the NAFTA investment rules-based system operates (Rugman 1994). Quadrant 3 presents the biggest challenge for the MAI, and its success will be determined largely by the ability of negotiators to make in-roads in this quadrant; the biggest challenges and gains are located here, where economic integration and sovereignty pressures conflict.
- *Quadrant 4*: A high sovereignty and nationalist view of the MAI, in which regulation of MNEs is advocated on distributional grounds and performance requirements are enacted by screening agencies such as Canada's FIRA. For a critical analysis of such investment reviews and the economic costs of regulation of FDI, see Rugman (1980, 1996) and Safarian (1993). Here an international accord, such as the MAI, is required to replace individual country regulations which distort trade and investment patterns.

The matrix is a simple device to capture key elements of the policy debate about market access issues, FDI and deep integration. It helps to demonstrate that the essence of the MAI is to link economic and political issues. The MAI could improve efficiency in all four quadrants since we are now at the stage of needing effective rules for international production.

The MAI at the OECD

The structure of the MAI at the OECD follows that of NAFTA, and is built upon the following platform:

- principle of national treatment, with lists of exempted sectors
- transparency, i.e. all regulations on investment are identified as are all exemptions to the principle of national treatment
- dispute settlement mechanisms, to permit individual investors (and companies) to appeal against government regulations and bureaucratic controls
- movement towards harmonization of regulations, although in the areas of competition policy and tax policy not much progress can be expected in the MAI (and none was achieved in NAFTA).

In the draft MAI all these four areas have been addressed. A reading of the draft shows that its structure is based upon NAFTA's investment provisions, as was predictable. The MAI's aim is to make domestic markets internationally contestable, by providing a basic set of rules for FDI, signed by all member countries. The OECD in Paris was the correct venue to negotiate the MAI, as 98 per cent of all the world's FDI is conducted by MNEs based in the OECD's 28 member countries, i.e. all of Western Europe, North America, Japan, Korea, Australia and New Zealand. There was some opposition to the MAI in a few third world countries, but until the World Trade Organization can move on investment issues, there was no practical alternative to it as a venue for the MAI.

Another reason for the MAI being at the OECD is that it builds upon several existing OECD investment instruments, including a code of conduct for MNEs from 1975, Safarian (1993). The OECD has worked for the last quarter of a century to establish a binding set of legal rules for foreign investment and ensure market access for investment according to the principle of national treatment. Expert opinion has agreed that developing countries would benefit from an MAI as it would encourage long-term investment and support sustainable development (Fitzgerald, 1998). This study did not find support for the concern that developing countries would lose economic sovereignty due to an MAI. Nor was there any question of an MAI leading to lower environmental and labour standards, as argued by NGOs.

Numerous 'insider' accounts of the OECD negotiations for the MAI are unanimous in repeating the technical nature of the process, in which the national treatment principle and bargaining over the exempted sectors is the cornerstone of the agreement, for example see Huner and Ehinger in Ward and Brack (2000).

MAI and exempted sectors

The draft MAI is similar to the NAFTA investment regime in all substantive respects and even in most procedural detail. Its critics have misunderstood its technical details (as they did the FTA and NAFTA). For example, they claim that there are tighter mechanisms for 'standstill' and 'rollback'. Here 'standstill' means that countries cannot impose any new regulations to restrict investment; while 'rollback' means that countries agree to a timetable to reduce existing regulations on investment. These are technical and legal terms intended to make the MAI function effectively. These process-related issues do not add to the economic or political substance of the MAI in any way when compared to NAFTA. There are similar provisions in NAFTA. There is, in fact, a large overlap in the technical and legal procedures of the proposed MAI and the existing NAFTA. In turn, there was a very strong overlap between the investment provisions of NAFTA and those of the FTA of 1987.

One issue seized upon by NGOs is the first NAFTA based investor-state appeal case brought by US-owned Ethyl Corporation. This corporation is the sole manufacturer in Canada of a gasoline additive, MMT, which was banned by the Canadian government in 1997. Although this is the only case in the four years of NAFTA, and is highly unlikely to be successful, NGOs use it as a stick to batter the MAI. They generalize the specifics of this case to claim that foreign investors could use the expropriation provision of an MAI to claim compensation for loss of business when an environmental regulation is passed. They argue that any harm to any foreign-owned property or product would qualify for MAI protection.

This fear is misconceived. All an MAI can do is apply the principle of national treatment. Environmental regulations can be adopted by countries, before or after an MAI, without the MAI making any difference. The MAI simply requires that foreign-owned firms be treated in the same way as domestic firms in the face of new legislation. The issue of a monopoly foreign supplier is a different one, better handled by economic-based competition policy than by any aspect of the MAI. Of course, there is always the possibility that lawyers can litigate excessively as the MAI will produce a new set of multilateral investment laws. The issue of eminent domain (the power of a sovereign country to regulate) and 'taking' of laws is a matter for legal interpretations, which can differ between regimes.[6] However, the MAI cannot confer more legal power on a foreign-owned firm. All it can do is make a foreign firm equal to a domestic firm in law.

The opposition of NGOs and the left to the MAI is also inconsistent with the data on MNEs, FDI and triad based international economic activity. Evidence to support the lack of pure economic globalization appears in Hirst and Thompson (1999). They also argue that the nation state is not disappearing and that world free trade is a myth. In other words, MNEs have not created a free trade world and global capitalism does not exist. Indeed, the activities of governments in placing long lists of exceptions for the principle of national treatment in the MAI negotiation is clear evidence that their thesis is correct. The reality of today's complex system is that we are in between markets and states – there are triad-based forces of economic interdependence offset by strong regional and national government regulations. Such state power continues to discriminate against MNEs across many sectors, such as in transportation, communications, financial services and culture.

MAI and Canada

During the Canadian federal election campaign in May 1997, the Council of Canadians and various other left wing NGOs such as the Canadian Labour Congress, the Sierra Club of Canada and Citizens Concerned About Free Trade ran full page advertisements criticizing the MAI. An MAI was being negotiated in Paris at the OECD. Negotiations started in May 1995 and should have been completed in May 1997; May 1998 was an extended completion date, but final discussion was postponed indefinitely.

Maude Barlow's Council of Canadians states that 'the new MAI gives transnational corporations so much power that Parliament won't matter.' More specific statements include allegations that the MAI:

- 'cripples Canada's ability to create jobs'
- 'paves the way for a two-tiered health system'
- 'guts our ability to protect our environment'

---

[6] The MMT case has been discussed by Rugman, Kirton and Soloway (1999) and by Soloway (1999).

- 'leaves Canada's culture at the mercy of US entertainment mega-corporations'.

None of these statements by the Council of Canadians is accurate and all of them convey a totally misleading picture alleging that the MAI will introduce changes adversely affecting Canadian sovereignty and economic control. In reality, an MAI will not bring any significant economic or political changes to Canada. The reason is very simple; Canada already has an MAI with the United States – it is called the Free Trade Agreement.

The investment provisions of the FTA as signed on January 1st 1988 form the basis of the draft MAI. The NAFTA investment provisions of 1993 were based upon the FTA and these NAFTA investment provisions are identical in all major respects to those in the draft MAI. For example, both the FTA and NAFTA incorporate the key principle of national treatment, i.e. equal access for foreign (US) investors to the Canadian market (but according to Canadian rules). In return, Canadian investors have equal access to foreign (US) markets, within host country rules. Both the FTA and NAFTA have exemptions from national treatment for important Canadian sectors, including the big five of health care, education, social services, cultural industries and transportation.[7]

Any MAI would be negotiated along the same lines; countries can readily agree to the national treatment principle but will always disagree over the number and type of exempted sectors. It is clear that the Canadian government will continue to insist on exemptions for the five sectors, especially culture, and that the logic of the FTA/NAFTA will be used as a model for the MAI. The underlying structure of the FTA, NAFTA and MAI is now well understood by Canadians as a clever balance between the pressures of globalization (national treatment) and the need for sovereignty (exempted sectors), as illustrated in Figure 5.1.

The current challenge in international trade negotiations, somewhat paradoxically, is to negotiate investment rather than trade rules. This is because, through seven GATT rounds and important bilateral agreements such as the FTA, the best known barriers to trade, in the form of tariffs, have already been reduced to a trivial hurdle, even when calculating effective rates of protection (which takes into account the value added and labour component of the protected goods).

---

[7] For details, see Rugman (1994).

Today, the majority of international business is not done by trade in goods, but through services and investments. Over 70 per cent of North Americans work in the service sector, with only 30 per cent in manufacturing. So the new agenda for international agreements is to negotiate rules for trade in services and for international investment (Ostry, 1997). The 'shallow' integration achieved by reducing tariff barriers to trade in goods is being replaced by 'deep' integration through FDI, trade in services and the international networks of multinational enterprises (Brewer and Young, 1998).

The Economic Logic of the MAI

While the intellectual foundations of the MAI are to be found in the FTA of ten years ago, the economic and political dynamics of the MAI are also based on the FTA. In terms of inward and outward foreign direct investment, 70 per cent of Canada's is with the United States, and this is already governed by the FTA and NAFTA. So an MAI will not bring any changes to investment rules for the great majority of Canada's FDI. An MAI cannot create any major new pressures on jobs, health or culture. As for the environment, NAFTA was the first international trade and investment agreement which explicitly considered environment, both in its text and through a new side agreement. A NAFTA-based Commission on Environmental Cooperation, based in Montreal, is beginning to research, assess and help improve cooperation on environmental issues in Mexico, as well as in Canada and the United States. While the draft MAI contained no environmental provisions, Canada retains the benefits of NAFTA's environmental measure for over 70 per cent of its trade and investment linkages.

From a Canadian perspective, the long-term underlying logic of the FTA, NAFTA and MAI is, of course, driven by the extraordinary high level of integration between the Canadian and US economic systems. For the last 20 years, over two thirds of Canada's trade has been with the United States. Indeed, Canadian exports to the United States have increased from 64 per cent in 1981 to 73 per cent in 1987 (at the time of the FTA) to 82 per cent by 1996.

It is perhaps less well known that while Canada's inward FDI follows a similar course (in 1996, 68 per cent of the stock of all inward FDI was from the United States), Canada's outward FDI is now much more diversified. In 1996, only 54 per cent of all Canadian outward FDI stock was in the United States. As much as 66 per cent of Canada's outward FDI stock was in the

United States in 1987, but in the last few years it has diversified to the EU (now 20 per cent) and Asia (although there is still only 1.6 per cent in Japan). While these data still confirm the tremendous economic inter-dependence of Canada and the United States, they explain why an MAI will be of benefit to Canadian business as it continues to diversify into Europe and Asia.

A multilateral agreement on investment is not bad news. It is a good news story. The other side of the national treatment coin is that Canadian outward FDI will be encouraged by an MAI. Indeed, as a non-member of the triad (the United States, European Union and Japan) Canada is a small, open economy dependent on access to triad markets. Today this access is more often achieved through FDI than through trade (although FDI and trade are highly positively correlated). While 54 per cent of Canada's FDI stock is in the United States (and thereby already has national treatment), the MAI will be very useful in setting stable rules for the rapidly increasing stock of Canadian FDI in non-US areas, especially in the EU and Asia. An MAI, in this sense, should help Canada continue to diversify its outward FDI away from the United States. Investment rules to ensure Canadian business has stable access to the EU in resource-based sectors such as forestry products, (where there has been a wave of protectionism in the last four years), will be of particular relevance in an MAI. It should also help to open up the Japanese, other Asian and Latin American markets for Canadian FDI.

While an MAI can help reduce Canada's economic dependence on the United States, it is important to keep in mind the 'regional' nature of business in North America. Canadian-based MNEs are doing well in the US market, and they have developed as viable parts of business networks and economic clusters on a North American regional basis. Today there is no such thing as a Canadian business – only North American businesses. Although Canada remains one tenth the size of the US economy, Canada has access to the US market via FDI, to the extent that the ratio of bilateral outward to inward FDI is 76 per cent – at least seven times larger than would be expected from their relative sizes. An MAI will provide stable rules to help Canadian businesses experience the same sort of market access in Europe and Asia.

The Canadian-owned MNEs that are doing well in the highly com-petitive global US market include Nortel, Alcan, Noranda, Moore, International Thomson, Bombardier, Bank of Montreal, and so on. In addition, the US MNEs in Canada, such as GM, Ford, Chrysler, IBM and Du Pont, contribute to Canada's economy by providing jobs and paying taxes. Together the 50 largest Canadian-owned MNEs in the United States and US-owned MNEs in Canada account for 90 per cent of all two way FDI and well over 70 per cent of all bilateral trade. The three US-owned auto assemblers themselves lead a cluster that accounts for one third of all US-Canadian trade. These points were known during the FTA negotiations in 1985-1987, and the story of North American economic integration is reflected in the FTA and NAFTA, and now in an MAI.

One of the exemptions in any MAI will be national security. This loophole has been built in by the United States to subsidize high tech consortia and continue current discriminatory practices against the US subsidiaries of foreign MNEs. This is a type of 'conditional' national treatment affecting research and development which NAFTA also permits. It remains one of the areas where misguided advocates of national competitiveness and strategic trade policy pin their hopes for an industrial/science policy.

An MAI is designed to prevent such discriminatory measures by triad members. It is in the economic interests of smaller countries like Canada to criticize conditional national treatment by others and to refrain from using it themselves. The latter is a simple choice, since a national industrial/science policy for Canada is doomed to economic failure as it protects small market Canadian-based businesses and discourages more useful inward FDI. But the major point to keep in mind is that an MAI is highly unlikely to change current NAFTA-based practice permitting research and development subsidies and conditional national treatment. Thus Canada is not much affected by an MAI in the area of science and technology.

Conclusions on the MAI

In general, because investment takes place long-term, business people need to be assured that political risk is low. New and capricious investment regulations deter FDI and so reduce global economic efficiency. The worst excesses of left-wing economic nationalism can be offset through the investment provisions of an MAI.

Even the MAI at the OECD was a good news story. All the substantive concerns raised by the Council of Canadians were dealt with first in the satisfactory negotiations for the FTA, and were then reaffirmed in NAFTA. The North American Free Trade Agreement is such an advanced trade and investment pact that it was used as the model for the OECD's MAI, and would also be relevant for an MAI at the WTO. An MAI will help to open up markets in the world economy on the same terms that Canada obtained for access to the US market.

Corporate Strategy and the Multilateral Agreement on Investment

The multilateral agreement on investment, whenever and wherever it is eventually concluded, will have an impact on the corporate strategy of multinational enterprises. In this section, I assess the impact of the MAI on the large MNE. I do this within the framework of the competitive advantage matrix, which brings together firm-specific advantages (FSAs) and country-specific advantages (CSAs). The major impact of the MAI will be to change the nature of regulation as it affects the CSAs of these MNEs. Most of these large MNEs are already anticipating an MAI and are well positioned to benefit from it.

A multilateral agreement will provide for a receptive climate for FDI. Through its national treatment and most favoured nation (MFN) provisions, the MAI will give equal treatment to domestic and foreign investors when domestic laws are applied. It will preserve the rights and interests of foreign investors and prevent discriminatory treatment against FDI. An effective and binding dispute settlement mechanism will cover all aspects of the MAI. Yet it is not an agreement which impedes governments from carrying out their agendas. There is room for country specific reservations and exceptions to the principle of national treatment, and in some areas (mostly service sectors such as health, education, culture and social science) there will continue to be discrimination against foreign firms. Since most of these services are local, not global, an MAI will make sense, provided that there is national treatment for manufacturing and business services, which are much more globalized sectors.

I am going to use the 'competitive advantage matrix' of Rugman and Verbeke (1990) which consists of both firm and country specific advantages, to study the impact that the future MAI will have on the strategies of a set of global firms. The matrix builds on work by Kogut (1985). It can be used to look at the influence that the MAI will have on multinational enterprises' strategies and positioning in that matrix. I then analyze ten such MNEs and their probable positioning before and after the realization of the future MAI.

Competitive and Comparative Advantages

The design of competitive strategies by firms is based upon the interaction between country-specific advantages (CSAs) and the firm-specific advantages (FSAs). The location or country-specific advantage is first. It can consist of either natural factor endowments or manmade advantages. Second, is the firm-specific advantage which stems from the firm's proprietary characteristics, be they production or marketing oriented.

As developed by Rugman and Verbeke (1990) the competitive advantage matrix of Figure 5.2 stresses the vigour (strong or weak) of both FSAs and CSAs respective to firms and nations. Where CSAs are strong, a firm can rely on gaining advantage from its location and resources alone. This occurs in Cell 3. Alternatively, when FSAs alone are robust, the CSAs are not paramount for a firm to be competitive (Cell 2). In Cell 1 there are strong CSAs and strong FSAs.

The international arena and the firms' strategies based on strong and/or weak CSAs and FSAs give rise to their positioning in the matrix. Yet, if and when the MAI comes through, it will alter the CSA axis of the present matrix, and consequently the way companies are situated in it. A big MAI (with few exempted sectors) would move many MNEs up the CSA axis, for example, if telecom regulations are removed the firms move up from regulated (weak CSAs) to unregulated (strong CSAs). From the point of

FIGURE 5.2

THE COMPETITIVE ADVANTAGE MATRIX OF CORPORATE STRATEGY

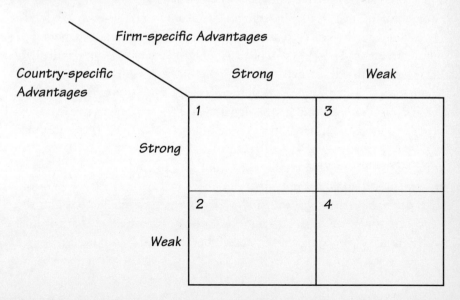

view of the MNEs' strategic planners, a highly regulated sector, like telecom, offers weak CSAs, but a set of multilateral rules will improve access for the MNEs and provide strong CSAs.

The MAI and the Competitive Advantage Matrix

Like government regulations or other international treaties, the MAI is also a set of rules and procedures covering in principle all forms of investments and the various economic sectors. It will subsequently bring about wide institutional changes in the investment environment. It will have a particular bearing on CSAs which, unlike FSAs, are outside the control of corporations; firms do not control the natural or artificial resources of nations. Concurrently, the MAI will bring modifications to the Competitive Advantage Matrix, shown in Figure 5.2, for two prevailing reasons.

Firstly, 'excessive regulation has long been an entry barrier in many industries' (Sjoblom, 1998). Along with the MAI comes deregulation, since it is an agreement that affects trade policies. It rids countries of protectionist measures and shelter-based trade barriers. The trend is towards less government intervention and favouritism resulting in a dramatic increase in competition. Indeed, as mentioned earlier, the national treatment and MFN provisions contained in the MAI aim for non-discrimination between all foreign and domestic firms. Under the MAI, artificial cost advantages and many government-support mechanisms which currently hinder competition will be removed. The agreement will propel global competition to peaks it has never yet attained.

Investment, especially in equipment, plants and other fixed assets, necessitates long-term commitments requiring a stable environment and legal certainties. The MAI will provide for that secure and sound milieu via more standardized markets. Furthermore, it renders domestic markets 'internationally contestable' enabling firms to challenge unfair treatment (Lawrence 1996). Consequently, signatories of the agreement can expect to attract greater investment flows given that, for example, 'there are huge regional differences in cost structure and growth rates in the world' (Sjoblom, 1998). Some nations constitute desirable home bases because of their resources and, by signing the MAI, they will attract new competition. This new competitive era will very probably cater more effectively for the ever increasing consumer expectations for higher quality, lower price and a wider choice of products and services. The MAI will be a powerful engine for prosperity.

The logic of the matrix in Figure 5.2 suggests that the MAI will undeniably bring changes to it rendering some CSAs either stronger or weaker: FDI and international trade can either improve or deteriorate a nation's specific advantages such as productivity. In fact, 'they expose a nation's industries to the test of international standards of productivity' (Porter, 1990). Firms will benefit from stronger CSAs with a deep MAI. These modifications to the institutional environment will consequently bring about changes in the strategies of firms.

Corporate Strategic Response and the MAI

The MAI will be an external force which will alter the way firms conceive of global/triad competition. Firms that seize and exploit the new opportunities will be able to profit and gain market advantage from the amendments stemming from the MAI. 'Complacency and a lack of appreciation [of those changes] could be a major threat to firms' growth' (Turpin, 1998). The MAI will have the effect of enhancing efficiency, thus increasing productivity and competitiveness. Across the nations, firms should be aware of the MAI factor. For example, desirable markets previously avoided by some corporations unwilling to penetrate insecure environments will be invaded. The same goes for companies operating in sheltered home industries (protected by governments' interventions) which will have to face new and intense competition.

Because of diminished government insulation and the upgrading of efficiency and productivity, some firms will have to confront major issues and rethink their strategies. For instance, firms established in attractive home bases which mainly derive their competitive performance from strong CSAs will have to redirect their energy to building strong FSAs as well. However, the MAI will not have such a strong impact on firms in 'advanced industries and economies where competition is already very much globalized and technology oriented' (Porter, 1990). It will serve as a catalyst stimulating higher competition and performance, but not in all countries and industries. Better access to industries which are already marketing oriented and high tech will not necessarily cause turmoil. However, it may have the effect of shortening products' life cycle, accelerating the pace of innovation and promoting new levels of international competition. Leadership, dynamism, creativity, and a better use of technology and marketing skills will be crucial – they may even be necessary for a firm's survival. Consequently managers should beware of new product substitutes. Strategically, firms will have to concentrate on what they do best to enhance and upgrade their competitive advantage.

Survival or agonizing death will be one important issue that managers will need to confront. There will be new-born as well as retiring competition with the MAI. Firms must seek higher international flexibility balanced by economies of scale and scope. They will have to exploit these potential economies along their value chains. What's more, to achieve sustainable competitive advantage managers will have to make use of knowledge and learning across triads. Some companies will need to rely on manoeuvres such as cross border mergers and acquisitions or even alliances. Others will have to resort to behaviours such as aggressive price cutting.

Smaller firms face an even greater challenge. Understanding the metamorphosis the triad markets will undergo is crucial for firms emerging from smaller domestic markets. A good number of smaller companies will have to form relationships with other organizations, such as joint ventures and some form of consortia. Resorting to collaboration will enable them to prevent the slow loss of their competitive advantages and increase their market power. Undeniably smaller firms, like the bigger ones, will have to re-evaluate their strategy in part or in whole. Either way, the intensity of the corporate strategic response to the MAI fallout will greatly depend on where in the matrix a firm is positioned.

Firm Strategy and the MAI

A firm's current strategic positioning will definitely affect how it perceives the MAI. Irrespective of their current competitive positions, corporations will need to realign because of the MAI. Whether they operate in multiple home bases or in a single domestic base, firms will have to seek a new balance of proprietary advantages (FSAs) and those derived from geographical locations (CSAs).

The MAI poses the biggest threat for those firms operating within Cell 3, classified as weak FSAs-strong CSAs. The MAI is modelled as providing strong CSAs, that is it lowers barriers to entry and provides a safer legal environment. Strong CSAs can offset weak FSAs. The MAI prevents firms in Cell 3 with weak FSAs from having to exit the market. Yet those corporations who anticipate the MAI should direct their energies towards the creation of more appealing FSAs, for example, by developing sharper marketing skills, or using research and development more intensively and efficiently. This would move them to Cell 1. They also have to make sure that their products will not be overtaken by substitutes and they must take up the chance of this major policy change to move quickly and pre-empt future competitors.

A similar line of reasoning applies for firms located in Cell 2, which is characterized as strong FSAs and weak CSAs. The impact of the MAI on the CSA axis is minimal since the competitive advantage of firms depends on their strong FSAs. In Cell 1 (strong FSAs and CSAs) the MAI also does not bring dynamic changes. For corporations positioned in Cell 1, categorised as strong FSAs and CSAs, the MAI produces little change. Here the triad competitive battle is as ferocious as ever. The markets and industries (mainly for manufacturing) are already highly competitive and internationally oriented, a situation of 'hypercompetition' (D'Aveni 1994). The development and international exploitation of core competencies is an ongoing requirement for firms in Cell 1. The matrix indicates that firms should not take any of the CSAs and FSAs for granted, but should rethink their joint positioning.

The present and future strategies of ten MNEs

The future MAI will affect multinational enterprises for they are the vehicles for FDI. The actual strategic positioning and possible repositioning of ten MNEs, including four Canadian MNEs, in diverse industries such as food products, telecommunication and pharmaceuticals will now be briefly presented.

Nestlé (Switzerland)

Nestlé calls itself the 'World's Largest Food Company' dedicated to providing 'a complete range of food products' (Nestlé website). Over 8,500 products are sold in more than 100 countries. At Nestlé, managers focus on products for which they have built strong brand name FSAs. Since it is based in a very small home market, Nestlé needs free trade and open markets, so it supports investment codes such as the MAI. Thus its strategy gives priority to the support of CSAs built upon open trade policies. While Nestlé is currently in Cell 1 it could fall to Cell 2 if the MAI is unsuccessful and government regulations affecting food products (e.g. health codes) are introduced. Nestlé's competitive advantages in branding, marketing in general and production, along with its policies of extensive decentralization, important investments in R&D and accelerated innovation will allow the company to remain positioned in that cell.

Seagram (Canada)

Seagram is a leading MNE in the spirits and wine industry as well as fruit juices and entertainment. Through eight decades, it has built an extensive international presence across the triads for itself. Seagram draws on very strong brand names and marketing FSAs. Additionally, in the decade Seagram has initiated many acquisitions and joint ventures, yielding a number of strategically located plants allowing the company to benefit not only from strong FSAs independent of CSAs. Seagram is therefore positioned in Cell 2 of the matrix for its drinks products. The MAI will exclude culture, so Seagram's entertainment business (films and records) will not benefit from strong CSAs, keeping the firm in Cell 2.

Bayer (Germany)

Bayer is an international chemical, pharmaceutical and health care group running operations in almost every country of the world. It is research based and highly technology oriented in its core activities; Bayer believes in success through innovation. It has strong commercial expertise and has achieved global presence through successful marketing. At the moment Bayer would be positioned in Cell 2 given that its competitive advantages are its strong FSAs, regardless of CSAs. With or without the MAI, Bayer will remain in its Cell 2 position.

Electrolux (Sweden)

Electrolux is said to be the world leader in the market for home and commercial appliances, and power devices for gardening and forestry. Electrolux grew almost exclusively through acquisitions, winning its dominance as world leader through proprietary characteristics (Bartlett and Ghoshal, 1995). Benefiting from a strategy of both niching and cost leadership, it is positioned nowadays in Cell 1 because it also profits from geographic location. When the MAI becomes a reality, if Electrolux maintains and even pushes its FSAs to higher ground it will remain in the same position internationally.

Alcan (Canada)

'Alcan is the parent of a world-wide group of companies involved in all aspects of the aluminium industry' (Alcan website). It runs its activities including bauxite mining, alumina refining, power generation, and research and technology in over 30 countries through subsidiaries and related companies. Today Alcan is largely benefiting from strong CSAs with regard to Canada's richness in raw materials. Alcan focuses not only on being a low cost producer but also on developing high tech processes and products through research. Thus it is based in Cell 1. If its FSAs were to fade away and its products became commodities then it would move to Cell 3. Given its current strategic priorities for the foreseeable future such as 'implement full business potential', 'aggressively seek out opportunities', 'focus on new market opportunities' and 'continue to provide premium quality products', there is a good chance it will stay in Cell 1.

Exxon (USA)

Exxon is the 'third largest US-based world-wide petrochemical company' (Exxon website). It is mainly engaged in two categories of activities of the oil and gas business: refining and marketing, and exploring and production. These activities enable Exxon to be a world-wide supplier of high quality products and services. At Exxon, new products are continuously being developed to meet the needs of the changing triad system, putting emphasis on marketing and customer technical support. Hence, not only does it exploit cost advantages of scale and scope throughout the world (strong CSAs), it also obtains a competitive edge through controlled attributes (strong FSAs). For all those reasons, Exxon is a Cell 1 firm. Given management's current strategy, Exxon could further benefit from the rules-based codes of the MAI, reaffirming its Cell 1 position.

Glaxo Wellcome (UK)

Glaxo Wellcome is one of the world's leading industrial pharmaceutical companies with significant contributions to biomedical research and development. Glaxo Wellcome focuses extensively on R&D, manufacturing, sales and marketing in geographical regions from Europe to Asia Pacific. The merger of Glaxo and Wellcome gave rise to a company with a broad and well balanced portfolio, but one based in Europe. Building on strong FSAs, independently of CSAs, has been the firm's strategy. Hence it is positioned in Cell 2. Today, management is taking major steps to expand the company's position into the North American triad, by merging with SmithKline Beecham and talking of moving head office to New Jersey. R&D operations are well established and will help expansion of the company in the future, enabling Glaxo Wellcome to retain its position in Cell 2.

Northern Telecom (Canada)

Northern Telecom is strong on marketing skills, R&D in high-tech, product innovation leadership and high quality service to customers world-wide. These FSAs of Northern Telecom (now Nortel Networks) provide its competitive advantages. Geographical balance and network integration allow the company to benefit partly from CSAs, although domestic regulation of telecom puts it in Cell 2. Nortel's motto says it all: 'Faster. Better. More reliable and cost effective than ever before.' Nortel swears by innovation, agility and speed to build its global presence. Given the mindset of management at Nortel, constant anticipation of future customers' needs and world changes, the firm will be well prepared to outmanoeuvre competition when and if the race for market shares is triggered by liberalization in telecom (set off by the MAI which will provide stronger CSAs, moving Nortel up to Cell 1). Management intends to intensify Nortel's FSAs so it can claim to be a business with world class performance providing cutting edge services. Thus, with the MAI, Nortel could consolidate its position in Cell 1.

Unilever (UK/Netherlands)

Unilever is in the food industry, operating, specifically, in five food categories: culinary, frozen foods, ice cream, tea and yellow fats. 'These categories represent business of enormous size and importance' (Unilever website). Moreover, Unilever is presently benefiting from strong regional brand equity and promotion of innovation and excellence, particularly in North America and Europe, yielding vigorous regional FSAs. These FSAs, rather than strong CSAs, have allowed Unilever to compete worldwide and to position itself in Cell 2. In fact, over many decades, Unilever has built an international network and very recently management has reorganized the firm to gain greater market presence through innovation centres. These centres are meant to 'probe consumer preferences more deeply and reduce lead times'. Chances are Unilever will remain in its current successful position in Cell 2 if it continues to play its cards correctly.

Bombardier (Canada)

Bombardier is an MNE with activities in five different fields namely transportation, recreational products, aerospace, services, and financial and real estate services. All of these are nationally regulated and need to be liberalized by an MAI. To overcome country regulations, Bombardier has reached its present scale through diversification and acquisitions in countries including Mexico, Austria, France and Belgium. It is one of the market leaders because it excels in design, manufacturing and marketing. It derives its advantages mostly from strong FSAs rather than CSAs, thus it is positioned in Cell 2. Bombardier recently operated its new grouping into five activities in order to benefit from optimal research allocation and integration of functions. This reorganization will allow the company to pursue further worldwide growth within a liberalized set of rules under an

MAI. Bombardier would then move from its current competitive position in Cell 2 to Cell 1.

Conclusions on Corporate Strategy and the MAI

Worldwide, international investment is growing more rapidly than ever and becoming one of the most powerful forces in the international economy. The MAI will be a complex blend of rules and measures governing FDI. Its major provisions will establish a secure, stable and non-discriminatory climate for FDI in the sectors liberalized. Many sectors, especially in services, will be exempted. The impact of the MAI on the MNEs was analyzed here using the 'competitive advantage matrix' comprising both CSAs and FSAs. The CSAs will be modified if the MAI introduces broad national treatment provisions, thereby limiting the discriminatory impact of national regulations. This type of MAI will liberalize FDI, and provide strong CSAs, which will have consequences for the strategies of MNEs, given that they are the primary vehicle for FDI. Around the world, MNEs will continue to take part in a relentless competitive battle. MNEs need FSAs based on leadership, dynamism, strong marketing and technology expertise, R&D investments and an accelerated pace of innovation. Such strategic behaviour in response to an MAI will enable MNEs to enhance their competitive advantages in the new millennium.

6

The New Regionalism: The North American Free Trade Agreement

Introduction

AS an example of the strength of triad-based production and FDI, it is useful to consider the economic interdependence of Canada, the United States and Mexico. Both Canada and Mexico now have over 80 per cent of their trade with, and over 60 per cent of their FDI stocks in, the United States. Canada is the largest and Mexico the third largest trading partner of the United States.

The North American Free Trade Agreement (NAFTA) of 1994 recognized the extent of this economic integration. It served as a model agreement for the dispute settlement panels of the WTO and for the Multilateral Agreement on Investment. I investigate NAFTA as a regional counter to globalization in this chapter. First, I shall present some basic trade and investment data on the economic rationale for NAFTA.

Data on North American economic interdependence

The economic interdependence of Canada with the United States has a parallel in that Mexico is also now economically integrated with the United States. As demonstrated in Table 6.1, in 1997, Canada had 90 per cent of its exports going to the United States, while Mexico had 86 per cent going to the United States. In contrast, there is very little trade between Canada and Mexico – less than one per cent of Canada's exports go to Mexico and only 2 per cent of Mexico's exports go to Canada.

In terms of FDI stocks, a similar pattern emerges of bilateral economic interdependence of both Canada and Mexico with the United States. In Table 6.2 the following points emerge:

- The United States has 18.4 per cent of its total outward FDI stock in 1997 with Canada and Mexico (which is remarkably high given that Canada is under one tenth the size of the United States and EU and

Table 6.1: Intra-NAFTA Trade, 1997

Exports in billions of US$

From/to	World	US	Canada	Mexico
US	687.6	-	150.1	71.4
Canada	196.7	188.3	-	0.9
Mexico	110.4	94.5	2.2	-

Source: IMF, Direction of Trade Statistics Yearbook, 1999

Exports as a percentage of total exports, 1997

From/to	US	Canada	Mexico	North America
US	0	21.8	10.4	32.2
Canada	90.1	-	0.5	90.6
Mexico	85.6	2.0	-	87.6

Source: IMF, Direction of Trade Statistics Yearbook, 1999

that Mexico is under one twentieth the size of these triad blocks).

• Canada has 54.3 per cent of its outward FDI stock in the United States and Mexico in 1995.

• Mexico does not report stock data on FDI, but a majority of its outward flow of FDI is to the United States (Rugman, 1994).

• Leaving out Mexico, in 1995, 19 per cent of the stock of FDI of Canada and the United States was intra-NAFTA, while 40.7 per cent was in the EU.

Behind these aggregated data lies the reality of the interdependence of major manufacturing sectors. For example, the North American automobile industry has been completely integrated across the US-Canada border for nearly 40 years, under the terms of the auto pact. Now Mexico is becoming integrated with the United States. Given the linkage of autos to related sectors such as steel, speciality chemicals, electronics, plastics, etc., there is a very high degree of intra-NAFTA trade and FDI by sector. In time, the services sector will also become more integrated, starting with transportation and financial services – both of which are still formally

Table 6.2: NAFTA's Outward Stocks of FDI

United States Outward FDI Stock (US$)

	1987	1989	1991	1993	1995	1997
	in billions of US dollars					
NAFTA	62.7	72.2	83.2	85.1	95.4	125.3
EU	126.2	161.1	203.3	244.5	315.4	369.0
ASEAN	9.1	9.5	14.4	20.6	30.3	37.5
World	314.3	381.8	467.8	564.3	717.6	680.7

Source: OECD, International Direct Investment Statistics, 1998

United States Outward FDI Stock (percentage)

	1987	1989	1991	1993	1995	1997
	as percentage of World FDI Stock					
NAFTA	19.9	18.9	17.8	15.1	13.3	18.4
EU	40.2	42.2	43.5	43.3	44.0	54.2
ASEAN	2.9	2.5	3.1	3.7	4.2	5.5
World	100.0	100.0	100.0	100.0	100.0	100.0

Source: OECD, International Direct Investment Statistics, 1998

Canada Outward FDI Stock (CAN $)

	1987	1989	1991	1993	1995	1997
	in billions of Canadian dollars					
NAFTA	46.3	52.9	63.6	68.2	87.7	na
EU	10.9	15.7	23.8	24.4	33.3	41.1
ASEAN	2.9	2.6	2.9	3.0	3.3	na
World	70.6	84.3	109.1	122.4	161.5	193.7

Source: OECD, International Direct Investment Statistics, 1998

Canada Outward FDI Stock (US $)

	1987	1989	1991	1993	1995	1997
[in billions of US dollars]						
NAFTA	35.62	44.08	57.82	52.46	62.64	na
EU	8.385	13.08	21.64	18.77	23.79	29.36
ASEAN	2.231	2.167	2.636	2.308	2.357	na
World	54.31	70.25	99.18	94.15	115.4	138.4

Source: OECD, International Direct Investment Statistics, 1998

Canada Outward FDI Stock (percentage)

	1987	1989	1991	1993	1995	1997
	as a percentage of outward FDI Stock to the world					
NAFTA	65.6	62.8	58.3	55.7	54.3	na
EU	15.4	18.6	21.8	19.9	20.6	21.2
ASEAN	4.1	3.1	2.7	2.5	2.0	na
World	100.0	100.0	100.0	100.0	100.0	100.0

Source: OECD, International Direct Investment Statistics, 1998

Intra and Extra NAFTA* Stocks of FDI (US $)

	1987	1989	1991	1993	1995	1997
	in billions of US dollars					
NAFTA*	98.32	116.3	141.0	137.6	158.0	na
EU	134.6	174.2	224.9	263.3	339.2	398.4
ASEAN	11.331	11.67	17.04	22.91	32.66	na
World	368.6	452.1	567.0	658.5	833.0	819.1

Source: OECD, International Direct Investment Statistics, 1998

Intra and Extra NAFTA* Stocks of FDI (percentage)

	1987	1989	1991	1993	1995	1997
	as percentage of outward FDI to the world					
NAFTA*	26.7	25.7	24.9	20.9	19.0	na
EU	36.5	38.5	39.7	40.0	40.7	48.6
ASEAN	3.1	2.6	3.0	3.5	3.9	na
World	100.0	100.0	100.0	100.0	100.0	100.0

Source: OECD, International Direct Investment Statistics, 1998
*Data on FDI stock for Mexico are not available

exempted from the national treatment provision of NAFTA. In the next section these institutional details of NAFTA will be explored in detail, as they reflect the complexity of this agreement.

The North American Free Trade Agreement

The North American Free Trade Agreement is a complex international agreement between Canada, the United States of America and Mexico. It provides a set of rules and the institutional framework to govern the trade and investment relationships of the three countries. It also has a mechanism for the accession of new members and it introduces new dispute settlement procedures (for both trade and investment disputes) not previously seen in international economic agreements.

The key trade-related provisions of NAFTA are:

- the elimination of all tariffs between the member countries (over three timelines)
- the introduction of new rules of origin to determine the tariff-free status of certain products such as vehicles and clothing.

The key investment-related measure of NAFTA is:

- the introduction of the principle of national treatment, which prohibits discrimination in the application of laws involving parties from the member states; except in certain sectors where the discriminatory laws are listed as derogations from the principle of national treatment.

I will now discuss these trade and investment measures in more detail.

Trade-related measures

The three members of NAFTA agreed, without exception, to abolish tariffs on all goods traded between them. Consequently, NAFTA is a classical 'free trade area' and satisfies the requirements of the GATT for substantial trade liberalization. The tariffs have been abolished, by sectors according to the GATT harmonized tariff schedules, in three categories:

- Category A: Tariffs abolished immediately upon the implementation of NAFTA on 1 January 1994
- Category B: Five equal cuts of 20 per cent a year over a five-year period, starting 1 January 1994
- Category C: Ten equal tariff cuts of 10 per cent a year over a ten-year period, starting 1 January 1994.

For a few sectors a 'C' category was introduced whereby tariffs will be cut over a 15 year period. Examples of Category A goods include computer parts and most advanced manufactured products; Category B includes many food products; and Category C includes pharmaceuticals, footwear, textiles and clothing.

The NAFTA tariff negotiations mainly took place between Mexico and the United States, and between Mexico and Canada. There were no tariff negotiations between Canada and the United States, since the tariff schedules already negotiated over the 1986-8 period for the Canada-USA Free Trade Agreement were carried óver into NAFTA without any changes. The business leaders of the three member countries were consulted about the tariff category in which they wished their businesses to be included and the final classifications matched these business requests almost exactly.

This has important implications, since those sectors more fearful of the adjustment costs involved were mainly placed in Category C, giving them a ten year period to adjust to trade liberalization. This period of the tariff phase-out in itself provides a type of adjustment assistance, which was determined by the input and requirements of the business sectors themselves. Some of the previously more vulnerable sectors, such as vehicles and textiles, also received new protection in the form of rules of origin. These are paper trails required by customs authorities to authorize duty-free access of the final traded product. Such access may be denied if the product contains too many inputs (and too much labour value) from outside NAFTA membership. The rules of origin follow complex formulae, the ultimate effect of which is to deny duty-free access to the US market of any vehicle and apparel product manufactured in Mexico which has any significant component or input from non-NAFTA countries.

Investment-related measures of NAFTA

NAFTA incorporates the principle of national treatment for foreign direct investment for the three members. Before NAFTA, both Canada and Mexico imposed discriminatory measures on FDI. In Canada, the Foreign Investment Review Agency from 1974-85 screened FDI to assess 'net benefit' to the Canadian economy. In Mexico, FDI had to be a minority of any enterprise until the mid-1980s. While the USA has no such formal agencies to prevent FDI, it has been using an informal review and monitoring system for over 15 years. The Committee on Foreign Investment in the United States (CFIUS) continues to have an informal screening role and its powers are periodically increased by Congress.

NAFTA will affect the North American investment regime through two types of provision. The first type deals explicitly with FDI issues. These appear in the following chapters:

- Chapter 11 of the Agreement, which outlines the basic rules for the treatment of FDI and the resolution of disputes between investors and states

- Chapters 12 and 14, which deal with investment issues related to the provision of services and financial services, respectively
- Chapter 17 on intellectual property rights.

The second type of provision in NAFTA which will affect the North American investment regime consists of investment-related trade measures. These include the rules of origin and measures related to duty drawback and deferral.

While NAFTA was a step ahead in establishing national treatment for portfolio investment as well as FDI, it took half a step back by exempting many key sectors from this discipline. For example, the annexes to NAFTA list 50 US laws as reservations from it. For Canada, the number is 48, for Mexico, 89. Exempted sectors include the US transportation sector, Canadian cultural industries and the Mexican energy sector. Furthermore, subnational levels of government had two years from 1 January 1994 to list additional state or provincial reservations. As well as the FDI reservations, NAFTA has restrictive rules of origin for vehicles and textiles that effectively discriminate against 'outsiders' and protect the 'insider' multinational enterprises of the three member states. These developments will make it harder to break down 'triad power' as NAFTA helps North American MNEs in these protected sectors, at the expense of their European and Japanese competitors.

Viewed in this light, NAFTA is a mixed deal with these strong elements of protection offsetting the tariff cuts and related moves towards freer trade. It is a regional free trade agreement, of benefit to insiders, not outsiders. The reason for this is the lobbying process by which MNEs took part in the negotiations. In all three countries, the business sector was not just consulted; it wrote the agenda. The capture of the trade negotiating process by MNEs, especially US MNEs, indicates a troublesome trend since several sectors, such as US vehicles and US textiles are inefficient. Agreements like NAFTA, and the latest GATT round, freeze these inefficiencies in place and prevent global competition.

Unresolved issues: deepening and broadening of NAFTA

Several unresolved issues in NAFTA will lead to the development of its institutional fabric, for example, through the work and decisions of bureaucracies and committees which it has established. Prominent among these are the new environmental and labour commissions set up after the text of NAFTA was negotiated to win approval in the US Congress. The labour and healthcare commission is basically an agency to appease US labour interests concerned about potential job losses to Mexico. Labour adjustment is funded by the US government, and the healthcare commission will probably have much less business than anticipated since the economic impact of NAFTA on US employment is largely neutral. The environmental commission is potentially much more important, as it will seek to increase environmental standards and enforcement in Mexico through a series of cases and reports which will probably influence public opinion. However, it has no power to enforce its decisions, so its role is also somewhat limited.

Over a dozen official committees have been established by NAFTA to work towards a deepening of the agreement, for example in the vehicle sector and in financial services. Here the most important new institutional provisions revolve around the caseloads of binational panels which can be established to review Chapter 19 appeals of anti-dumping (AD) and countervailing duty (CVD) laws. In the Canada-USA Free Trade Agreement there were 50 such cases of AD and CVD over the 1989-93 period, and this precedent of the review of unfair trade law decisions has been continued in NAFTA. Binational panels have also been established under Chapter 20 to review any other disputes under NAFTA. Finally, there are new dispute settlement mechanisms for investors. In all these areas NAFTA has the potential to become more of a common market than a free trade area.

In terms of broadening NAFTA's membership, there is an accession clause whereby each of the three member countries must approve entry. In November 1994, the three countries agreed to negotiate Chile's membership. However, in 1997 Congress refused to delegate 'fast track' negotiating authority to President Clinton, so the accession of Chile was stalled. There is no immediate prospect of any of the Latin American countries joining NAFTA; if they do apply for membership the approval process could take several years.

In conclusion, more work remains to be done in terms of improving the institutional fabric of NAFTA by a deepening process, than in terms of the very limited possibilities of broadening its membership. It appears that NAFTA, although limited to its three member countries, could become a very useful model, especially in terms of its investment provisions, for the Asia Pacific regional trade agreement and a potential trade agreement across the Atlantic.

The Origins of NAFTA-based regional free trade

On 4 October 1987 the negotiations for the Canada-US Free Trade Agreement were completed in Washington DC. In November 1988 the Mulroney government was re-elected to implement the FTA, which started on 1 July 1989. The major theme of this section is that the FTA served as a model for all subsequent important trade and investment agreements:

- FTA as a model for NAFTA – especially on FDI (but environment was added in the side agreement)
- FTA as a model for GATT/WTO – trade in services (but intellectual property was added)
- FTA as a model for MAI – exempted sectors
- FTA as a model for APEC
- FTA is not a model for Britain – e.g. UK/EU.

A second theme is that the institutional process of the FTA serves as a model. Consultations were held with the business sector through Canada's International Trade Advisory Committee (ITAC). The ITAC members helped get fast track approval for the FTA in April 1986 and helped to 'sell' the FTA in the election of 1988. The Trade Negotiation Office (TNO) was an effective bureaucracy and Mulroney a great leader for the FTA. The Sectoral Advisory Group on International Trade (SAGITS) was also important.

Outline of the FTA

The FTA elements negotiated on 3 October 1987 in Washington DC between Derek Burney for Prime Minister Mulroney and Howard Baker for President Reagan were as follows:

- tariff cuts by A, B, C, involved timing (with ten years to make the scheduled C cuts, five year for the B ones with A taking immediate effect) thus adjustment measures were featured in the FTA
- the Canada-US auto pact of 1965 (a form of managed trade) was retained
- FDI – national treatment with exempted sectors
- culture, health, social services, education, transportation and energy
- services – professional services, but exempted financial services, and telecom; temporary entry for professionals

- government procurement
- Chapter 19 panels.

Evaluation of the FTA

Canada's negotiating objective in the FTA was to achieve enhanced access to the US market, at a time when Canadian business faced increased obstacles to trade, especially in the form of a new type of 'administered' protection. (Administered protection in the triad is discussed in Chapter 9.) This was due to the over-enthusiastic administration of US countervailing duty and anti-dumping measures. Such measures do not exist within the EU, although Brussels can administer them against other countries. Canada attempted to extract an exemption from these unfair trade laws (in return for collapsing its own CVD and AD system), but the US negotiator could not get the authority to do this. In the final deal of October 1987, it was agreed, in Chapter 19 of the FTA, to set up binational panels to review CVD and AD decisions.

In the five years of the FTA these panels were a great success. As shown in Figure 6.1, between 1989 and 1994 there were 132 appeals of US CVD and AD decisions by all other countries in the world except Canada. These countries did not have Chapter 19 panels, so their appeals went to the US Court of International Trade (CIT), which made 42 remands of decisions: that is, about one third were successful. In contrast, Canada made 18 appeals under the Chapter 19 provisions and achieved nine remands from the binational panels, a success rate of one half. While the economic impact of these cases cannot be assessed just by counting the numbers of cases, appeals and remands, the higher success rate of appeals is some indication of the overall success of the FTA in achieving enhanced US market access for Canada.

Figure 6.1: Anti-Dumping and Countervailing Duty Appeals by Canada and Rest of the World 1989-1994

	CANADA FTA, Chapter 19	Rest of World CIT
Appeals	18	132
Remands	9	42

Source: US G.A.O. US-Canada Free Trade Agreement, (1995).

The Process of Negotiations

Arguably, the single most important event in postwar Canadian history was the 1988 election on the issue of free trade and the implementation of the Canadian-US Free Trade Agreement (FTA) on 1 January 1989. The 1988 election saw the defeat of Canadian economic nationalism and the triumph of continentalism. The subsequent negotiation of the North American Free Trade Agreement has built on the model of the FTA.

While the FTA is a critical document, it is still widely misunderstood, if not misrepresented. Hart (1994) explains the details of the FTA, and the negotiating process behind them. He offers an unusual insider perspective on the process of bilateral trade negotiations and the ability of trade bureaucrats to set Canada's political and economic agenda, when coupled with a government dedicated to the pursuit of free trade.

Michael Hart refutes the Doern and Tomlin (1991) thesis that the United States out-negotiated Canada. Their thesis is based on an evaluation of Canada's 'wish list' at the start of the negotiations and their interpretation of what was achieved; they see a gap, especially in terms of the process of the negotiations. But Hart demonstrates that Doern and Tomlin are wrong in their assessment that the United States out-negotiated Canada in terms of process and political strategy. He states that the positive outcome of the FTA outweighs the actual negotiating process, and that the primary Canadian goal of enhanced access to the US market was achieved. Hart makes a convincing case that Canada out-negotiated the United States on the details of the FTA. Canada had a focused team and a clear strategic objective. This objective, of enhanced access to the US market for Canadian business secured by binding dispute settlement procedures, was achieved. The United States was disorganized, and its negotiator, Peter Murphy, had no clear vision or even a mandate other than to keep the Canadians busy while making as few concessions as possible until a final, political, deal could be made.

Michael Hart worked for Canadian chief negotiator Simon Reisman and the other senior members of the Trade Negotiations Office: Gordon Ritchie, Charles Stedman and Alan Nymark. It is clear from his book that the trade bureaucracy actually makes trade policy since process is what matters. Insiders own the show. In the case of the FTA, Reisman, as chief negotiator, had a clear mandate from the Prime Minister and Cabinet to deliver a trade agreement. Control of the negotiating process brought complete power to the insider trade bureaucracy erected by Reisman in the TNO. There was consultation with business groups and with ministers and a final political fix but, in the end, the trade team wrote the FTA.

Yet, at critical stages, the Canadian trade bureaucracy was stopped cold in its tracks by overarching political issues which were only solved by the total commitment to free trade of the Prime Minister. Examples are the problems in securing 'fast track' approval for the FTA in the Senate in April 1985; the frequent lack of engagement by Murphy which required the Prime Minister to go one on one with President Reagan; and the need for Reisman to suspend negotiations in September 1987 in order to have the politicians cut a deal. Indeed, without Brian Mulroney's personal belief in the benefit of free trade and his willingness to fight for it, despite opposition within Cabinet and the muted enthusiasm of even his trade ministers, there would have been no FTA. The hero of free trade is Brian Mulroney, not Simon Reisman or the TNO. The latter were agents of the Prime Minister. There was a strong congruence of their agendas but the FTA owes as much to the political courage of Mulroney as the brilliant technical work of Reisman's team.

In terms of the latter, Hart demonstrates that Canada did its homework and was well prepared for the free trade negotiations. The government, trade bureaucracy and leading negotiators were all converted to the need for market access to the United States, and this grouping was strong enough to marginalize the economic nationalists opposed to free trade. Of particular interest in Hart's discussion is the displacement of old style external affairs trade veterans opposed to free trade (John Holmes, John Halstead, George Ignatieff, Ken Wardroper and Michael Dupuy) by the young turks (Derek Burney, Don Campbell, Gerry Shannon, Michael Hart, etc.) in favour of free trade.

In contrast to the careful preparation of the Canadians, the US side is portrayed as ill prepared for trade negotiations, being quite ignorant of Canada and lacking in any 'big vision'. In particular, US chief negotiator Peter Murphy is portrayed as a cartoon figure, a technical trade engineer with red hair but no real mandate and no clout with Congress (he apparently dealt with Congress only through Senator Lloyd Bentsen's finance committee counsel). Yet Reisman appears to have underestimated Murphy, and took too long to realize that his 'big deal' vision of the FTA would not fly with him. The reality was that a trade deal with Murphy and the US Congress would be a technical war of attrition. That they persisted with the technical details is a tribute to the professional expertise of the TNO, but it made most of the 15 months of negotiations in the 1986/1987 period frustrating and semi-redundant.

The 22 plenary negotiating sessions were an exercise in frustration, with

Murphy unable to engage in serious discussions. Instead he kept to a narrow US technical agenda of 'irritants' and failed to deliver a big comprehensive agreement. There was no substantive movement on the 'deal breaker' of dispute settlement, disappointing US proposals on trade in services and on government procurement, and an unacceptable proposal on investment, which Reisman refused to consider. This raises the question of the value of Reisman sticking to the negotiations with Murphy, when it became clear that Murphy had no clout with Congress, or even with the Administration. Murphy was a technical American trade official, apparently with about as much political clout in Washington as someone like Michael Hart would have in Ottawa.

Reisman make the nearly fatal mistake of agreeing that Murphy alone would deal with Congress. When it became known that Murphy did not have access to more than one member of Congress, Reisman should have adopted a proactive lobbying strategy with the key trade committee members in the Senate and House. As it was, the Canadian Ambassador in Washington, Allan Gotlieb, helped to save the day by conducting a useful insider lobbying campaign which provided vital intelligence for the final political push when Derek Burney (acting for the Prime Minister) cut a last minute deal with Howard Baker (acting for the President).

From this it emerges that the negotiations started and ended too soon. Canada did its homework but was overprepared. The United States never did its homework, failed to engage in the negotiations, and was only saved in the end by the intervention of the President's top political team who cut a last minute deal. When I say the negotiation ended too soon I also mean that the TNO was abolished too soon. The TNO was not on guard in 1988, after the FTA had been signed, but before it was approved by Congress. The enabling legislation of the FTA in Congress contained many subtle changes (e.g. on investment related issues, R&D, dispute settlement etc.) that should have been caught by a Canadian side aware of the critical importance of the details. But only Alan Nymark was left of the TNO team to watch over the Congress. Reisman, Ritchie, Stedman and all others in the TNO either left the government or were reassigned.

Also valuable were consultations with both the provinces and the private sector. These groups had an impact on the negotiations. Excellent work was done by Alan Nymark with the premiers and Gordon Ritchie with the private sector's International Trade Advisory Committee and SAGITS. My own experience on ITAC was that there was a useful two way exchange of information with Reisman, Ritchie, the trade minister and the Prime Minister on both strategic and technical issues, and that the private sector's role was critical at two stages. First, in lobbying for the 'first-track approval', which was partly achieved by ITAC members calling senior US business contacts to influence critical senators. Second, in 'selling' the FTA, which was done mainly through the Canadian Alliance for Trade and Job Opportunities (which was founded as a result of an ITAC discussion). The FTA exists today because it was 'sold' through the personal belief and commitment of business leaders who articulated the FTA to the business community (and later to the entire country in the 1988 election), reflecting their participation and stake in it.

Economic Integration and the FTA

The ten years of the FTA can also be assessed using basic economic data on trade and investment linkages. This section looks at the aggregate economic data. It can be supplemented by sectoral data, as reported elsewhere by Lipsey, Schwanen and Wonnacott (1994).

At the time of the FTA a very high degree of economic interdependence between Canada and the United States already existed, as Table 6.3 reveals. In 1987, 71.5 per cent of Canada's exports went to the United States; by

Table 6.3: Direction of Canada's Trade

Country/Region	Exports To				Imports From			
	1987 (US$b)	% of total	1996 (US$b)	% of total	1987 (US$b)	% of total	1996 (US$b)	% of total
United States	71.5	72.0	164.8	82.3	59.6	65.9	114.6	67.4
EU*	7.2	7.3	10.8	5.4	10.2	11.3	16.7	9.8
Japan	5.3	5.4	7.4	3.7	5.7	6.3	7.6	4.5
Total (Triad)	84.0	84.7	183.0	91.4	75.5	83.5	138.9	81.7
Mexico	0.4	0.4	0.9	0.4	0.9	1.0	4.3	2.5
All Others	14.2	14.5	16.2	8.1	14.0	15.5	26.8	15.7
Total**	98.6	99.6**	200.1	99.9**	90.4	100.0	170.0	99.9**

Notes:

*EU in 1987 refers to 12 countries in the EC, EU in 1996 additionally includes Sweden, Finland and Austria, which joined in 1996.

**Percentages do not add up to 100 due to rounding.

Sources: IMF, *Direction of Trade Statistics Yearbook*, 1991; IMF, *Direction of Trade Statistics Quarterly*, June 1997.

1996 Canadian imports+exports to US / total Canadian imports+exports = 0.755

1996 the figure had risen to 82.3 per cent. In 1987, 65.9 per cent of Canada's imports were from the United States; by 1996, the figure was 67.4 per cent. In contrast, the United States has about one fifth of its trade with Canada, which is its largest trading partner, while Japan is its second largest and Mexico its third. Canada's trade with Mexico forms about one per cent of its total trade; in 1996 exports to Mexico were 0.4 per cent and imports from Mexico were 2.5 per cent of Canada's total.

Foreign direct investment indicates a similar pattern of tight economic integration. As Table 6.4 shows, in 1987, 70 per cent of the stock of FDI in Canada was US owned; in 1996 it was at 68 per cent. In 1987, 66 per cent of all of Canada's outward stock of FDI was in the United States, but by 1996 this had fallen to 54.4 per cent.

Table 6.4: Direction of Canada's FDI, by Stocks

Country/Region	Outward				Inward			
	1987 (Cdn$b)	% of total	1996 (Cdn$b)	% of total	1987 (Cdn$b)	% of total	1996 (Cdn$b)	% of total
United States	48.9	65.9	92.9	54.4	74.0	69.9	123	68.0
EU*	12.6	16.9	34.7	20.3	21.3	20.1	38	21.2
Japan	0.4	2.7	2.7	1.6	3.0	2.8	7	3.6
Total (Triad)	61.9	83.3	130.3	76.3	98.3	92.8	167.5	92.8
All Others	12.2	16.7	40.5	23.7	7.6	7.2	12.9	7.2
Total	74.1	100.0	170.8	100.0	105.9	100.0	180.4	100.0

Source: Statistics Canada, Canada's International Investment Position, 1926-1996, Catalogue no. 67-202.

As Table 6.5 shows, in 1996 20.3 per cent of Canada's outward stock of FDI was in the EU and 8.7 per cent in Asia (including Japan and China). The 54.4 per cent is an important statistic; it shows that in the ten years of the FTA, Canada's reliance on the US market for outward FDI fell from about two thirds to just over one half of total outward FDI; in other words, FDI became more diversified.

Table 6.5: Canadian Direct Investment Abroad, 1996

Country/Region	Stock of Investment Abroad (Cdn. $m)	% of total
North America	**107,780**	**63.1**
United States	92,907	54.4
Bermuda	3,417	2.0
Bahamas	2,390	1.4
Mexico	1,078	0.6
Other N.A.*	7,988	4.7
South/Central America	**8,251**	**4.8**
Brazil	2,747	1.6
Other South/Central America***	5,504	3.2
Asia	**14,900**	**8.7**
Japan	2,718	1.6
Australia	3,301	1.9
Singapore	2,384	1.4
Hong Kong	2,344	1.4
Indonesia	1,410	0.8
Other Pacific Rim**	2,743	1.6
Europe	**35,912**	**21.0**
EU	34,701	20.3
Switzerland	1,211	0.7
Middle East	**1,078**	**0.6**
Subtotal	167,921	98.8
Total	**170,845**	**100.0**

Source: Statistics Canada, *Canada's International Investment Position*, 1926–1996, Historical Data Series, Catalogue no. 67–202

Notes:

*Other North America: Netherland Antilles, Antigua and Barbuda, Barbados, Belize, British Virgin Islands, Cayman Islands, Cuba, Dominica, Dominican Republic, French West Indies, Grenada, Guadeloupe, Haiti, Saint Lucia, Trinidad, Tobago.

**Other South/Central America is South and Central America except for Brazil.

***Other Pacific Rim: Brunei, Papua New Guinea, China (mainland), Philippines, French Oceania, Thailand, New Zealand, Vietnam.

Another interesting statistic emerges in Table 6.6. Canada's outward stock of FDI in the United States has increased from US$49 billion in 1987 to US$93 billion in 1996, growing at 7.6 per cent a year on average over the decade. At the same time, the US stock of FDI in Canada also increased, but at a slower rate (of 5.6 per cent per year); it was US$74 billion in 1987 and US$123 billion in 1996. The ratio of Canadian FDI in the United States to US FDI in Canada was 66 per cent in 1987 which had increased to 76 per cent by 1996. As the Canadian economy is only one tenth the size of the US, this means that Canadian MNEs are doing well to access that market, and even better since the FTA. It also means that Canada's outward FDI stock in non-US countries is growing much more rapidly, as Table 6.5 told us that (despite the increase in the ratio of Table 6.6) Canada's share of all outward FDI in the United States actually fell from 66 to 54.4 per cent over the ten years.

Table 6.6: Foreign Direct Investment Between Canada and the United States 1987–1996

A Year	B Canadian FDI in the U.S. (Cdn. $m)	C US FDI in Canada (Cdn. $m)	D (B)/(C) %
1987	48,876	74,022	66.0
1988	51,025	76,049	67.1
1989	56,578	80,427	70.3
1990	60,049	84,089	71.4
1991	63,379	86,396	73.4
1992	64,502	88,161	73.2
1993	67,770	90,477	74.9
1994	76,781	102,035	75.2
1995	86,466	112,485	76.9
1996	92,907	122,722	75.7
Average Rate of Increase	7.5	5.8	

Source: Adapted from Statistics Canada, Canada's International Investment Position, 1926-1996, Catalogue no. 67-202.

Further liberalization of international investment and the environment will be the main items on the agenda at the next round of the WTO. In both areas, building a coalition of market-opening groups is vital to counter the opposition of self-appointed and unaccountable NGOs.

In terms of investment, the delay in reaching a multinational agreement on investment at the OECD in 1998 can be blamed on the opposition of left wing, poorly informed NGOs, especially in North America. Although Mel Hurtig's National Socialist Party, running on a platform of economic nationalism, secured less than half of one per cent of the Canadian popular vote in the 1993 Federal Canadian election, the Council of Canadians, chaired by Maude Barlow, continues to oppose NAFTA and the MAI. The Council was influential in the mobilization of NGOs in Europe, using the Internet to spread uninformed and insular criticisms of the MAI. It was also effective in the media; supporters of the MAI were not prepared, as they had been during the FTA debate in the Canadian election of November 1988.

NGOs of this kind oppose efforts to liberalize trade and investment by writing general rules on environmental issues. NAFTA's environmental provisions have been attacked, even though it is the first international trade agreement which actually incorporates environmental issues, and has established an organization – the Commission on Environmental Co-operation – to monitor them. The propaganda of unrepresentative NGOs opposed to trade and environment agreements must be countered by detailed arguments supported by the analysis of market-oriented research groups, and effectively communicated in the media. International business must in future reach a multinational agreement on investment, and establish rules for open trade and investment across areas such as the natural environment, which have become new issues.

7

The Evidence on
Triad Economic Activity

THE theme of triad-based regional economic activity (and the regional nature of the production processes of multinational enterprises) is supported by the evidence. In this chapter, I shall explore the aggregate economic data on trade and foreign direct investment. In Chapter 8, I will look at specific multinational firms along with sectoral data. Both these chapters present self-reinforcing sets of data, all of which support the lack of globalization and the importance of regional-triad production.

Triad trade data

Trade data for 1996 confirm that most economic activity is triad-based. The triad made 57.3 per cent of world exports in 1996, and 56.5 per cent of imports. Exports and imports to the non triad areas were about 43 per cent of the world total. These data are reported in Table 7.1.

Figure 7.1 again reveals that the world's trade is controlled by the triad. According to data for 1997, the triad's exports total US$ 4,200.9 billion, with the majority of the EU exports of US$ 2,092.3 being internal, as will be shown shortly. The EU exports only 7.6 per cent of its total to the United States (US$ 158.1 b.) while the United States exports 20.5 per cent of its total to the EU (US$ 140.8 b.) and 9.5 per cent to Japan (US$ 65.6 b.). Japan exports 28 per cent of its total to the United States (US$ 118.4 b.) and 15.6 per cent to the EU (US$ 65.7 billion).

The 'core' triad members can be expanded by adding Canada and Mexico to the United States, which gives us NAFTA, and then constructing a group of countries for 'Asia'. This group consists mainly of Japan, Australia, New Zealand, China, Taiwan, Hong Kong, India, Indonesia, Malaysia, Philippines, Singapore, Thailand but also of smaller Asian Pacific economies. This gives us the 'broad' triad. This yields Figure 7.2.

Figure 7.2 confirms that the world's trade is controlled by the triad. Note again that NAFTA and Asia are used rather than the United States and Japan. According to data for 1997, the triad's exports total US$ 4,145.8 billion, with 60.6 per cent of the EU exports of US$ 2,092.3 being internal,

Table 7.1: Ten Years of Triad Trade

| | Exports to | | | | Imports from | | | |
| | 1987 | | 1996 | | 1987 | | 1996 | |
	US$ bill.	% of total	US$ bill.	% of total	US$ bill.	% of total	US$ bill.	% of total
United States	252.9	10.5	679.5	12.7	424.1	17.1	791.2	15.0
EU*	1,049.1	43.7	1,926.6	36.0	1,049.6	42.3	1,882.1	35.6
Japan	231.3	9.6	456.9	8.5	150.9	6.1	317.6	6.0
Triad	1,533.3	63.9	3,063.0	57.3	1,624.6	65.5	2,990.8	56.5
All Others	867.2	36.1	2,284.7	42.7	854.9	34.5	2,299.9	43.5
Total	**2,400.5**	**100.0**	**5,347.7**	**100.0**	**2,479.5**	**100.0**	**5,290.7**	**100.0**

Notes: *EU numbers are for exports and imports of every member to the rest of the world. Thus, EU union exports and imports include intra-EU figures. Triad countries include United States, EU, Japan.

Source: Adapted from International Monetary Fund, *Direction of Trade Statistics Yearbook*, (Washington DC: IMF, 1994) and International Monetary Fund, *Direction of Trade Statistics Quarterly*, (Washington DC: IMF, June 1997).

FIGURE 7.1:

EXPORTS IN THE CORE TRIAD

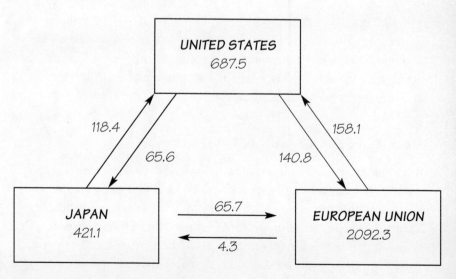

Note: Data are for 1997, in US$ billion.
Source: International Monetary Fund. *Direction of Trade Statistics, 1999.*

FIGURE 7.2:

EXPORTS IN THE BROAD TRIAD

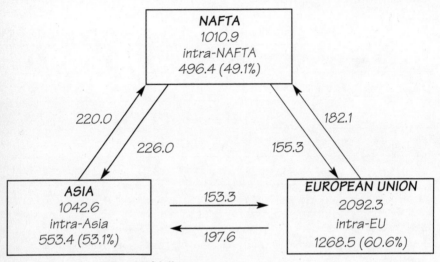

Note: Data are for 1997, in US$ billion.
Source: International Monetary Fund. *Direction of Trade Statistics, 1999*.

at US$ 1,268.5 billion. The EU exports only 8.7 per cent to NAFTA (US$ 182.1 billion) and 9.4 per cent to Asia (US$ 197.6 billion). NAFTA exports 15.4 per cent of its total to the EU (US$ 155.3 billion) and 22.4 per cent to Asia (US$ 226.0 billion). Asia exports 21.1 per cent of its total to NAFTA (US$ 220.0 billion) and 14.7 per cent to the EU (US$ 153.3 billion).

In summary, the extent of intra EU exports is 60.6 per cent. For NAFTA internal trade it is 49.1 per cent and for Asia it is 53.1 per cent. The majority of world trade in each triad is within the internal markets of the triad, and most of the rest is between themselves.

Most European trade is internal

Most of the EU's trade is internal, as shown above. Appendix Table 7.1, where over 60 per cent of all exports by the 15 EU member states are intra-regional, confirms this in more detail. Another 13 per cent go to other parts of Europe, mostly Eastern Europe. Only 7.6 per cent of the EU exports go to the United States and 2 per cent to Japan. The picture for EU imports is very similar (see Appendix Table 7.2). So, there is overwhelming evidence that European trade is internal, and only just over 10 per cent goes to other triad members. This confirms the point that the vast majority of trade by the EU is intra-regional, not inter-regional.

Table 7.2 demonstrates the sectoral percentages of internal European trade; and that the vast majority of EU trade is internal for all 15

Table 7.2: European Union, Exports by Commodity, 1997 as a percentage of total exports of specific commodity

Commodity	intra-EU trade
Beverages and tobacco	57.2
Pulp and waste paper	81.5
Textile fibres	60.7
Petroleum	65.9
Gas, natural and manufactured	87.7
Electric current	71.2
Chemicals	60.9
Iron and steel	67.0
Machinery and transport equipment:	57.3
Power generating machinery	48.2
Office machines and computers	74.8
Telecommunications	54.7
Electrical machinery	57.9
Road vehicles	68.7
Footwear	62.8

Source: Eurostat, External and Intra-European Union Trade, *Statistical Yearbook, 1958-1997*

Notes: Textile fibres are other than wool and include their wastes when not manufactured into yarn or fabric. Petroleum includes petroleum products and related materials. Chemicals includes related products and are divided as: organic chemicals; inorganic chemicals; dyeing, tanning and colouring materials; medicinal and pharmaceutical products; essential oils and resinoids and perfume materials: toilet, polishing and cleansing preparations; fertilizers, plastics and chemical materials and products. Telecommunications includes sound recording and reproducing apparatus and equipment.

manufacturing sectors. In 1997, the latest year for which trade data are available, the internal export percentages are: 88 for gas; 82 for pulp and paper; 75 for office machines and computers; 71 for electricity; 69 for cars and trucks; 67 for iron and steel; and so on. The lowest percentage of intra-EU trade is for telecommunications at 54.7 per cent.

When European trade is broken down by country the evidence is, again, of intra-regional trade. The data for the United Kingdom, in Appendix Table 7.3, indicate that 53 per cent of exports go to other members of the EU, 12.2 per cent to the United States, and only 2.6 per cent to Japan.

A similar story emerges for the British manufacturing sector. In Appendix Table 7.4, 12 of the 15 sectors make more than half of their exports to the EU – only beverages and tobacco (at 41 per cent), textile fibres (at 46 per cent) and power generating machinery (at 42 per cent) have a majority of non-EU sales.

German trade figures follow the same pattern. In 1997, Germany's exports to the rest of the EU came to 55.5 per cent, with a total figure of 73 per cent to all of Europe. Only 8.6 per cent of its exports go to the United States and 2.3 per cent to Japan. See Appendix Table 7.5.

The sectoral breakdown for Germany is not readily available, but the aggregate figures again suggest that, like the UK, virtually all its sectors make the majority of their sales to the rest of the EU.

These data lead to the firm conclusion that EU trade is mainly intra-regional and that the amount of inter-regional trade is much smaller. Indeed, on average, the EU's inter-regional triad trade is about one fifth of its intra-regional trade.

Triad foreign direct investment data

There is abundant evidence that foreign direct investment as well as trade, is dominated by the triad. The latest available aggregate data on stocks of foreign direct investment to the triad is for 1997, and is published in the latest UNCTAD *World Investment Report 1999*. This specialist United Nations agency has been responsible for gathering data on FDI and making policy recommendations, based on economic analysis, for the last 20 years. It was once based in New York but moved to Geneva in the early 1990s.

From Figure 7.3 we can see the dominance of the core triad members as sources of foreign direct investment. These data are reporting the aggregate stocks of FDI, that is they reveal the historical value and wealth of foreign subsidiaries to the home country. They do *not* represent an annual flow of FDI (as do the trade data earlier in this chapter, for example).

FIGURE 7.3:

TOTAL OUTWARD FDI STOCKS IN THE CORE TRIAD

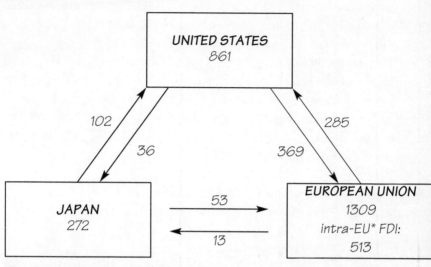

Note: Data are for 1997, in US$ billion.
Source: United Nations, *World Investment Report*: (Geneva: UN Publications, 1999),
OECD, *International Direction of Trade Statistics*, (Paris, OECD, 1998)
*Data are for 1996

By 1997, the EU was the largest engine of FDI, with an aggregate outward stock of US$ 1,309 billion. The outward stock of the United States (leaving aside its NAFTA partners for a moment) was US$ 861 billion. Finally, Japan's outward stock was US$ 272 billion. The combined value of the core triad members is US$ 2,442 billion, which is 71 per cent of the world's total stock of FDI in 1997 of US$ 3,473 billion.

The most important number in Figure 7.3 is that for internal EU FDI, at US$ 513 billion. This is a larger number than for any single inter-triad stock of FDI. It shows that 39 per cent of all EU FDI is internal.

The data in Figure 7.3 yield several important insights (all data are in US$ billion).

- The total stock of outward FDI in the triad amounts to the sum of internal figures in the boxes, i.e. 2,442.
- The total amount of inter-triad outward FDI stock is the sum of the six arrows between the three triad boxes, i.e. 858.
- The difference is the stock of outward FDI in the triad which is both internal triad FDI and FDI by the triad to the rest of the world; these

two amounts total 1,584. That is 64 per cent of the total outward stocks of the triad.

- The total world stock of outward FDI for 1997 (not reported in Table 7.3) is 3,473. The total triad stock of non inter-triad FDI is 1,584. This is 45 per cent of the world's stock.
- The total triad FDI is 2,442 (consisting of the inter-triad FDI stock of 858 plus the non inter-triad FDI stock of 1,584) which is 71 per cent of the world's total stock of outward FDI.
- The amount of FDI originating in the non-triad countries is equal to the world stock (of 3,423) less the triad stock (of 2,442) which is 981. This is 27 per cent of the world's total.

When the two NAFTA partners are added to the US stock of outward FDI then the NAFTA total increases to 999.1, as shown in Figure 7.4

FIGURE 7.4:

TOTAL OUTWARD FDI STOCKS IN THE BROAD TRIAD

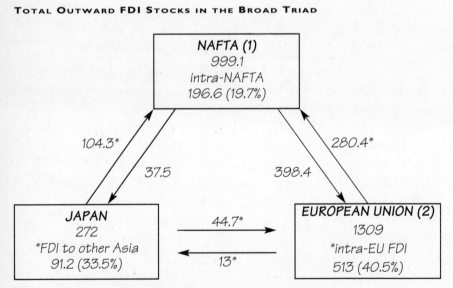

Note: Data are for 1997, in US$ billion.
Source: United Nations, *World Investment Report*: (Geneva: UN Publications, 1999), OECD, *International Direction of Trade Statistics*, (Paris, OECD, 1998)

*Data are for 1996, (10 Data include FDI originating in Mexico. (2) EU data only include: Austria, Finland, France, Germany, Italy, Netherlands, Sweden, United Kingdom. Data for other EU countries are not available. Data for Netherlands are for 1995.

- The amount of internal-triad FDI in Figure 7.4 is very large, since the internal EU FDI stock alone is 513. The amount for North America is 196 and the amount for Asia is 91.2. Thus the internal FDI stock in NAFTA is 20 per cent of its total, while for Asia it is 33.5 per cent.

The conclusions are that:

a) the triad dominates FDI

b) as much as 40 per cent of FDI is internal to each triad member than is inter-triad

c) inter-triad FDI is very large, particularly between the EU and the United States

d) only a quarter of the world's FDI is not controlled by the triad.

The Asian and NAFTA triads

The data for the three-partner NAFTA and for the broad Asian triad, based on Japan, basically confirm the analysis of the EU given in this chapter so far.

Japan

Tables for Japanese exports and imports by region appear in Appendix Tables 7.6 and 7.7 respectively. They show that in 1998 about 40 per cent of Japan's exports and 52 per cent of its imports were intra-regional to Asia and Oceania. About 36 per cent of Japanese exports went to North America and 27 per cent of imports came from there. Finally, 18 per cent of Japan's exports went to the EU compared with 14 per cent of Japan's imports from there.

In Appendix Table 7.8 there is a breakdown of Japanese exports by major commodity sector. For 1997 the following sectors have high amounts of intra-regional trade:

petroleum	86 per cent
textile fibres	76 per cent
iron and steel	71 per cent
chemicals	58 per cent
electrical machinery	52.3 per cent

In contrast only 12 per cent of road vehicles were exported to other Asian countries, but 41 per cent to the United States.

China

China is a paradox. Over the last ten years it has accounted for the second fastest rate of growth of inward FDI flows (after the United States). Yet its stock of the world's FDI is still only two per cent. As the world's largest potential market, in terms of population, China is taking a long time to generate effective demand. It has a 'dual' economy with rapid growth in the coastal cities and slower access to market capabilities in the central cities. FDI flows through Hong Kong account for a large percentage of all FDIs.

NAFTA

In Appendix Table 7.9 it is reported that 40 per cent of the exports of the United States, Canada and Mexico are intra-regional, i.e. within NAFTA. A further 15 per cent go to the EU and only 7 per cent to Japan, but 22 per cent to Japan and other Asian countries, including Oceania. For imports, in Appendix Table 7.10 it is shown that, again, 40 per cent of imports are intra-NAFTA, 16 per cent are from the EU, 11 per cent from Japan and 32 per cent from Japan and other Asian countries, including Oceania.

Appendix Tables 7.11 and 7.12 report exports and imports for the United States alone. Thirty two per cent of US exports (1997) are intra-regional. This is remarkable as Canada is only one tenth the economic size of the United States, and Mexico only one twentieth. A further 20 per cent of US exports go to the EU and 10 per cent to Japan.

As regards US imports, 29 per cent come from Canada and Mexico (its NAFTA partners), 10 per cent from the EU and 14 per cent from Japan. A total of 39 per cent of the United States' imports come from all of Asia, including Japan.

Definitions and Measures of Global Performance

In addition to the publicly available aggregate data on trade and FDI reported so far in this chapter and the Appendix, it is possible to unveil the performance of MNEs by reworking their firm-level accounting data. In general, once an MNE has been identified, it is useful to measure its activities and performance over time. Abundant data sources are available for the largest MNEs, virtually all of which are publicly held and listed on the stock markets. Their annual reports and other information produced for investors are a rich source of information for analysts.

This financial, economic and organizational information can be used in several ways. While the tables in this book are mostly based on country-level classifications of trade and FDI, the actors behind this economic activity are the MNEs, and their own performance is of interest. We can manipulate firm-level information further by using published company accounts. For discussion of the basic research methodology see Rugman (1980, 1981, 1996).

The following data enable us to construct an index of multinationality:

1 Ratio of foreign to total operations (F/T) measured by:
   - sales
   - assets
   - employees
   - R&D
   - stock market capitalization

The best measures require separate sets of data on 'parent' MNE and all 'subsidiaries' operating (so 'capitalization' is impossible unless data exist in multiple listings across national stock markets).

2 Measure of geographic 'scope', e.g.:
   - number of countries in which the MNE has a foreign subsidiary, preferably weighted by (F/T)
   - number of foreign direct investments made by the MNE over a constant time frame, e.g. five, ten years, or in total
   - number of joint ventures (JV); strategic alliances; network partners, etc.
3 Company data on the extent of 'centralization' versus 'decentralization' in the MNE's strategic decision making, which needs to be linked to the MNE's strategic intent; the so-called 'transnational' MNEs need a decentralized strategy where country managers are decision makers. Some researchers have obtained subsidiary managers 'event' and 'decision' data from interviews and questionnaires (Birkinshaw, 1997; Birkinshaw and Hood, 1998; Bartlett and Ghoshal, 1998). Some MNEs now operate as networks and new forms of data on organizational linkage are required.
4 A combination of 1 and 3 above, with weights for each approach, explained by a detailed methodology which is applied to a data set such as the Global 500.

Building on the logic of these statements as an extension to earlier work on the performance of MNEs in Rugman (1980, 1981, 1996), I have collaborated with Michael Gestrin and Rory Knight to produce *The Templeton Global Performance Index*. This is a data bank of the largest 500 MNEs in which their return on foreign assets is calculated in a careful and novel manner, as explained in the next section.

The Templeton Global Performance Index

Most studies of FDI have relied upon aggregate FDI data, which countries report publicly and upon which publications like the United Nations annual *World Investment Report* are largely based. Although useful for the analysis of broad FDI trends at the national level, these data are not useful when analyzing the internal dynamics behind MNEs strategic decision-making. To do this, firm-level data on the performance of foreign subsidiaries (foreign assets) are needed.

Until recently, such firm-level data have not been available for the simple reason that many MNEs have not reported such information. However, as a result of recent changes in accounting requirements across most OECD countries, the great majority of MNEs do now report detailed data on their foreign operations. This takes the form of geographic segment disclosures, usually found in the notes to a company's consolidated accounts.

Segment reporting consists of the disaggregation of certain items in a company's consolidated accounts, according to its lines of business and the geographic areas in which it operates. Segment accounts usually cover some combination of assets, revenues and profits, depending upon the regulatory requirements of the jurisdiction in which the company is based. The choice of definition of each item also tends to vary across jurisdictions and to the extent that the applicable regulatory requirements allow for discretion in the choice of definition. The main purpose of segment reporting is to provide investors and creditors with more detailed information on a firm's operations. These data can be used to generate a number of performance measures for a company's international activities.

Returns on foreign assets

One of the most commonly used measures of performance is the rate of return on assets (ROA). Using geographic segment data it is possible to calculate ROA for FDI (the return on foreign assets, or ROFA). The rate of return on assets measures a firm's performance in terms of the earnings it generates with the assets under its control, irrespective of how these are financed (Stickney and Weil, 1997, p.278). It is usually calculated as:

(1) ROA = (Net income + interest expense net of income tax savings)/average total assets

ROA gives some idea of operational, as opposed to financial, performance. As Stickney and Weil write, 'ROA attempts to measure the success of a firm in creating and selling goods and services to customers' (p.278).[1] In equation 1, 'interest expense net of income tax savings' is added to the numerator to account for the fact that firms compute net income after subtracting their interest expense on debt. The effect of interest expense as a deduction in the calculation of taxable income also needs to be taken into account, in order to arrive at an income measure that is not biased by including a portion of the financing costs faced by the firm.

Return on assets can be disaggregated as the product of two other operational performance ratios, the profit margin and the asset turnover ratio.[2] The former is defined as net income (before interest expense and related tax effects) divided by total sales. This ratio reflects the effectiveness of firms in managing operating expenses (e.g. production, marketing and distribution costs). The asset turnover ratio is defined as sales divided by average total assets. This ratio can be interpreted in terms of a firm's effectiveness in generating sales with a given stock of assets (or its effectiveness in controlling levels of investment for a given level of sales).[3]

The appeal of performance measures such as these relates mainly to the ready availability of relevant data, which can be easily calculated and interpreted. Consequently, accounting data are extensively used in research on various aspects of company performance.

By using geographic segment disclosures, it is possible to calculate measures of performance such as ROA and profit margins for the foreign operations of MNEs. In many cases these measures can be calculated directly from the data contained in annual reports. The *Templeton Global Performance Index*

---

[1] For purposes of measuring financial performance, the rate of return on common shareholders' equity (ROE) and earnings per common share are more appropriate ratios in that they take into account the sources and costs of financing assets that generate earnings. For calculations of the performance of MNEs using ROE see Rugman (1980, 1996). For a more detailed explanation of accounting measures of a firm's financial performance, see Stickney and Weil, 1997, Chapter 6.

[2] ROA = (net income plus interest expense net of income tax savings/sales) multiplied by (sales/average total assets)

[3] For a more thorough treatment of the calculation, analysis and interpretation of such ratios, see e.g. Pendlebury and Groves, 1994, Stickney and Weil, 1997, and Vause, 1997.

(Gestrin et al, 1998, 2000), for example, is based upon the calculation of the ROFAs generated by a sample of MNEs from the Fortune Global 500.

Relative returns on foreign assets

The relative performance of a company's foreign and domestic operations is another useful measure of its international performance that can be generated using geographic segment disclosure data. The underlying logic of such a comparison is that the international strategies of most companies are based upon core competencies developed in their home market.[4] Differences between home country and international performance reflect upon a company's ability to use these competencies in foreign markets through what could be described as a distinct foreign asset competency.

RELROFA is the ratio of the share of foreign profits in total profits to the share of foreign assets in total assets. It can be expressed as:

$$RELROFA = (FP/TP)/(FA/TA)$$

Where: FP = foreign profits
TP = total profits
FA = foreign assets
TA = total assets

This 'ratio of ratios' provides a measure of the extent to which foreign profits are commensurate with the assets committed to their generation. For example, if foreign profits account for 30 per cent of total profits and foreign assets account for 60 per cent of total assets, RELROFA equals 0.5. In other words, the return on foreign assets is half the value of the return on total assets. Any RELROFA with a value below one indicates that the rate of return of the foreign assets is lower than the rate of return on total assets and, by extension, domestic assets. Values above one indicate the opposite.

RELFOPM is similar to RELROFA except that it applies to the differential between foreign and domestic operations in terms of operating margins. RELFOPM can be expressed as:

$$RELFOPM = (FP/TP)/(FR/TR)$$

Where: FR = foreign revenues
TR = total revenues

---

[4] On average, approximately 65 per cent of the assets of multinational enterprises in the Fortune Global 500 are located in home countries.

The FDI performance of the world's largest MNEs

As an example of the type of analysis that can be conducted using firm-level data on the performance of FDI, data on the average ROFAs for a broad set of nine industries are presented in Table 7.3. These data come from The *Templeton Global Performance Index* (Gestrin et al, 1998). Pharmaceuticals stand out as a clear leader in terms of global performance, followed by electronics. Problems of overcapacity, controlling costs, high levels of global competition and a recent wave of investments in emerging markets are among the reasons behind the automotive industry's poor performance. This information can only be calculated using firm-level data.

Table 7.3: Selected industry average returns on foreign assets

Industry globalization rank	Industry (number of companies)	Average ROFA
1	Pharmaceuticals (14)	10.84
2	Entertainment and publishing (4)	9.62
3	Electronics (18)	6.91
4	Retail (11)	6.04
5	Computers and associated products (12)	5.42
6	Food, beverage and tobacco (14)	5.26
7	Energy (26)	5.11
8	Chemicals (4)	4.37
9	Automotive (17)	3.03

Source: Gestrin et al (1998)

Firm-level data on the performance of FDI can also be used to compare performance by home-country[5] (Table 7.4). For example, according to Gestrin et al (1998), British and United States companies were the best performers with average returns on foreign assets of 7.78 and 6.24 per cent, respectively. Companies from Japan and Australia finished last with average annual returns on foreign assets of 1.25 and 0.31, respectively.

[5] The country in which they are legally registered.

Table 7.4: Average annual returns on foreign assets by home-country, 1996-1997

Home country	Average ROFAs	No. of companies covered
Britain	7.78	23
United States	6.24	97
Rest of Europe	5.11	12
Canada	3.16	6
Germany	2.95	6
France	2.75	12
China	2.10	1
Japan	1.25	42
Australia	0.31	4

Source: Gestrin et al (1998)

Further details of *The Templeton Global Performance Index*, which is updated annually, are available from the author.

Appendix Table 7.1: Intra-Regional Trade in Europe: Exports

EU Exports by Region, percentages, 1991–1997

	1991	1993	1995	1997
	percentage of total exports			
EU	66.8	61.7	62.4	60.6
Total Europe	76.4	72.1	73.4	73.1
US	6.4	7.3	6.7	7.6
North America	7.6	8.6	7.7	8.7
Japan	2.0	2.0	2.1	1.9
Total Asia	7.3	9.0	9.7	9.4
Other countries	8.6	10.3	9.2	8.8
Total	**100.0**	**100.0**	**100.0**	**100.0**

Notes: Other countries refers to developing countries in Africa, the Middle East, the Western Hemisphere (excluding Mexico), North Korea, and Cuba.

Statistical discrepancies are the result of rounding.

Source: IMF, *Direction of Trade Statistics Yearbook*, 1999

Appendix Table 7.2: Intra-Regional Trade in Europe: Imports

EU Imports by Region, percentages, 1991–1997

	1991	1993	1995	1997
	percentage of total imports			
EU	62.8	59.6	61.1	59.4
Total Europe	71.8	69.6	71.8	70.3
US	7.6	7.9	7.4	8.3
North America	8.6	8.8	8.4	9.3
Japan	4.6	4.8	4.0	3.7
Total Asia	9.4	11.7	11.6	11.3
Other countries	10.1	9.9	8.2	9.1
Total	**100.0**	**100.0**	**100.0**	**100.0**

Notes: Other countries refers to developing countries in Africa, the Middle East, the Western Hemisphere (excluding Mexico), North Korea, and Cuba.

Statistical discrepancies are the result of rounding.

Source: IMF, *Direction of Trade Statistics Yearbook*, 1999

Appendix Table 7.3: UK Exports by Region

UK Exports by Region, 1991-1997

	1991	1993	1995	1997
	percentage of total exports			
EU	60.5	52.1	53.9	52.7
Total Europe	69.7	58.2	59.8	59.4
US	10.9	12.9	12.2	12.2
North America	12.8	14.8	13.6	13.6
Japan	2.2	2.2	2.5	2.6
Total Asia	10.6	2.3	13.0	13.1
Other countries	6.9	14.8	13.6	14.0
Total	100.0	100.0	100.0	100.0

Notes: Other countries refers to developing countries in Africa, the Middle East, the Western Hemisphere (excluding Mexico), North Korea, and Cuba.

Statistical discrepancies are the result of rounding.

Source: IMF, *Direction of Trade Statistics Yearbook*, 1999

Appendix Table 7.4: UK Exports by Industry Sector, 1997

UK, Exports by Commodity Sector, as a percentage of total exports of specific commodity, 1997

Commodity	EU	Total Europe	US	North America	Japan	Total Asia & Oceania
Beverages and tobacco	40.5	46.4	11.4	13.3	4.2	23.1
Pulp and waste paper	86.5	88.1	3.1	3.3	0.5	6.8
Textile fibres	46.4	56.2	7.6	9.1	2.4	13.1
Petroleum	75.0	79.5	16.1	18.1	0.0	0.6
Gas, natural and manufactured	91.8	95.5	0.2	0.2	–	0.3
Electric current	100.0	100.0	–	–	–	–
Chemicals	56.7	64.7	10.1	13.2	2.7	12.0
Iron and steel	58.6	67.8	8.0	10.0	0.8	13.6
Machinery and transport equipment	53.3	60.5	13.8	15.5	2.6	13.4
Power generating machinery	41.8	47.9	28.8	32.7	1.4	18.4
Office machines and computers	68.1	74.2	12.2	13.0	4.6	9.4
Telecommunications	60.5	69.1	7.7	9.1	0.8	14.5
Electrical machinery	57.5	63.7	11.7	13.2	2.2	16.7
Road vehicles	63.8	69.9	10.4	11.3	4.6	11.4
Footwear	51.1	57.6	22.5	24.7	3.5	10.8

Source: UK Government Statistical Service, Overseas Trade Statistics of the United Kingdom with the World, 1997

Appendix Table 7.5: German Exports by Region

Germany Exports by Region, percentages, 1993–1997

	1993	1995	1997
	percentage of total exports		
EU	56.8	57.0	55.5
Total Europe	72.8	73.2	73.0
US	7.7	7.5	8.6
North America	9.1	8.5	10.0
Japan	2.6	2.6	2.3
Total Asia	10.8	11.7	10.6
Other countries	7.3	6.6	6.4
Total	100.0	100.0	100.0

Notes: Other countries refers to developing countries in Africa, the Middle East, the Western Hemisphere (excluding Mexico), North Korea, and Cuba.
Statistical discrepancies are the result of rounding.
Source: IMF, *Direction of Trade Statistics Yearbook*, 1999

Appendix Table 7.6: Japan's Exports by Region

Japan's Exports by Region, percentages, 1991–1998

	1991	1993	1995	1997	1998
	percentage of total exports				
Asia	37.0	40.8	45.5	44.5	37.9
Oceania	2.7	2.7	2.4	2.4	2.5
Asia and Oceania	39.7	43.5	47.9	46.9	40.4
EU	18.8	15.7	15.9	15.6	18.4
Other Europe	4.1	3.0	1.5	1.9	2.1
Total Europe	22.9	18.8	17.4	17.5	20.5
US	29.1	29.2	27.3	27.8	30.5
Other North America	5.1	4.9	4.3	4.7	5.1
North America	34.2	34.1	31.6	32.5	35.7
South America	1.3	1.6	1.5	1.8	1.9
Africa	1.9	2.1	1.7	1.3	1.5
Total	100.0	100.0	100.0	100.0	100.0

Source: Adapted from Japan Information Network (JIN), Statistics
(http://jin.jcic.or.jp/stat/)

Appendix Table 7.7: Japan's Imports by Region

Japan's Imports by Region, percentages, 1991–1998

	1991	1993	1995	1997	1998
	percentage of total imports				
Asia	43.5	45.5	46.1	48.4	46.2
Oceania	6.6	6.3	5.5	5.3	5.6
Asia and Oceania	50.1	51.8	51.6	53.7	51.8
EU	13.4	11.4	15.5	18.4	13.9
Other Europe	4.8	3.8	3.5	4.1	2.8
Total Europe	18.2	15.2	19.0	22.5	16.8
US	22.5	23.0	22.4	22.3	23.9
Other North America	4.5	4.3	4.0	3.7	3.5
North America	27.0	27.2	26.4	26.0	27.4
South America	3.0	2.6	2.8	2.6	2.6
Africa	1.6	1.6	1.4	1.4	1.4
Total	100.0	100.0	100.0	100.0	100.0

Source: Adapted from Japan Information Network (JIN),
Statistics (http://jin.jcic.or.jp/stat/)

Appendix Table 7.8: Japan Exports by Commodity Sector

Japan, Exports by Commodity Sector, as a percentage of total exports of special commodity, 1997

Commodity	Asia	EU	North America
Beverages and tobacco	–	–	–
Pulp and waste paper	–	–	–
Textile fibres	76.2	–	–
Petroleum	86.0	–	–
Gas, natural and manufactured	–	–	–
Electric current	–	–	–
Chemicals	57.7	15.6	19.6
Iron and Steel	70.9	2.9	13.5
Machinery & transport equipment	37.0	16.7	33.0
Power generating machinery	31.1	–	41.3
Office machines and computers	22.9	27.5	46.9
Telecommunications	–	15.7	34.3
Electrical machinery	52.3	15.1	26.8
Road vehicles	12.3	16.2	41.0
Footwear	n/a	n/a	n/a

Source: JETRO, *White Paper on International Trade Japan*, 1998

Appendix Table 7.9: NAFTA Exports by Region

NAFTA Exports by Region, percentages

	1991	1993	1995	1997
	percentage of total exports			
NAFTA	36.5	40.8	38.4	39.8
EU	20.7	17.2	16.2	15.4
Other Europe	3.4	3.3	2.5	2.7
Total Europe	24.0	20.4	18.7	18.0
Japan	9.4	8.4	8.6	7.3
Total Asia and Oceania	23.8	23.3	25.0	22.4
Other Exports	15.7	15.4	17.9	19.9
Total Exports	100.0	100.0	100.0	100.0

Appendix Table 7.10: NAFTA Imports by Region

NAFTA Imports by Region, percentages, 1991–1997

	1991	1993	1995	1997
	percentage of total imports			
NAFTA	35.4	36.5	37.7	39.8
EU	17.2	16.2	15.9	15.9
Other Europe	2.1	2.4	2.5	2.5
Total Europe	19.3	18.6	18.4	18.4
Japan	15.6	15.3	13.9	11.4
Total Asia and Oceania	34.0	34.5	35.1	32.3
Other Imports	11.4	10.3	8.8	9.5
Total Imports	100.0	100.0	100.0	100.0

Appendix Table 7.11: US Exports by Region

US Exports by Region, percentages, 1991–1997

	1991	1993	1995	1997
	percentage of total exports			
EU	25.7	22.0	21.2	20.5
Total Europe	29.3	25.9	24.1	23.7
North America	28.1	32.6	29.5	32.2
Japan	11.4	10.3	11.0	9.6
Total Asia	29.7	30.0	33.0	30.1
Other countries	13.0	11.5	13.4	13.9
Total	100.0	100.0	100.0	100.0

Notes: Other countries refers to developing countries in Africa, the Middle East, the Western Hemisphere (excluding Mexico), North Korea, and Cuba.
Statistical discrepancies are the result of rounding.
Source: IMF, *Direction of Trade Statistics Yearbook*, 1999.

Appendix Table 7.12: US Imports by Region

US Imports by Region, percentages, 1991–1997

	1991	1993	1995	1997
	percentage of total imports			
EU	6.3	6.8	8.1	9.7
Total Europe	8.5	9.7	10.9	12.5
North America	24.7	25.7	27.4	28.8
Japan	18.7	18.4	16.5	13.8
Total Asia	41.2	41.7	41.8	39.1
Other countries	25.6	23.0	19.8	19.7
Total	100.0	100.0	100.0	100.0

Notes: Other countries refers to developing countries in Africa, the Middle East, the Western Hemisphere (excluding Mexico), North Korea, and Cuba.
Statistical discrepancies are the result of rounding.
Source: IMF, *Direction of Trade Statistics Yearbook*, 1999.

8

The Evidence on Multinational Enterprises

The Triad MNEs

The United Nations has identified over 45,000 MNEs, but the largest 500 account for 80 per cent of all the world's foreign direct investment. Of these, 434 are from the triad blocs of the United States, European Union, and Japan. Table 8.1 shows the world's 500 largest MNEs by country/bloc. There are 179 from the United States, 107 from Japan and 148 from the 15 member countries of the EU. Total annual sales of these 500 firms are in

Table 8.1: The World's 500 Largest Multinationals, 1999

Country	No. of MNEs
United States	179
European Union	148
Japan	107
Canada	12
Switzerland	11
South Korea	12
Australia	7
China	10
Brazil	3
Norway	2
Taiwan	1
India	1
Malaysia	1
Mexico	2
Russia	2
South Africa	1
Venezuela	1
Total	**500**

Source: Adapted from Fortune, 'The Fortune Global 500', 24 July 2000

excess of US$11 trillion and they collectively employ over 35 million people. These firms are engaged in operations such as autos, chemicals, computers, consumer goods, financial goods, industrial equipment, oil and steel production. Clearly, the large industrial MNEs have a significant impact on international business and the world economy.

The change in the make up of the 500 largest MNEs over the last ten years is shown in Table 8.2. This confirms that well over 80 per cent of the 500 largest MNEs are always from the triad, with a reasonably steady increase in the EU proportion and most variation in the Japanese proportion.

Table 8.2: Changes in the Fortune Global 500

Country/Block	1990	1991	1992	1993	1994	1995	1996	1997	1998	1999
United States	164	157	161	159	151	153	162	175	185	179
EU	129	134	126	126	149	148	155	155	156	148
Japan	111	119	128	135	149	141	126	112	100	107
Switzerland	11	10	9	9	14	16	14	12	11	11
South Korea	11	13	12	12	8	12	13	12	9	12
Canada	12	9	8	7	5	6	6	8	12	12
Brazil	3	1	1	1	2	4	5	5	4	3
Australia	9	9	9	10	3	4	5	7	7	7
China	0	0	0	0	3	2	3	4	6	10
Others	50	48	46	41	16	14	11	10	10	11
Total	500	500	500	500	500	500	500	500	500	500

Source: Fortune, 'The Fortune Global 500', 24 July 2000
Note: Finland and Sweden were included as Others prior to 1996 and as EU from 1996, when they became members.

The names of the largest MNEs in the triad, as well as those from Canada are listed in the four Appendix Tables, see Nos. 8.1 to 8.4.

Triad-based mergers

Multinational firms do not succeed with global strategies, they use regional/triad strategies. The business world of automobiles, telecoms and pharmaceuticals is organized by triad, not globally.

Another piece of evidence supporting regional strategies is the recent spate of mergers and acquisitions (M&A) by large multinational enterprises. Table 8.3 lists the largest 25 such M&As over the last three years. These are mainly examples of M&As across the triad blocks of Europe and North America. They are especially noticeable in sectors such as autos, telecoms and pharmaceuticals.

Of these 25 M&As, five were by US-based MNEs acquiring European MNEs, while five were the reverse–European-based MNEs acquiring US

Table 8.3: 25 Largest Cross-Border M&A Transactions 1997-1999

	Acquiring MNE	Triad Home Base	Acquired MNE	Triad Base of Acquired MNE	US$b
1	AirTouch Communications	US	Vodafone Group PLC	UK	65.9
2	British Petroleum Co PLC	UK	Amoco Corp.	US	55.0
3	US West Inc.	US	Global Crossing Ltd.	Bermuda	51.1
4	Daimler-Benz AG	Germany	Chrysler Corp.	US	40.5
5	BP Amoco	UK	ARCO	US	33.7
6	Zeneca Group PLC	UK	Astra AB	Sweden	31.8
7	Hoechst AG-Chemicals & Fibres Div.	Germany	Rhône-Poulenc SA-Chemicals & Fibres Div.	France	28.5
8	Hoechst AG-Life Sciences Div.	Germany	Rhône-Poulenc SA-Life Sciences	France	21.2
9	Zurich Versicherungs GmbH	Switzerland	BAT Industries PLC Financial	UK	18.4
10	YPF SA	Argentina	Repson SA	Spain	17.1
11	British Aerospace	UK	Marconi Electronics	US	13.0
12	Scottish Power PLC	UK	Pacific Corp	US	12.6
13	Frontier Corp.	US	Global Crossing Ltd.	Bermuda	12.5
14	Total SA	France	Petrofina SA	Bermuda	11.5
15	TransAmerica Corp.	US	Aegon NV	Netherlands	10.8
16	Wal-Mart Stores	US	ASDA Group PLC	UK	10.7
17	Universal Studios Inc	US	PolyGram NV (Philips Electronics)	Netherlands	10.3
18	Roche Holding AG	Switzerland	Corange Ltd.	Bermuda	10.2
19	Allianz AG Holding Berlin	Germany	AGF	France	10.2
20	Deutsche BankAG	Germany	Bankers Trust New York Corp.	US	9.1
21	Northern Telecom Ltd. (BCE Inc)	Canada	Bay Networks Inc	US	9.0
22	Texas Utilities Co.	US	Energy Group PLC	UK	8.8
23	Case Corp.	US	New Holland	Netherlands	8.7
24	VIAG AG	Germany	Alusuisse-Lonza AG	Switzerland	8.6
25	ICI PLC	UK	Quest International, 3 others	Netherlands	8.0

Source: Adapted and updated from United Nations, *World Investment Reports 1998, 1999.*

MNEs. Another four involved acquisition of MNEs registered in Bermuda, one was a Canadian take-over of a US firm, and the final ten were intra-European mergers. While the overall message from this set of data is not all that clear, it offers little support for the globalization thesis, and more for the inter-penetration of triad markets and the consolidation of internal triad-based economic activity.

Telecom mergers

The telecommunications industry is facing wide restructuring around the world. Initially, it was dominated by domestic companies under heavy government regulation. Today, a wave of mergers and acquisitions and strategic alliances is transforming the industry, creating regional networks that compete for a rapidly growing market.

Vodafone Airtouch is the result of a merger between Vodafone, the biggest UK wireless carrier, and Airtouch, the largest independent mobile operator in the United States. The merger was strategic for the European market. Vodafone had investments in France, Sweden, Germany, Greece and the Netherlands, Airtouch was positioned in Germany, Italy, Belgium, Spain, Portugal and Eastern Europe. The move allowed them to consolidate their interests in Germany and to access each others' markets in the rest of Europe. It also gave Vodafone access to the US market and increased the new company's reach in Asia.

The Vodafone Airtouch merger was followed by the consolidation of the new company's mobile phone assets in the US with those of Bell Atlantic. PrimeCo, their joint venture, now had twice as many mobile subscribers as AT&T and has become a serious competitor in the US market.

In November 1999, a Vodafone Airtouch bid for Mannesmann was met by opposition from German management. This led to the launch of a hostile takeover. Vodafone Airtouch would merge with Mannesmann's Telecommunication division, divesting itself of Mannesmann's engineering and automotive divisions. France Telecom would acquire Orange, the UK wireless operator presently owned by Mannesmann. The merger between Vodafone Airtouch and Mannesmann would create the largest mobile telecommunications operator with over 42 million customers around the world and the potential to expand further into a rapidly growing wireless market. In Europe, it would be the largest telecommunications company, with a presence in eleven EU countries. The German company owns D2, the number one mobile phone operator in Germany. Mannesmann itself has been expanding over the last few years and has acquired stakes in a number of European countries. As well as Orange in the UK, it has a controlling stake in Omnitel, the second largest mobile operator in Italy. Minority stakes in Cegetel (France), which provides mobile services through tele.ring in Austria and SFR in France are part of the company's strategy to expand into the greater European market.

Vodafone Airtouch already has minority stakes in Mannesmann's D2 and Omnitel. If the merger goes through, the new company will have controlling interests in key players in some of the largest markets in Europe. (In early 2000 the merger succeeded).

US telephone companies in Europe

AT&T and the seven regional phone companies in the United States, popularly known as the 'Baby Bells,' are well known for their reliable equipment for high-quality service. Now they are taking their expertise to Europe and gaining international market share. Currently most of the major US deals in the EU consist of strategic alliances with local companies. Here are four examples:

- Ameritech has interests in Europe totalling over $6 billion. It purchased WLW, a European provider of business information, which allowed it to take over operations in 10 European countries. In Denmark, this 'Baby Bell' owns 34.7 per cent of Tele Danmark, which provides all kinds of telecommunication services. In Norway it holds a 19.7 per cent stake of NetCom which services Norway's cellular market. The company also has joint ventures with Deutsche Telekom to provide local phone lines, cellular, long distance, and cable TV in Hungary. It has joined a six way partnership with Tele Danmark, and Singapore Telecom, among others, to provide telecommunication services to Belgium.
- Bell Atlantic and US West are part of a joint venture that has been awarded a contract to work with the state telephone company in the Czech Republic and in Slovakia to build and operate cellular and data networks and to modernize the basic telephone network.
- MCI WorldCom provides an integrated telecommunication network linking major cities throughout the continent, such as Paris, London, Brussels, Frankfurt, Amsterdam and Stockholm and it is expecting to triple the size of its pan-European network by the end of 1999.
- Bell South has a 22.5 per cent share of the E-plus consortium in Germany which today services 98 per cent of Germany's population.

In Denmark the company has a 46.5 equity share in a joint venture with Sonofon to provide digital cellular services to 500,000 Danes.

AT&T is also playing a big role in the EU market. In 1998 it decided to merge its international operations with British Telecom into a US$11billion enterprise. The company currently has 3,000 international employees, up from 100 in 1984. It has joint ventures or alliances in 44 countries around the world. AT&T also makes a great deal of money on its long distance service between the United States and Europe. Four of the 10 countries that have the most long distance traffic with the United States are Britain, Germany, France, and Italy. Over 50 per cent of these long distance calls travel on AT&T equipment.

EU firms are well aware of their US competitors and are now striking back. In many cases they are forming alliances with US companies and/or other European firms. In 1999 Telecom Italy was holding talks with Deutsche Telekom over a possible merger. France Telecom, Deutsche Telekom and Sprint formed Global One, a joint venture to provide voice and data telecommunications. Global One employs 3,800 people in more than 65 countries. While US telecommunications companies are finding the EU to be an attractive market, there is growing local competition that may severely limit the market opportunities for AT&T and the Baby Bells.[1]

Mergers in automobiles

Virtually every month there is news of a major merger between multi-national enterprises. The most startling was the takeover of Chrysler by Daimler-Benz in 1998, a deal worth over US$ 40 billion. The US 'big three' auto producers – GM, Ford and Chrysler – have become a 'big two', with Chrysler rapidly being absorbed within the management structure of Daimler. 'How do you pronounce Daimler-Chrysler? – the Chrysler is silent', was a popular joke in 1999.

This merger links two parts of the triad. It gives Daimler access to the North American market, matching the European presence which GM and

---

[1] This section is adapted from Andrew Kupfer, 'Ma Bell and Seven Babies Go Global,' Fortune, November 4, 1991; Mark Lewyn, 'There's Less and Less Static on These Lines,' Business Week, January 8, 1990, p. 101; Gary Slutsker, 'The Tortoise and the Hare,' Forbes, February 1, 1993, pp. 66-81; http://www.ameritech.com/; http://www.bellatlantic.com/; http://www.wcom.com/; http://www.att.com; http://www.sprint.com; 'European Telecoms in a Tangle,' Economist, April 24, 1999.

Ford have established over the last 40 years. By giving Daimler access to Chrysler's supplier and distribution networks throughout North America, the merger positions Daimler-Chrysler as a rival 'flagship' to both GM and Ford. In doing this, Daimler-Benz is pursuing a regional strategy for North America, not a global strategy.

Partly in response to Daimler's take-over of Chrysler, in late 1998 Ford acquired Volvo cars (but not the Volvo trucks division). This allowed Ford to complete a line of 'high-end' luxury cars, such as Jaguar and Aston-Martin, which complement its core brand models and basic platforms. Ford has long been successful in linking the European and North American regional markets, but it still does not produce a global car.

Two other car producers merged in 1998. Volkswagen made an agreement with BMW to acquire Rolls Royce Motors. This completed the sale of the British car industry to the Germans, since BMW had previously acquired Rover. No aspects of global strategy are apparent in these mergers – rather they reflect consolidation within the regionally isolated market of Western Europe. In early 2000 BMW sold most of Rover to a British company and also sold Land Rover to Ford.

Table 8.4: Largest Motor Vehicle Companies

Company	Country	Revenues US$ billion	Activity
General Motors	United States	161	
Daimler-Chrysler	Germany	155	Merger
Ford Motor	United States	144	Acquired Volvo
Toyota Motor	Japan	98	
Volkswagen	Germany	76	Acquired Rolls Royce
Nissan Motor	Japan	51	Acquired by Renault
Fiat	Italy	51	
Honda Motor	Japan	49	
Renault	France	41	Acquired Nissan Motor
Peugeot	France	38	Joint ventures with Renault, Fiat and Ford
BMW	Germany	36	
Mitsubishi Motors	Japan	27	
Volvo	Sweden	27	Acquired by Ford
Mazda Motor	Japan	16	

Source: Adapted from Fortune, 'The Global 500, August 2, 1999.

Finally, Nissan was acquired by Renault. The French management team introduced cost saving and efficiency measures into the Japanese firm, leading to some of the largest job losses in Japanese history. Again, this is an inter-triad move, by the European firm into Nissan's the Japanese home-base. There are interesting second order global repercussions, since Nissan is an active producer in North America, where its operations are somewhat more efficient. These mergers are recorded in Table 8.4.

Consolidation in the automobile industry has largely occurred through US firms buying up EU producers, but making strategic alliances with Japanese producers. The 'big five' of world automobile production are:

- General Motors
- Ford
- Toyota
- Daimler-Chrysler
- Renault-Nissan – Renault owns 36.8 per cent.

This is how their mergers and alliances stack up:

- General Motors (United States) has made three European acquisitions:
    Opel (Germany)
    Vauxhall (UK)
    Saab (Sweden) – 50 per cent ownership
    It also has an alliance with Fiat (Italy)

- GM has four joint ventures in Asia:
    Suzuki (Japan) – GM owns 10 per cent
    Isuzu (Japan) – GM owns 49 per cent
    Toyota (Japan)
    Subaru/Fuji Heavy Industries (Japan) – GM owns 20 per cent

- Ford Motors (United States) has four European acquisitions:
    Jaguar (UK)
    Aston Martin (UK)
    Volvo Cars (Sweden)
    Land Rover (UK), from BMW

- Ford has two joint ventures in Asia:
    Mazda (Japan) – Ford owns 33.4 per cent
    Kia (Korea)

- Toyota (Japan) has a joint venture with General Motors (United States)

- Daimler-Benz (EU) has merged with Chrysler

- Renault (EU) has acquired Nissan.

This pattern of mergers and joint ventures is part of a strategy of inter-triad consolidation, driven by the need for market access to other parts of the triad. The big two US auto assemblers now have a considerable presence in Europe. They have also helped to bring Japanese manufacturing quality production processes to their US home base, through strategic alliances with Japanese partners. Daimler-Benz has achieved a major presence in the North American market through its acquisition of Chrysler. Renault has taken over Nissan (which is badly in debt) and may achieve some access to North America through Nissan's presence there.

The Ford ownership of 33.4 per cent of Mazda Motors has not been an easy relationship. There have been three presidents in the last three years, with Mark Fields succeeding James Miller in December 1999 as President of Mazda Motor Corporation. The first President, Henry Wallace, also only lasted a year. The companies are still to finalize production of their first car using a shared platform. For Ford to be successful in Asia it needs to operate a regional strategy with Mazda. Ford needs to build on Mazda's engine technology and production expertise to manufacture a vehicle to compete with the rival Nissan/Renault and GM/Suzuki, GM/Isuzu, GM/Subaru groups, as well as with Toyota. Ford also is attempting to restructure Mazda's distribution network in Japan, and the rest of Asia. The success of this will be determined locally rather than due to any so-called global business skills of Ford.

Nissan is going through a dramatic restructuring, driven by the need to reduce its net debt of ¥.700 b. It has lost market share to rival car producers like Toyota, GM, Ford and Daimler-Chrysler, all of whom began restructuring long before Nissan. Renault have appointed Brazilian, Carlos Ghosn as Chief Operating Officer of Nissan, to force through con-solidations by five plant closures in Japan and cuts in Nissan's Japanese and global workforce of 14 per cent (21,000 jobs). In addition purchasing costs are to be cut by 20 per cent over three years, with the number of key suppliers being reduced by a half to 600. In addition, Nissan's dealership structure is being overhauled. Nissan is one of the first Japanese companies to suffer plant closures. For a country where lifetime job security was a given, the late 1990s have been an unpleasant introduction to international competitive realities.

Pharmaceuticals mergers

Aventis, the joint venture between Rhône-Poulenc of France and Hoechst of Germany, will see both companies' life sciences divisions merging to become one of the largest pharmaceutical and agricultural companies in the world. With sales of US$20 billion in 1997 and a US$ 3 billion R&D budget, Aventis will be able to market and develop products in an industry increasingly dominated by huge mergers. The joint venture is the first step to a full merger, when the companies have divested themselves of other operations.

Aventis is just one of a wave of mergers, joint ventures and strategic alliances in the pharmaceutical industry (see Table 8.5). In 1995, Glaxo and Wellcome and then Pharmacia and Upjohn merged to create two of the world's largest pharmaceutical companies. Bayer and Roche merged their US operations and Roche has been busy acquiring Genetech in 1990 and the Corange Group in 1997. Switzerland's Ciba-Geigy and Sandoz merged in 1996 to create Novartis. In 1999, British company Zeneca merged with Swedish Astra to create AstraZeneca. In 1999 Pharmacia & Upjohn proposed a merger with Monsanto and Pfizer was attempting a hostile takeover of Warner-Lambert, who preferred to merge with American Home Products (AHP).

Pharmaceutical mergers tend to be difficult to secure. Before finally agreeing to merge in January 2000, Glaxo Wellcome and SmithKline Beecham previously called off a merger in 1998, due to top management differences, angering shareholders and creating large stock market losses. The new company is called GlaxoSmithKline. Glaxo Wellcome had attempted a merger with US pharmaceutical company Bristol-Myers Squibb, but managers were unable to reach an agreement. AHP is also on the look out for a partner. In 1998 talks with SmithKline Beecham proved unfruitful. By 1999 AHP was holding talks with Warner-Lambert. Pfizer then bid for Warner-Lambert and appeared to outbid AHP in late 1999.

These mergers are the result of an industry driven by innovation and market expansion. Large pharmaceutical companies can achieve economies of scale in R&D while increasing their overall R&D budget. Bringing a successful new drug to market can cost as much as US$ 500 million and for each successful product in the pipeline there are many that fail in development. Costs are expected to increase even further in the future with

Table 8.5: Largest Pharmaceutical Companies

Company	Country	Revenues US$ million	Merger Activity
Merck	United States	26,898	
Johnson & Johnson	United States	23,657	
Novartis	Switzerland	21,874	Merger of Ciba Geigy and Sandoz
Bristol-Myers Squibb	United States	18,284	Failed merger with Glaxo Wellcome
Roche Holding	Switzerland	17,016	Acquired Genetech and Corange Group
Pfizer	United States	14,704	Hostile takeover in progress with Warner-Lambert in 1999
American Home Products	United States	13,463	Is seeking to acquire Warner-Lambert
SmithKline Beecham	United Kingdom	13,396	Merger with Glaxo Wellcome, January 2000
Glaxo Wellcome	United Kingdom	13,232	Merger of Glaxo and Wellcome in 1995. In January 2000, merged with SmithKline Beecham.
Abbott Laboratories	United States	12,478	
Warner-Lambert	United States	10,214	Potential merger in progress with Pfizer, or AHP
Eli Lilly	United States	10,051	
AstraZeneca	United Kingdom	9,133	Merger of Astra and Zeneca, 1999

Source: These data on revenues are for 1998 as adapted from Fortune, 'The FortuneGlobal 500,' August 2, 1999. The information on merger activity reflected the situation in mid January 2000.

the genomics revolution. Access to markets and distribution systems is also facilitated by partnering with a well-established rival. The large pharmaceutical companies are fighting to choose partners for a strategic game of innovation.

Mergers in small, open economies

Another way of looking at the issue of mergers is to consider it from the viewpoint of a non-triad economy, such as Canada. Although Canada is a member of the G7, it is a 'small' and 'open' economy, dependent on the demand side of international markets for its firms to achieve economies of scale or brand recognition. Canada's large firms are actually small in triad terms – for example, they are under one tenth the size of the largest US firms. What is the context for anti-trust or competition policy in such a situation?

Competition policy and concentration in Canada

Mergers and acquisitions in Canada do not have deleterious effects on competition. Business restructuring is necessary for Canadian companies to compete effectively in the global market. The emergence of large multinational enterprises has changed the thinking of Canadian managers. To secure access to the US market, the private sector in Canada supported negotiation and implementation of the Canada-US Free Trade Agreement of 1988. This was followed by the North American Free Trade Agreement in 1993. Now, strategic planners in Canadian corporations of all sizes are geared up to operate in an integrated North American market – the first step towards doing business on a global/triad scale. An inevitable result of the FTA and NAFTA has been the restructuring of Canadian business. This has led to consolidation and to mergers and acquisitions.

Larger business units are being created in a bid to survive intense competition from multinationals based in the United States, Europe and Japan, and Canadian corporations are developing strategies to compete either on price, by differentiation or by finding niches in goods and service markets. The wave of mergers and acquisitions in Canada over the last ten years is part of an efficient process by which the Canadian economy can prepare itself to survive into the twenty-first century.

Increased market concentration

Despite the economic logic of corporate concentration, early in 1999 the Canadian Minister of Finance, Paul Martin, disallowed the potential mergers of the Royal Bank of Canada with the Bank of Montreal and the CIBC with the Toronto-Dominion Bank. Yet ten years ago similar concerns were being raised about some of the 'mega-mergers' of that time. Back in 1989, Molson Cos. Ltd merged with Carling O'Keefe Breweries, giving them over 53 per cent of the Canadian beer market and only one domestic competitor, Labatts (now bought out by a Belgian brewer, Interbrew). Canadian Airlines International and Wardair Inc. airlines joined to compete against Air Canada on domestic routes. Imperial Oil Ltd merged with Texaco Canada.

In each of these three cases, Canadian market concentration increased to an extraordinary degree, and any conventional measure of the domestic concentration ratio shot into the perceived danger zone. Yet none of these mergers really threatened competition in Canada.

This is because Canada is not an economic island. Rather, it is a relatively small economic unit in a sea of global competition. The Molson-

Carling joint beer venture ranked only sixth in size among North American beer firms and about twelfth on a world scale. Similarly, the size of Canada's airlines and oil firms is small in global terms. In late 1999 Air Canada bought Canadian Airlines, following the failure of Onex to buy Air Canada. The federal government had waived the competition policy guidelines to allow such a merger.

Clearly, old fashioned thinking about domestic concentration ratios is irrelevant in today's interdependent global economic system. Canada's competition watchdog, the Bureau of Competition Policy, has not been undoing such mergers. One of its mandates is to assess the impact of any merger from the viewpoint of Canada's international competitiveness. From this perspective, Canada's corporate sector is not overly concentrated. More concentration in a relatively small open economy like Canada will lead to greater economic efficiency.

Merging to efficient relative size

The relative size of Canadian firms on a global scale is seen by comparing tables 8.6 and 8.7. Table 8.6 identifies the ten largest industrial companies in Canada, ranked by sales for 1996. The average size of these ten firms was about US$13 billion.

Table 8.6: The Largest Canadian MNEs

Rank	Firm	Industry	Sales (US$ m.)
1	Nortel Networks	Network Communications	21,287.0
2	George Weston	Food and Drug Stores	14,033.9
3	CIBC	Banks: Commercial & Savings	13,441.2
4	Royal Bank of Canada	Banks: Commercial & Savings	13,146.1
5	Transcanada Pipelines	Energy	12,415.2
6	Seagram	Entertainment	11,784.0
7	Bank of Montreal	Banks: Commercial & Savings	11,139.3
8	Bank of Nova Scotia	Banks: Commercial & Savings	11,118.6
9	Sun Life Ass. of Canada	Insurance: Life, Health (mutual)	10,511.1
10	Toronto Dominion Bank	Banks: Commercial & Savings	10,470.3
Average (10 Largest)			**12,934.6**

Source: Adapted from *Fortune*, 'The Fortune Global 500', 24 July, 2000

Table 8.7: The World's Largest Industrial Firms

Rank	Firm	Revenues (US$m.)
1	General Motors	16,558.0
2	Wal-Mart Stores	166,809.0
3	Exxon Mobil	163,881.0
4	Ford Motors	162,558.0
5	Daimler-Chrysler	159,985.7
6	Mitsui	118,555.2
7	Mitsubishi	117,765.6
8	Toyota Motor	115,670.9
9	General Electric	111,630.0
10	Itochu	109,068.9
Average (10 largest)		**140,248.2**

Source: Adapted from *Fortune*, 'The Fortune Global 500', 24 July, 2000.

In contrast, table 8.7 identifies the ten largest industrial companies in the world, again based on 1996 sales which have been converted into US dollars. The average size of these firms is US$140 billion – over ten times larger than the Canadian set. The average size of the world's largest 50 firms is also well over ten times that of Canada's largest 50 firms. Even after the mega-mergers, the new banks in Canada would not be of any significant size on a global scale.

Even when foreign-owned companies in Canada – such as the big three US auto companies in table 8.7 – are thrown out of the picture, the largest Canadian owned firms are still about one-tenth the size of the largest US (or world) firms. The reason is very simple – companies in Canada reflect the economic size of the nation relative to its largest market (the US takes about 80 per cent of Canadian trade and 54 per cent of its foreign direct investment). In short, Canada is one-tenth the size of the United States and so are its companies.

In our integrated North American and global economic systems, Canada's companies are merging to their efficient relative size. Mergers and acquisitions merely reflect the reality of doing business in this environment and should not cause Canadians to worry.

The larger Canadian companies become, the better equipped they are to pursue successful competitive strategies against foreign rivals. Today, successful multinational enterprises pursue three types of strategy:

- Price competitive, through global economies of scale and learning curve effects
- Product differentiation, through advertising and turning products into familiar brands
- Niche seeking on a geographic or product line basis.

The trend towards corporate concentration helps Canadian-owned multinationals in all three areas. Bigger firms have greater potential for cost savings through large-scale of production and more opportunities to assemble an optional set of brand name products which they can produce worldwide. Niche strategies can be pursued by both large and small firms; however, they are most useful to larger firms when coupled with the development of scale or differentiation strategies.

Canada loses Head Offices

A recent concern expressed in Canada, for example by Tom d'Aquino, CEO of the Business Council on National Issues, is that the mergers and acquisitions are reducing the number of head offices in Canada. Examples that occurred in 1999 were that Canada's largest forestry company MacMillan Bloedel was bought by US competitor, Weyerhaeuser and the head office moved out of Vancouver. Canada's Nova Chemicals has moved from Alberta to Pittsburgh. In an even more interesting case Alcan, probably Canada's most successful post war resource-based firm, merged with Pechiney and Algroup to create the world's second-largest aluminium company (after Alcoa and Reynolds). The Alcan President, Jacques Bougie will be the CEO of the new group, but the head office will leave Montreal for one in New York, if the merger is approved.

These mergers are part of a pattern of North American triad-based consolidation. Unfortunately, Canada will probably continue to lose head office jobs. Instead of Mr d'Aquino being concerned about losing a few members of his BCNI, he should rather be pleased that the merged companies are now competitive on a triad basis. There will be more jobs for Canadians as partners in these competitive business groups, or as key suppliers, or as other partners with the very largest MNEs, many of whom will be controlled from the United States rather than Canada. With free trade and NAFTA, Canada is integrated with the United States. The lesson from international business is that the ownership of capital is much less important than its performance.

More deregulation needed

To enhance the efficiency of Canada's largest companies further, more deregulation of the Canadian economy is needed. The beer industry is still handicapped by interprovincial barriers to trade, while the transportation sector faces severe regulation. Development of energy and other industrial sectors would be helped by a more stable climate for private sector investment. In the services sector, domestic banking reform is necessary to reflect the realities of global competition, which demand larger and more efficient banking units. As in telecom, there is no longer any feasible way of isolating Canadian business from foreign competitors.

The Canadian federal government appears to understand the need to foster corporate development, so more privatization of the economy and declining government regulation can be expected. This will not, in itself, increase corporate concentration in Canada, but neither will it hinder such a necessary process. Even more corporate concentration in Canada is required to do business in world markets. A successful economic future means looking outward with mergers and acquisitions in the service sector as well as in manufacturing.

Table 8.8: The global distribution of assets of the world's leading automotive MNEs (per cent)

	North America	Japan[1]	Europe
US MNEs[2]	64.3	11.6	24.3
Japanese MNEs[3]	26.5	66.3	7.2
European MNEs[4]	2.8	4.7	92.5

Footnotes:-
[1] For US and European MNEs data are for Asia
[2] General Motors, Ford, Dana, Johnson Controls
[3] Mitsubishi Motors, Nissan, Fuji Heavy Industries, Denso, Mazda Motor, Honda, Toyota
[4] Renault, Peugeot
Source: Michael Gestrin, Rory Knight and Alan Rugman (1998), *The Templeton Global Performance Index*. Oxford: Templeton College, University of Oxford.

Automobile assets are regional, not global

Using data on the world's largest 500 MNEs, Gestrin, Knight and Rugman (1998) find a strong concentration of assets in the home triad base of the large automobile firms.

As Table 8.8 shows, 92.5 per cent of the assets of Renault and Peugeot are held in Europe, i.e. they have virtually no foreign assets in the form of foreign subsidiaries. The large Japanese MNEs have 66.3 per cent of their assets in their home base, with 26.5 per cent in the United States and 7.2 per cent in Europe. The large US MNEs have 64.3 per cent of their assets at home 24.3 per cent in Europe and 11.6 per cent in Japan.

These data demonstrate that the large automobile firms have regionally-based assets (subsidiaries) within their home triad base. There is no evidence of global production whatsoever for EU firms, while US and Japanese firms have about one third of their assets in other triad markets.

Automobile sales are of locally produced vehicles

In Japan, Table 8.9 shows that 95.6 per cent of all new motor vehicle registrations in 1998 were of Japanese-made vehicles and only 4.4 per cent were of imported cars. For passenger cars alone in 1998, registration of domestically produced vehicles was 93.5 per cent.

Table 8.9: Triad-based Automobile Data

(a) Motor Vehicle Registrations in Japan (1998)

	units
Japanese made	5958144
Imports	275869
Total	6234013
Percentage of registrations that are for Japanese-made motor vehicles	95.57%
Passenger Cars Registrations in Japan (1998)	
Japanese	3827196
Imported passenger cars	265948
Total passenger cars	4093144
Percentage of registrations for passenger cars that are produced domestically	93.50%

Source: http://www.toyota.co.jp/e/data/databank-m/f2102.html
originally from JADA, JMA, JAIA

(b) United States (1996)

	thousands
Passenger car production	6083
Imports from Canada	1688
sum above	7771
New passenger car retail sales	8527
North American produced	7254
Imports	1273
Percentage of US retail sales of those that are produced in North America	85.07%

Source: Statistical abstract of the United States 1998.

(c) Canada (1998)

	units
Total Canadian sales of new motor vehicles	23201535
Produced in North America	21165239
Foreign produced	2036296
Percentage of Canadian sales of new motor vehicles that are produced in North America	91.22%

Source: Statistics Canada, Cansim Database, Labels D2366 and D2367.

In the United States new passenger car retail sales in 1996 were 8,527,000 while production of North American cars was 7,254,000; it follows that 85 per cent of all US sales of cars were of cars produced (or at least assembled) in North America.

In Canada, 91.2 per cent of all new motor vehicle sales in 1998 were of cars produced or assembled in North America.

Data for Europe-wide car registrations and production were not available.

Appendix Table 8.1: The 25 Largest US MNEs, 1999

Rank	Firm	Industry	Revenues (US$m.)
1	General Motors	Motor vehicles and parts	176,558.0
2	Wal-Mart Stores	General Merchandisers	166,809.0
3	Exxon Mobil	Petroleum Refining	163,881.0
4	Ford Motor	Motor vehicles and parts	162,558.0
5	General Electric	Diversified Financials	111,630.0
6	Int. Business Machines	Computers, Office Equipment	87,548.0
7	Citigroup	Diversified Financials	82,005.0
8	US Postal Service	Mail, Package, Freight Delivery	62,726.0
9	AT&T	Telecommunications	62,391.0
10	Philip Morris	Tobacco	61,751.0
11	Boeing	Aerospace	57,993.0
12	Bank of America Corp.	Banks: Commercial & Savings	51,392.0
13	SBC Communications	Telecommunications	49,489.0
14	Hewlett Packard	Computers, Office Equipment	48,253.0
15	Kroger	Food and Drug Stores	45,351.6
16	State Farm Insurance Co.	Insurance: P & C (mutual)	44,637.2
17	Sears Roebuck	General Merchandisers	41,071.0
18	American International Group	Insurance: P & C (stock)	40,656.1
19	Enron	Energy	40,112.0
20	Tiaa-Cref	Insurance: Life, Health (mutual)	39,410.2
21	Compaq Computer	Computers, Office Equipment	38,525.0
22	Home Depot	Speciality Retailers	38,434.0
23	Lucent Technologies	Network Communications	38,303.0
24	Procter & Gamble	Soaps, Cosmetics	38,125.0
25	Albertson's	Food and Drug Stores	37,478.1

Source: Adapted from *Fortune*, 'The FortuneGlobal 500', 24 July, 2000

Appendix Table 8.2: The 25 Largest European MNEs, 1999

Rank	Firm	Country	Industry	Revenues (US$m.)
1	Daimler-Chrysler	Germany	Motor vehicles and Parts	159,985.7
2	Royal Dutch/Shell Group	Britain/Netherlands	Petroleum Refining	105,366.0
3	AXA	France	Insurance: Life, Health (stock)	87,645.7
4	BP Amoco	Britain	Petroleum Refining	83,566.0
5	Volkswagen	Germany	Motor vehicles and Parts	80,072.7
6	Siemens	Germany	Electronics, Electrical Equip.	75,337.0
7	Allianz	Germany	Insurance: P & C (stock)	74,178.2
8	ING Group	Netherlands	Insurance: Life, Health (stock)	62,492.4
9	Deutsche Bank	Germany	Banks: Commercial & Savings	58,585.1
10	Assicurazioni Generali	Italy	Insurance: Life, Health (stock)	53,723.2
11	E. On	Germany	Trading	52,227.7
12	Fiat	Italy	Motor vehicles and Parts	51,331.7
13	Nestlé	Switzerland	Food	49,694.1
14	Credit Suisse	Switzerland	Banks: Commercial & Savings	49,362.0
15	Metro	Germany	Food and Drug Stores	46,663.6
16	Total Fina Elf	France	Petroleum Refining	44,990.3
17	Vivendi	France	Engineering, Construction	44,397.8
18	Unilever	Britain/Netherlands	Food	43,679.9
19	Fortis	Belgium/Netherlands	Banks: Commercial & Savings	43,660.2
20	Prudential	Britain	Insurance: Life, Health (stock)	42,220.3
21	CGNU	Britain	Insurance: P & C (stock)	41,974.4
22	Peugeot	France	Motor vehicles and Parts	40,327.9
23	BNP Paribas	France	Banks: Commercial & Savings	40,098.6
24	Renault	France	Motor vehicles and Parts	40,098.6
25	Zurich Financial Services	Switzerland	Insurance: P & C (stock)	39,962.0

Source: Adapted from *Fortune*, 'The Fortune Global 500', 24 July, 2000.

Appendix Table 8.3: The 25 Largest Japanese MNEs, 1999

Rank	Firm	Industry	Revenues (US$m.)
1	Mitsui	Trading	118,555.2
2	Mitsubishi	Trading	117,765.6
3	Toyota Motor	Motor vehicles and Parts	115,670.9
4	Itochu	Trading	109,068.9
5	Sumitomo	Trading	95,701.6
6	Nippon Telegraph and Telephone	Telecommunications	93,591.7
7	Marubeni	Trading	91,807.4
8	Nippon Life Insurance	Insurance: Life, Health (mutual)	78,515.1
9	Hitachi	Electronics, Electrical Equip.	71,858.5
10	Matsushita Electric Equipment	Electronics, Electrical Equip.	65,555.6
11	Nissho Iwai	Trading	65,393.2
12	Sony	Electronics, Electrical Equip.	60,052.7
13	Dai-Ichi Mutual Life Insurance	Insurance: Life, Health (mutual)	55,104.7
14	Honda Motor	Motor vehicles and Parts	54,773.5
15	Nissan Motor	Motor vehicles and Parts	53,679.9
16	Toshiba	Electronics, Electrical Equip.	51,634.9
17	Fujitsu	Computers, Office Equipment	47,195.9
18	Sumitomo Life Insurance	Insurance: Life, Health (mutual)	46,445.1
19	Tokyo Electric Power	Utilities: Gas & Electric	45,727.7
20	NEC	Electronics, Electrical Equip.	44,828.0
21	Meiji Life Insurance	Insurance: Life, Health (mutual)	33,966.6
22	Mitsubishi Electric	Electronics, Electrical Equip.	33,896.2
23	Bank of Tokyo-Mitsubishi	Banks: Commercial & Savings	32,623.6
24	Mitsubishi Motors	Motor vehicles and Parts	29,951.3
25	Ito-Yokado	Food and Drug Stores	28,670.9

Source: Adapted from *Fortune*, 'The Fortune Global 500', 24 July, 2000.

Appendix Table 8.4: The Largest Canadian MNEs, 1998

Rank	Firm	Industry	Revenues (US$ m.)
1	Nortel Networks	Network Communications	21,287.0
2	George Weston	Food and Drug Stores	14,033.9
3	CIBC	Banks: Commercial & Savings	13,441.2
4	Royal Bank of Canada	Banks: Commercial & Savings	13,146.1
5	Transcanada Pipelines	Energy	12,415.2
6	Seagram	Entertainment	11,784.0
7	Bank of Montreal	Banks: Commercial & Savings	11,139.3
8	Bank of Nova Scotia	Banks: Commercial & Savings	11,118.6
9	Sun Life Assur. of Canada	Insurance: Life, Health (mutual)	10,511.1
10	Toronto-Dominion Bank	Banks: Commercial & Savings	10,470.3
Average:			12,934.6

Source: Adapted from *Fortune*, 'The Fortune Global 500', 24 July, 2000.

Strategies for Triad Firms

IN this chapter, I examine the end of globalization from the point of view of senior managers of MNEs and smaller firms. I look at their strategies for their triad home-base and also how to access other triad markets. Today, these firm-level strategies need to be constantly rethought in the light of 'triad wars' and other, related, government and regulatory influences. Use of the 'flagship' model is a potential solution for triad based regional business networks (Rugman and D'Cruz, 2000).

Strategies for managers

The end of globalization requires new thinking by managers of MNEs and other organizations. Trying to design and implement a global strategy is no longer appropriate. Instead, a triad strategy is required. This will include a large element of localization, as regional barriers to trade and investment preclude simplistic strategies of foreign expansion. Entry to other triad markets is likely to be difficult and frequently subject to bargaining and negotiation.

Once managers realize that there is no single global market, that consumers are not all the same, then every production and distribution decision needs to be rethought. There are limits to time and space. Distance matters. Geography matters. Regions are the unit of analysis for decision making.

The managers of non MNEs (often smaller firms) also need to rethink their strategies. Small firms and entrepreneurs should not leap into foreign markets; they are risky and the risk needs to be addressed. To reduce risk, smaller businesses should hook into a regional triad producer; for example, by becoming a key supplier to a large automobile MNE, or working as a distributor and/or intermediary with the national health system for an MNE pharmaceutical producer. They must maintain good relations with government officials who can help smaller companies achieve market access to regional partner markets and also to other triad markets. Think regional, act local, forget global.

Managers must do the following to develop a successful regional/triad strategy:

- develop a competence, capability, competitive or firm-specific advantage (whatever current strategic management term is preferred) on a regional basis
- expand from a secure country home-base into geographically close and culturally similar regions as a first step
- after securing the benefits of production and distribution in a home triad base, expand into at least one of the other triad markets, especially into the triad home base of their major competitor
- work with local, national and regional governments to secure the commercial feasibility of the home market and to have them help open up the other triad markets
- develop internal organizational structures which allow the top management team on a local, national and regional basis to develop
- when expanding into another triad, use managers from that region and move them up quickly to the top management team – their knowledge of the new triad's culture and markets is likely to be the key ingredient for success in this new region
- develop an ethical corporate philosophy which is shared by all senior managers and employees – share the passion for success throughout the company – make it a regional learning organization

Economies of scale in the triad

A more sophisticated definition of globalization is based on economies of scale. If there were no barriers to trade and investment, then a firm could sell its products anywhere in the world. It would be able to achieve production and distributional efficiencies in a single world market under conditions of free trade. As its production volume increased to utilize fully its plant and resources, then global economies of scale would be realized.

In practice, virtually all potential economies of scale are achieved within triad markets – there are few, if any, residual scale benefits from globalization. For example, the rationale for the Single European Market, in the Cecchini Report (1988) is precisely for EU firms to achieve effective economies of scale within the single market. The EU market is now as big as that of the United States, where firms traditionally roll out products and services across the regions for this reason. Only in Japan is there a hint of an argument for external scale economies. In consumer electronics it is the home market advantage in quality as well as scale which has helped Japanese firms achieve global market share.

It is, however, important to note that the free trade and global economies of scale argument provides a rationale for home production and selling worldwide by the export mode. Yet we observe a massive amount of FDI. Firms would not need to resort to FDI if markets had free trade. Basically, FDI (and therefore the MNE) is a substitute for free trade, Rugman (1981). The triad-based barriers to free trade are the reason that FDI is induced as a mode of entry. We also observed (in Chapter 7) that 80 per cent of FDI is undertaken by triad-based firms. Further, only a minority of all their FDI is inter-triad, which suggests that barriers to free trade remain even within the triad. As FDI is a substitute for exporting, this strongly indicates that economic globalization is a myth. Instead, we need to understand that the activities of MNEs, who do the FDI, and also the exporting, are triad-based.

Again, it is often observed that a growing proportion of international business is in the form of international joint ventures (IJV) and strategic alliances. It is frequently stated that MNEs no longer rely on FDI alone, but resort to these non-equity, new forms of international business. This is only partly true. The misinterpretation arises from data showing a rapid growth of IJVs. While most international joint ventures involving technology are triad based, those in the resource and basic manufacturing sectors are much less concentrated in the triad. Careful examination of the data shows that many new IJVs are formed to do business in China, Russia, Eastern Europe, parts of Asia and Africa. All these economies have restrictive government regulations which prohibit majority-owned FDI. Local governments intervene in the market and require local partners. As MNEs expand their activities in these newer markets, the number of international joint ventures grows. Often, FDI would be the better way to operate, but MNEs are forced into IJVs by the restrictions of the host government. This is another example of the lack of globalization, not evidence for it.

Protectionist strategies

One of the biggest problems in international business in the triad is the ability of domestic producers to lobby their home governments to erect barriers to trade. In the past, textile, apparel and shoe industries were able to obtain protection from cheaper imports through tariffs, quotas and special measures. Now multilateral trade agreements under the GATT and WTO (and also regional and bilateral ones such as NAFTA and APEC) outlaw such blatant instruments of protection. They have been replaced by more subtle ones.

Prominent as a new type of protectionist device is the use of 'unfair trade laws', especially anti-dumping (AD) and countervailing duty actions

(CVD). The economic logic of AD and CVD makes some sense. It is unfair for a foreign producer to 'dump' a product in your country below its price at home, or the cost of producing it. Similarly, subsidized foreign products should be offset by a countervailing duty of equivalent effect. The problem lies with the administration of the trade laws, which is subject to political lobbying.

A variety of studies have found that the bureaucrats who administer AD and CVD laws are subject to capture by the home industries, who then use AD and CVD cases as harassment tools against often economically efficient foreign rival producers. It was found by Rugman and Anderson (1987) that the United States administration of AD and CVD was used in a biased manner against Canadian producers, especially in resource-based industries (such as softwood lumber, fishing and agriculture). Thus in the Canadian-US Free Trade Agreement of 1989, and then in NAFTA, five person binational panels of trade law experts were set up to review the decision of the US (and Canadian) trade law agencies.

In a subsequent study, Rugman and Anderson (1997) found that these binational panels were able to remand back (i.e. successfully challenge) the decision of the US agencies twice as often in cases involving Canada, as in AD and CVD cases involving the rest of the world. In related work it has been found that the EC is just as bad as the United States, in that the EC brings in questionable AD measures, especially against Asian countries. Indeed, one of the unresolved problems is how smaller countries can secure access to the protected markets of triad economies such as the United States and EU. In Japan's case there are similar arguments (including from its triad rivals) that there are entry barriers in place preventing market access.

Administered protection in the triad

For the last 20 years trade wars have been fought between the members of the triad: between Europe and the United States; between Europe and Japan; and between the United States and Japan. The United States' major weapon has been the process of countervailing duties, available to domestic industries which can make a legal case that competitive foreign produced products are subsidized by foreign governments. EU firms have chosen the use of anti-dumping duties as their instrument of protection. In this section I discuss how the CVD and AD systems work. First, the data shown in Table 9.1 are useful.

Table 9.1: World Countervailing Duty Actions, July 1980 to June 1995

Country/Area	Actions	Percentage of world	Definitive duties	Percentage of world
United States	360	56.4	148	79.6
Chile	153	24.0	6	3.2
Australia	69	10.8	15	8.1
Canada	22	3.4	12	6.5
Brazil	11	1.7	1	0.5
New Zealand	7	1.1	–	–
European Union (EU)	6	0.9	3	1.6
Peru	4	0.6	–	–
Austria	2	0.3	1	0.5
Argentina	2	0.3	–	–
Japan	1	0.2	–	–
Mexico	1	0.2	–	–
Total	**638**	**100.0**	**186**	**100.0**

Source: Adapted from GATT, *Basic Instruments and Selected Documents* (BISD), supplements 27-41.

From Table 9.1 it is strikingly apparent that CVD is a specialist weapon for US firms. The United States has accounted for 56.4 per cent of all the world's CVD actions since 1980 (when the system was reformed). It has such effective trade lawyers that it accounts for 80 per cent of all the world's successful CVD actions, where duties are imposed. In contrast, firms in Chile launched 24 per cent of all the world's actions, but these only account for 3.2 per cent of the world's successful actions. Canadian lawyers are, proportionately, even better than US ones, as its firms account for 6.5 per cent of successful CVD actions, although they only launched 3.4 per cent of the world's total.

The EU and Japan do not have many firms which make use of CVD actions. The EU only had six actions and Japan one over the 1980-1995 period. Many more countries have firms which make use of anti-dumping actions, as reported in Table 9.2.

Table 9.2: World Anti-dumping Actions, July 1980 to June 1995

Country/Area	Actions	Percentage of world	Definitive duties	Percentage of world
United States	608	28.2	366	37.2
Australia	549	25.4	193	19.6
European Union (EU)	377	17.5	140	14.2
Canada	362	16.8	190	19.3
Mexico	81	3.8	40	4.1
New Zealand	41	1.9	15	1.5
Brazil	30	1.4	9	0.9
Poland	24	1.1	–	–
Finland	15	0.7	2	0.2
India	14	0.6	–	–
Korea	12	0.6	5	0.5
South Africa	9	0.4	1	0.1
Sweden	8	0.4	–	–
Austria	8	0.4	–	–
Argentina	6	0.3	6	0.6
Peru	4	0.2	–	–
Japan	3	0.1	–	–
Chile	2	0.1	3	0.3
Turkey	2	0.1	11	1.1
Singapore	2	0.1	–	–
Colombia	1	0.0	2	0.2
Thailand	–	–	1	0.1
Total	2,158	100.0	984	100.0

Source: Adapted from GATT, *Basic Instruments and Selected Documents* (BISD), supplements 27-41.
*Data for July 1993 to June 1994 were not available.

Again, US firms are the most aggressive users of AD, accounting for 28 per cent of all actions since 1980, and 37 per cent of successful ones. Australia and, again, Canada are major users of AD, having 25 per cent and 17 per cent respectively of the world's actions. The EU has 17.5 per cent and 14.2 per cent of successful actions. These four economies (United States, Australia, Canada, EU) account for 88 per cent of all actions and 90 per cent of all successful actions. The other 18 countries listed are not major users of AD.

One interpretation of the data on the use of CVD and AD actions is that they are used as barriers to entry to triad markets by US and European firms.

An example is the US steel industry, which regularly initiates AD actions against Asian and European rivals, often multiple actions against various types of steel products. The administration of US trade remedy law has been found to be biased in favour of domestic plaintiffs so it serves as a form of administered protection, Rugman and Anderson (1987), Rugman and Gestrin (1991).

It is apparent that CVD and AD are protectionist tools used to deny access to triad markets. The targets are rival triad producers and developing countries. The CVD and AD process is a triad/regional one to segment markets and deny the actual benefits of global markets. Anti-dumping and countervailing duty measures are inconsistent with globalization.

Professional sports are local, not global

Professional sports organized on a triad, rather than a global, basis are an important 'service' sector today.

In North America, major league baseball, professional football, the National Hockey League and professional basketball are the main sports. Baseball, American football and basketball are embedded in the US home market. There are a few exports of these sports (especially to Japan) but they are not really inter-triad. Ice hockey originated in Canada, but is now bigger business in the United States. Several northern European countries also have ice hockey leagues (Russia, Sweden, Finland, Norway, even the UK) but they account for a fraction of the North American business. None of these four North American sports is global.

In Europe, professional football (soccer) is the big sport. As over 100 countries have football leagues, some people think of it as a global sport. It even has a World Cup every four years and is possibly the only sport which can make a claim to this title. (In contrast the US 'world series' for baseball has only been won twice by a non-US team – the Toronto Blue Jays in 1992 and 1993.) Yet even soccer is not a truly 'global' business as the main teams play in national leagues and then qualify for regional/triad competitions. For example, Manchester United won the 'triple' of the English football league, the FA Cup and the European Cup in the 1998/1999 season. It then competed with a Brazilian team for an intercontinental cup in November 1999. In turn, the Brazilian team qualified through its national league and Latin American playoffs.

The World Cup of football is a festival every four years in which participation is based on regional qualifications – basically from Europe, the Americas and East Asia. The nature of the competition is regional, not global. The football teams have strong regional brand names, with only a handful (like Manchester United) having a presence in other triad markets. And even for Manchester United, there is no interest in the United States.

Cricket and rugby are played mainly by British Commonwealth countries and have little or no presence in two parts of the triad (Japan and North America). The Olympic Games does bring together most of the nations of the world, but it is a festival at a rotating site, to which admission is by national championships. In other words, the national Olympic committees are the powers; there is no global Olympic business.

Formula One car racing gives the appearance of being global: races take place around the world, there are a set of ten or so racing teams and advertising sponsors appear to want global exposure. Yet, again, this is a regional business. Races take place mainly in Europe and most of the teams are European, with strategic alliances with US and Japanese producers. The legacy and history of the sport is mainly European. A few races take place in North America, where there are competing motor sports which are US-based, such as the Indianapolis 500.

Like professional tennis, Formula One is an annual carnival. There is a circuit of races, mostly in Europe. In tennis there are tournaments built around the 'grand slam' events in Australia, France, Wimbledon in the UK and the US Open. While the sponsors are MNEs, the organization and delivery of these national events is a local responsibility. Local groups host the visiting circus. Some of the inputs appear to be global – the drivers or players, the TV coverage, but the events are one off, local entertainments requiring local/regional strategies rather than global ones.

Professional golf has institutionalized triad rivalry in the form of the Ryder Cup which is competed for by US and European players. Although some of the better European players compete in some of the major US events, such as the Masters, US Open and PGA tournaments, the European tour is now a solid rival to the formerly dominant US tour. And to complete the triad, a newer Asian golf tour has developed. Again, there is no global golf business – instead it is triad-based and as it develops it becomes less global and more regional.

What are the implications for managers of this analysis of professional sports? First, work well within the national/local league. Second, aim to compete as a national champion in the regional competitions. Third, try to gain an extension of your brand name into at least one other triad market. However, do this through an 'export' activity rather than by foreign direct investment. This is because of the unique home base constraint of being a national champion – it means that sports business is a home business.

Airlines are local, not global

The airline industry is not global. Despite the rapid growth of international passenger traffic and the speed of travel, which is reducing the costs of geography, all airlines are tightly regulated. Each triad region has strong controls which prevent foreign competition. Foreign airlines do not have the right to pick up passengers in national markets, i.e. they are routinely denied national treatment (Rugman, 1994). In NAFTA, airlines were fully exempted from the national treatment provisions; an 'open skies' agreement was concluded between the United States and Canada. As a result, Air Canada has opened over 50 routes into the United States, using Toronto as a hub. In return, US airlines have more point to point access to Canadian cities, but cannot undertake 'domestic' carriage within Canada. The same denial of national treatment still applies to other transportation sectors – railways, trucking and shipping (the notoriously protectionist US Jones Act was exempted in NAFTA).

Law firms are local, not global

There have been mergers in law firms in recent years. For example, in September 1999 it was announced that the UK's largest law firm, Clifford Chance is merging with a US partner, Rogers & Wells and also with the German firm, Pünder, Volhard, Weber & Associates. This will create a new business of over US$ 625 million with 2,700 lawyers (including 566 partners). The driver behind this merger is the growing business in commercial law for work on mergers and acquisitions. There have been other mergers of UK with European firms (such as Lovells), to better serve EU clients, and of US and Canadian firms, to take advantage of NAFTA. The results of these mergers are better, triad-based, service firms.

There is no globalization of law firms, as their lawyers still qualify according to separate national, even sub-national regimes, and their administration of laws is either country or triad based. Even in the area of trade law, where WTO-based issues to deal with trade disputes arise, the lawyers engaged are home country experts. This is because the plaintiffs and defendants are always country-based, i.e. one firm in one country urges its government to use the WTO appellate system. As the political regime for law making is largely local, so the lawyers will remain local. MNE clients understand this and are used to engaging local lawyers as they expand the operations of their foreign subsidiaries, and enter new overseas markets.

There is no simple global strategy

Given the logic, and empirical evidence in this book about the lack of globalization, why do academics and business commentators think that a global strategy is a good idea? I think that the answer lies in the fallacy of a few 'big name' global businesses. Everyone thinks of McDonalds, Coca Cola and IBM as global players and then assumes that they have global strategies. Yet each of these three firms has been careful to avoid a simplistic global strategy and take pains to understand its local markets. Their top management teams are not global, but either home or host country based.

McDonalds is a global brand name, but its products are not homogeneous. In India there are vegetarian instead of beef burgers. In Asia, there are spicier foods than in North America. In Russia, McDonalds had to reconstruct the entire supply chain to provide inputs of good enough quality. Its managers are local and, indeed, follow a generalized fast-food production formula. But they are essentially operating as independent franchises, paying percentage royalties with a great degree of independence as to how they operate the business.

Coca Cola also has to adapt its product for local tastes. It varies the amount of syrup and other ingredients and its local bottling plants are largely independent operations, loosely linked to head office by quality inspectors but not by budget controls. In June 1999, the production problems at a Belgian plant led to a major loss of business for Coca Cola across Europe. To win back the market is a regional/triad challenge, not one that can be solved by the Atlanta head office.

IBM, of course, was always a reasonably decentralized company. It operated by country or region and attempted, in its heyday of the 1960s and 1970s, to balance product, trade and sales by region. Now it has reinvented itself as a services firm, with extremely localized and decentralized operations and delivery.

In the next chapter, I shall review the successful strategies of 20 well known MNEs. Here I shall consider next examples of two firms which have adopted a global strategy without success. What can we learn from their mistakes? I then contrast this with an MNE from Taiwan.

First, I have chosen Disney as a representative example of the viewpoint that US-style 'Hollywood' movies and pop culture is a global business. Yet, while there is a market for such US-produced 'cultural' products, big mistakes can be made by assuming that the rest of the world is always the same as the good old USA. Second, I look at the failure of Saatchi and Saatchi to expand on their growth and brand name success in advertising in the UK as they expanded to the United States. I find that their assumption that a global service business can operate on a standardized basis is incorrect; services are local, not global. As a contrast, I then consider the success of Acer of Taiwan in its expansion into the larger triad markets.

Strategic mistakes (1): Disneyland Paris

An example of the failure of globalization in strategy is the story of Euro Disney.

During the years 1988 to 1990 three US$150 million amusement parks opened in France. By 1991 two of them were bankrupt and the third was doing poorly. However, this track record did not scare off the Walt Disney Company's plan to open Europe's first Disneyland in 1992. Far from being concerned about the theme park doing well, Disney executives were worried that Euro Disneyland would be too small to handle the giant crowds. The US$ 5 billion project is located on 5000 acres in Seine-et-Marne, 20 miles east of Paris. Paris seemed to be an excellent location; there are 17 million people within a 2-hour drive of Euro Disneyland, 41 million within a 4 hour drive, and 109 million within 6 hours of the park. This includes people from seven countries: France, Switzerland, Germany, Luxembourg, the Netherlands, Belgium and Britain.

Disney officials were optimistic about the project, especially after the success of Tokyo Disneyland, where the amusement park could not accommodate the large number of visitors. The company's initial share of the venture was 49 per cent, at a cost US$160 million. Other investors put in US$1.2 billion, while the French government provided a low interest US$900 million loan, banks loaned US$1.6 billion, and the remaining US$400 million came from special partnerships formed to buy properties and to lease them back. The Walt Disney company was to receive 10 per cent of Euro Disney's admission fees, and 5 per cent of food and merchandise revenues, in addition to management fees, and 49 per cent of all profits.

The location of the amusement park was thoroughly considered. France and Spain, the two principal locations being considered, conscious of the park's capacity to create jobs and stimulate the economy, wooed the company. France offered both a central location in the heart of Europe and considerable financial incentives. Additionally, the French government promised to build a train line to connect the amusement park to the European train system. Thus, France was chosen as the site.

Yet things started to look gloomy from the first day. The inauguration was expected to attract 500,000 visitors but a mere 50,000 showed up. This was partly a result of French sentiments against the park. Vandalism during the first days of the operation and media criticism against the American operation began to upset investors. Furthermore, the company received complaints about high prices, labour policies and general policies that conflicted with European practices. Prices were so high due to the Franc exchange rate that it was cheaper for the English to go to Florida than to Euro Disney. Labour policy was in contradiction with French law, which led to a high turnover. By May 1992, only a month after the amusement park opened its doors, 3,000 employees had quit over pay and working conditions. Worker complaints ranged from managers having to speak English in meetings, even if most people at the meeting were French, to policies on personal grooming. Other conflicting policies were a result of Disney's previous experiences. In the United States, liquor was not sold outside of the hotels, or specific areas. The general area was kept alcohol free, including the restaurants. This was to maintain a family atmosphere. In Japan, the policy was accepted and worked out very well. However, Europeans were used to accompany any outing with some kind of alcoholic beverages. In particular, the French were accustomed to wine while the Germans wanted beer.

In 1994, after three years of heavy loses, Euro Disney was in such bad shape that it was expected it would have to be shut down. A variety of measures were taken to save the company. Prince Walid Talal purchased 24.6 per cent (reducing Disney's share to 39 per cent) of the company, injecting $500 million of much needed cash. Furthermore, Disney waived its royalty fees, the company worked a better loan repayment plan with the banks and new shares were issued. These measures allowed the company to buy time while it restructured its marketing and general policies to fit the European market.

In October 1994, Euro Disney officially changed its name to 'Disneyland Paris'. This made the park more French, while it capitalized on the romanticism that the word Paris conveys. Most importantly, the new name allowed for a new beginning, disassociating the park from the failure of Euro Disney. This was accompanied with measures to remedy past failures. The park changed its most offensive labour laws, reduced prices, and began being more culturally conscious. Now, alcoholic beverages are served in most areas in the park.

The company began operations by stressing the European origins of their founder, Walt Disney, and of many of their fairy tale characters. It also produced European specific attractions (such as European history movie shows, and a science fiction tour inspired by Jules Verne's stories). Now the company is increasing their efforts even further in this area. The reason is very simple, the company doesn't want to be seen as an American company, but one that can appeal to the European, specially the French.[1]

It seems that things might have begun to turn around for the ailing park. In 1995, for the first time ever, the company reported a slight profit. The trend continued for 1996 with profits doubling and no further losses have been reported. However, critics say that the signs are misleading and that these profits are not so much a result of an improvement in the general profitability of the company, but a result of Disney's waive of royalty fees, and the favourable payment plan from the banks. Nonetheless, prices have started to rise in the amusement park, and anti-Disney hostility has cooled off.

Strategic Mistakes (2): Saatchi & Saatchi

Another well known example of failure of a globalization strategy is that of Saatchi & Saatchi. This successful British advertising firm experienced a spectacular rate of growth in the 1980s, partly due to a series of successful acquisitions in Britain and Europe, based on easily obtained financing from the City of London. The high quality of their advertisements, including those for the Thatcher Government, and the clear vision of the Saatchi brothers enhanced their brand name in the British part of the European triad. But this led them to make a classic mistake.

They read an article by Harvard Business School professor Ted Levitt on the virtues of building a global business to get economies of scale.[2] The Levitt argument is the basic argument for globalization and it is the one that

---

[1] Adapted from Steven Greenhouse, 'Playing Disney in the Parisian Fields,' *New York Times*, February 17, 1991, Section 3, pp. 1, 6; 'Euro Disney Resignation,' *New York Times*, January 16, 1993, p. 19; William Heuslein, 'Travel,' *Forbes*, January 4, 1993, p. 178; Stewart Toy and Paula Dwyer, 'Is Disney Headed for the Euro-Trash Heap?', *Business Week*, January 4, 1994, p.52; Theodore Stanger et al, 'Mickey's Trip to Trouble,' *Newsweek*, February 4, 1994, pp.34-39; 'International Briefs: Revenue for Euro Disney Up by 17% in Quarter', *New York Times*, January 22, 1998; 'Euro Disney Theme Park Cuts Loss, Shares Fall', *Yahoo News: Reuters*, April 22, 1998
(http://www.clubblue.com/text/headlines/9...nment/stories/industry_eurodisney_1.html);
http://www.informatik.tu-muenchen.de/~schaffnr/etc/disney/his8891.htm;
http://www.informatik.tu-muenchen.de/~schaffnr/etc/disney/finhist.htm.
[2] Theodore Levitt, 'The Globalization of Markets', Harvard Business Review (May/June, 1983).

I have demonstrated is entirely wrong. Back in the late 1980s Ted Levitt was put on the Saatchi & Saatchi Board and the company proceeded to make its disastrous entry to North America through the purchase of Bates. The US market accounted for 55 per cent of the world market in advertising in 1988, Japan at 13 per cent, while all of Europe was only 24 per cent (with the UK having only 5 per cent of the world total).

The Saatchi brothers also wanted to build a global service supermarket for a set of multinational enterprise clients by expanding on from their core advertising business to include a communications/public relations division and also a consulting division. The objective of being a full service provider across the triad, using a common brand name, required skills in integration, co-ordination and leadership that the Saatchi organization did not possess. Their expansion to the United States was a major failure and lots of money was lost.

In the end, services are local. The creative part of advertising, communications and consulting are not easily acquired, retained and absorbed into a large and growing company. Big is not always beautiful, especially when standardization is not possible. As Saatchi & Saatchi learned, a service business is not global, but local. Although their clients were MNEs, even these MNEs were not really global in the sense of being standardized. Either country level or triad-based regional strategies are needed by service businesses.

Strategic Success: Acer Taiwan

Finally, it may be helpful to end this chapter on strategy for multinational enterprises with an unusual success story. There is an MNE from a non-triad base in Taiwan that has become the second largest producer of personal computers in the world. This is Acer, run by an imaginative, dedicated and entrepreneurial CEO, Stan Shin.

In November 1999 the Fellows of the Academy of International Business elected Mr Shin, as the international executive of the year. This is a company which has achieved global success, by penetrating the Asian, North American and European triads, from its small country base in Taiwan. Mr Shin is representative of a new breed of entrepreneurs from smaller countries who are succeeding in gaining market access to the triad.

Previous AIB executives of the year have been the CEOs of larger MNEs: Percy Barnevik of ABB, Giovanni Agnelli of Fiat, Akio Morita of Sony, Takuma Yamamoto of Fujitsu, Walter Wriston of Citicorp, Jacques Maisonrouge of IBM, then Air Liquide. Armand Hammer of Occidental

Petroleum and S.K. Chey of Sunkyong. Also two Canadians have been recognised for running MNEs from a small, open economy: David Culver of Alcan in 1990 and Jean Monty of Northern Telecom in 1996.

Acer Taiwan is the third largest PC manufacturer worldwide. It has 80 branch offices worldwide and distribution networks in over 100 countries. By 1998 the Acer Group had over 23,000 employees. It is the best known brand in Asia, and a large player in Latin America. In the United States, where IBM, Compaq and Dell dominate, Acer has earned the number two position in the PC consumer electronics market. By 1997, the company owned over 400 patents. Not bad for a company no one knew about prior to 1986.

In 1976, CEO Stan Shin and some of his friends managed to put together US$25,000 to start Multitech. With seven employees, the company began to develop small electronics such as pocket calculators and games. Slowly the company began to grow. Its initial entrance in the PC market was not direct. Multitech produced computers to be sold under other brand names. It was only in 1986, that the company launched its own brand name computer: Acer. While the company still supplies under other brand names such as Hitachi and Siemens, Acer has become the seventh best known brand in the world. In 1994, the company's revenues totalled US$3.2 billion.

The question is how could a small company from Taiwan gain market share on the more established computer manufacturers. The answer is entrepreneurial management drive and the discovery of niches. Shin found that small markets, which were not yet captured by the likes of IBM, were open to their products, so constant expansion and growth became the driving force behind Acer's success. After 25 years of growth, now Shin is planning to develop tailored PCs. Instead of a computer that can do everything, a more task-specific computer can be built at a low cost.

Acer's distribution system is also a novelty. With the product life of computer components at about three months, exporting overseas becomes a problem. Acer has manufacturing and assembling parts all over the world. The company distributes parts with long product lives by ship, while highly volatile products like semi processors, PCB and memory are shipped by plane. This allows for just-in-time production which Shin compares to the distribution system of a fast food chain with perishable and non-perishable ingredients.

The success of the company is highly correlated with the management structure created by Shin. Unlike traditional Chinese business, where management is highly hierarchical and controlled by the owning family,

Shin has decentralized management. Autonomy is important. Managers should think like owners so as to take advantage of all profit opportunities. Additionally, Acer has gone public. The Shin family stake is only about 10 per cent. Employees have the option of buying shares at extremely low prices. Acer functions as a coordinator for the group members, who themselves have the flexibility to implement the goals of the headquarters.[3]

To succeed in the long term the company has built alliances. To enter the United States the company formed a joint venture with Texas Instruments. To acquire specific technology, in 1987 Acer bought Counterpoint Computers, a US maker of multiuser systems. In 1990, Altos (US) and Kangaroo Computer (Dutch) were also purchased to acquire needed technology. Lately the company has been using a different strategy. Acer has cross-licensing agreements with IBM and Intel. This helps Acer gain access to IBM's technology and to the Intel brand name.

Acer is well positioned for the future. Its market share has been increasing steadily and the company has ventured well outside its borders to become a multinational enterprise. Investors seem to be optimistic about the future as the market value of Acer shares is constantly increasing. The company is an excellent example of a successful MNE from a smaller economy. In the next chapter I shall explain the reasons for the strategic success of twenty other MNEs, most of these from triad-based regions.

---

[3] Adapted from Stefan Simmons, 'Lessons from the Village Shop', *Der Spiegel*, November 4, 1998; Brian Dumaine, 'Asia's Wealth Creators Confront A New Reality', *Fortune*, December 8, 1997; Catherine Shepherd and Alejandro Reyes, 'Lords of High Tech', *Asiaweek*, November 7, 1997;
http://www.acer.com.tw/ai/factsht/fs_reen2.htm;
http://www.acer.com.tw/ai/newsrel/apifdab4.htm;
http://www.acer.com.tw/ai/newsrel/pribmlc2.htm.

10

Strategies of Twenty Triad-based Multinationals

Introduction

In this section, I discuss the strategies and structures of a set of 20 MNEs. All of these large MNEs have complex organizational structures and their business strategies have been analysed extensively by consultants and researchers from business schools. I use publicly available information published in my textbook of international business to discuss their core strategies and structures.[1]

Although these MNEs are often treated as global firms, all of them come from one of the triad home bases. The internationalization process has consisted of consolidating on that triad base and then moving into the other triad markets. All these organizations essentially operate triad/regional strategies.

Of the 20 MNEs discussed here, eleven are from the EU; three are from Asia, with two of these coming from Japan, and six are from North America, of which all but one are from the United States. I shall discuss them in this order, i.e. the European triad first, then the Asian and finally the North American.

These 20 triad-based MNEs are:

Name of MNE	Triad home base
Unilever	EU
IKEA	EU
Benetton	EU
Kingfisher	EU
Tate & Lyle	EU

---

[1] Alan M Rugman and Richard Hodgetts: *International Business: A Strategic Management Approach*, second edition, (London: Financial Times Management/Pearson Education,).

Rhône-Poulenc	EU
Nokia	EU
Ericsson	EU
Thames Water	EU
P&O	EU
Philips	EU
Matsushita	Asia – Japan
Fuji Xerox	Asia – Japan
HSBC	Asia
Xerox	NA
Procter & Gamble	NA
Hewlett Packard	NA
3M	NA
Enron	NA
Nortel Networks	NA – Canada

A general analysis of MNE strategies

The basic lessons of international management will not become redundant with the end of globalization. Indeed, virtually all top management teams in the large MNEs have long been aware of the threats to globalization and the inherent dangers of a pure globalization strategy. Not only is globalization a myth; a global strategy is a myth.

Most managers of MNEs pursue a regional triad-based strategy. They do well across the regions of their home triad market and then expand into nearby markets, gaining familiarity with international markets in a risk averse manner. The entry into rival triad markets is a deliberate strategic chess move. It is a decision based on careful analysis of market shares, growth potential, costs, revenues, factor conditions, political, cultural and related environmental issues.

One of our most powerful strategic tools in international business is the integration/responsiveness framework popularized by Bartlett and Ghoshal (1989). I have used this in different versions earlier in this book and will draw upon it now as a potentially synthesizing tool of analysis.

In Figure 10.1, I reproduce this basic international management strategy matrix. This is developed from the viewpoint of the manager of an MNE. The vertical axis represents the economic benefits of integration, yielding economies of scale. Here the MNE is centralized, closely integrated and internally co-ordinated and has a strong HQ office, with product-line managers in control.

FIGURE 10.1

THE INTERNATIONAL MANAGEMENT STRATEGY MATRIX

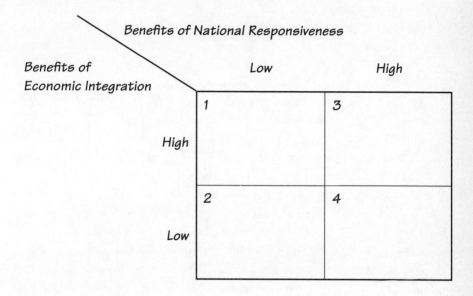

The horizontal axis represents the benefits of national responsiveness. This occurs when the subsidiaries of the MNE are embedded in the local culture of their host nations, and the MNE operates in a decentralized manner.

This matrix yields four generic strategies for MNEs:-

- Quadrant 1 – a pure integration strategy
- Quadrant 4 – a pure national responsiveness strategy
- Quadrant 3 – the transnational solution of a balance of integration and national responsiveness strategies
- Quadrant 2 – an unsatisfactory set of strategies with few or no benefits of either integration or national responsiveness.

As the twenty MNEs are analyzed in this chapter I shall place each of them in this matrix.

Unilever

Some of the best known MNEs have never adopted a globalization strategy. Unilever is a classic example. This mammoth food products, detergents, toothpastes and related consumer products company has always adopted a 'regional' strategy for its brands. Its overall strategic objective is to be close to its customer in local markets, so its managers operate largely on a decentralized regional/country basis, rather than in the centralized and hierarchical manner that would be typical of a purely globalized firm. Unilever has several hundred brands which are efficiently produced and co-ordinated, but the local marketing decisions are the essential ones.

The second largest consumer goods business in the world, Unilever employs 270,000 people worldwide. It has production plants in 70 countries and sells its products in 158 countries. With annual revenues of US$48 billion, it is considered one of the world's 50 largest MNEs. Its products include food and home and personal care products. Unilever was founded in 1929 through the merger of Margarine Unie (Dutch) and Lever Brothers (UK). The Lever Brothers already had operations in Africa and Asia, so that when Unilever was created, it immediately became an MNE with 20 per cent of its profits originating outside Europe. By 1980, this number had doubled, mainly due to expansion in Africa, South America and Asia.

Today, the company is a multicultural MNE with operations in five selected regions: Southern South America, Central and Eastern Europe, India, China, and South-East Asia. Its brands include Persil detergents, Flora margarine and Sure deodorants. In 1999, Unilever had as many as 1,600 brands, but it is moving to reduce this to 400 leading brands.[2]

Unilever has an advantage in national responsiveness against its main competitors in many of these regions. The Company has been in South America since its foundation, with companies in Chile (1928), Argentina (1928) and Brazil (1929). In 1927 it began operating in the Philippines, followed by Thailand in 1932 and India and Indonesia in 1933. Unilever started operations in China in the 1920s and when the government opened up in the 1980s, it was quick to sign joint ventures to re-enter the market. Today its sales in China total US$500 million.

Unilever's success in emerging markets is a result of its regional perspective. To sell to consumers from different cultures with different incomes, it must be able to adapt to local tastes. The company is committed to ensuring that managers understand the specific needs of their diverse customers. Differences in taste, culture, and income must all be taken into

---

[2] This is adapted from Deborah Orr, 'A Giant Reawakens', Forbes, January 25, 1999, pp. 52-54; 'Unilever to Purge Three out of Four Brands', The Times, September 22, 1999, p.45; 'Munching on Change – Unilever's food business', The Economist, January 6, 1996, pp. 56-61; http://www.unilever.com.

account, as in India and Brazil where there are large income disparities and, therefore, different markets for products.

In terms of Figure 10.1, Unilever is conducting a Quadrant 4 strategy. It is a nationally responsive, decentralized, locally-oriented producer. At the same time, it co-ordinates production and achieves worldwide 'best practice' in its network of subsidiaries. But it has not yet decided to move into Quadrant 3, in contrast to its traditional rival, Procter and Gamble.

IKEA

In less than 50 years IKEA has grown from a small, private, Swedish furniture retailer to a multinational business with 140 stores in 30 countries, with annual sales in 1997 of US$ 6 billion. This internationalization process is remarkable in that IKEA kept to the basic philosophy of its founder, Ingvar Kamprad, throughout its global expansion. Today it remains a private company.

Kamprad was a creative maverick in the furniture business. He redesigned the business system in the furniture industry by introducing knock-down kits that customers could take away from the store and assemble themselves. This saved on delivery and changed furniture from its traditional frosty 'showroom' mentality to a more 'fun' place with children's playpens, nurseries and cafés in IKEA stores. IKEA built on the fast growing informal suburban culture by providing lots of parking spaces and making a trip to IKEA an entertainment for the family.

This Scandinavian image of relaxed, informal yet efficient service, was extended to Switzerland in 1973, Munich in 1974, to ten more replica stores across Germany by 1980 and then throughout the rest of Europe, with entry to Britain in 1987. It opened in Australia in 1975 and Canada in 1976. Expansion to the United States started in 1985, through the Canadian IKEA operation. IKEA expanded into Eastern Europe in the early 1990s and into Shanghai, China in 1998.

IKEA also brought innovation to the logistics of furniture production. It set up groups of key suppliers to produce components at low cost. These subcontractors made money by getting large volume orders for standardized components from IKEA. The company kept tight control over product design and quality to maintain the IKEA brand name and distinctive identity of its furniture. It was able to expand rapidly because it did not have to establish its own expensive manufacturing facilities around Europe, but it retained centralized control over its subcontractors.

IKEA's marketing strategy has been to build on the Swedish home-base stereotype of clean and efficient service. Its furniture is well designed, modern, functional, durable, of high quality and is price competitive. Its image and brand name are well established and it has survived against several imitators. IKEA has moved from its Scandinavian base to being a strong regional player in Europe, and is now competing successfully across the triad.

IKEA is a successful multinational business because it has introduced a highly differentiated product into a traditional industry and has now built up a universally recognised brand name for high quality, inexpensive and attractive furniture. It has combined the generic strategies of differentiation, low cost and niching and has outsourced both production and delivery components of the value chain.[3] It has used a Quadrant 1 (Figure 10.1) strategy and kept to its home-based formula, despite the needs for national responsiveness in much of retailing. IKEA is therefore a strong exception to the usual Quadrant 4 retail strategies.

Benetton

Famous for its shocking advertisements, Benetton started in 1955 as a small business. Lucianno Benetton and his family started by selling coloured sweaters door to door in Treviso, Italy. Over time a regional network of family friends and agents set up a closely monitored set of distinctive retail outlets. Over a 15 year period Benetton built up 300 affiliated but independently owned outlets in Italy and a factory with new methods to dye and condition wool. Benetton was not directly involved in the retail outlets, who received high quality products at low costs. Part of the manufacturing savings are realized by outsourcing to neighbouring subcontractors.

Today Benetton has kept this loose network of independent production subcontractors and distribution agents but has now built up to a worldwide network of over 7,000 retail stores. Of these, Benetton only owns about 50 flagship stores. The great majority are operated by independent entrepreneurs. Over 80 per cent of production still takes place in Italy and the company is still 72 per cent owned by the Benetton family.

---

[3] www.IKEA.com Bartlett, Chris A. and Ashish Nanda, 'Ingvar Kamprad and IKEA', Harvard Business School Case 9-390-132. Joseph R. D'Cruz and Alan M. Rugman, 'Developing International Competitiveness: The Five Partners Model', *Business Quarterly* (Winter 1993).

Benetton is one of those worldwide companies that was partly successful because its production and design concept was built on a strong home base. It then expanded the marketing end of its business through closely monitored (but not owned) independent stores. These were able to use the Benetton brand name and distinctive colours and were supported by clever international advertising. All in all, a Quadrant 3, transnational strategy, has been developed.

Benetton does not advertise its clothes directly, rather it advertises a 'lifestyle'. The 'United Colours of Benetton' advertisements are designed for multicultural global consumers interested in fast cars and a fast lifestyle. Benetton goes in for cutting edge advertising that grabs public attention. This creates an image of new age awareness, as Benetton advertising has featured Formula 1 cars, AIDS, high art and 'attitude'.

How well this plays out across the triad is uncertain. For example, in 1988 Benetton had 700 retail stores in the United States, but by 1995 it only had 150. Is this because Benetton has too European an image to succeed in middle America? How can an Italian family firm understand the American lifestyle from its European bases?[4] Life in the future in Quadrant 3 will be tough. Benetton will need to keep working at its internal organizational capability in order to survive.

Kingfisher

In a recent study of the profitability of foreign assets a British retailer, Kingfisher, came top of the pack. Its average return on foreign assets was 32 per cent for 1996 and 1997, well above the average of 4.78 per cent for the world's top 500 multinational enterprises. What's more, in that period, Kingfisher only had 9 per cent of its total assets in foreign markets. By 1999 this had increased to 40 per cent.

Kingfisher is a company that is using its foreign assets to promote growth. Its first successful acquisition was of French electrical retailer Darty, followed in 1998 by a merger with French DIY retailer

---

[4] 'Benetton SpA: Industrial Fashion', (A) Harvard Business School Case No. 9-685-614. 'Benetton', (B) Harvard Business School Case No. 9-685-020.
INSEAD-CEDEP Case No. 01/97-4520, 1996; David Stillit 'Benetton: Italy's Smart Operator', *Corporate Finance*, June 1993; Anon. 'Benetton's Network', *Ivey Business Quarterly*, 1997.

Castorama. Kingfisher also has other operations across Europe; in Belgium, the Netherlands, and Germany. It has moved into Asia with the acquisition of an electrical retail chain in Singapore in 1998, and is also in Taiwan.

The Kingfisher Group was formed in 1989, and consists of the British Woolworths stores, Comet (electrical products), Superdrug and B&Q (home improvement stores). In 1998 its total sales revenues were £6.4 billion (about US$ 10 billion). There were 2,500 stores in 13 countries, principally in Britain and France. These retail brand stores operate in chains across Britain. The CEO, Sir Geoffrey Mulcahy, has led the drive for growth. He tried to consolidate Kingfisher's leading position in Britain by merging with the supermarket chain Asda in 1999 ; Asda is one of the UK's three biggest supermarket chains along with Tesco and Sainsbury. Instead, Wal-Mart bought Asda.

Sir Geoffrey Mulcahy has also provided leadership in the foreign expansion process through patience and strategic initiative. The merger with Castorama took five years to negotiate, as did the earlier one with Darty. The French managers and workers kept their jobs as 'retail is detail' and local knowledge is vital. All operations are in Quadrant 4 of Figure 10.1. While its foreign businesses operate autonomously, there are logistical savings and scale economies in purchasing that arise for the Kingfisher group as a whole. Sir Geoffrey has positioned Kingfisher to ride the wave of growth through profitable international expansion.

Another popular way of doing business in the EU is through the use of strategic alliances. Experts agree that four of the most important steps include:

1. Picking a compatible partner and taking the time to get to know and trust this company
2. Choosing a partner with complementary products or markets, rather than one who competes directly
3. Being patient and not rushing into a deal or expecting immediate results
4. Learning about the partner's technology and management but trying not to give away your own core secrets.

In some alliances one partner has taken advantage of the other by stealing technology or forcing the partner into a position where it had to sell out to the other. However, this will not happen if both sides make substantive contributions to the undertaking and each realizes that it needs the other. Moreover, even when alliances have not worked out, companies have found it in their best interest to continue looking for other partners for other deals.[5]

Tate & Lyle

The dominant firm in the sugar industry is Tate & Lyle plc, a British MNE founded in 1921 which based its early success on processing sugar from plantations in the Caribbean. The major sugar provider to Europe, it is also present in North America and now finds its fastest growing market in Asia, especially China, and in developing third world economies.

Tate and Lyle's firm-specific advantages are based on its brand name and reputation for quality and also on economies of scale in its very large sugar refinery plants. Since sugar producers (such as beet farmers in the United States) are highly protected, Tate & Lyle needs to be nationally responsive to local regulations as well as highly globalized, i.e. it has to operate as a 'transnational' firm in Quadrant 3 of Figure 10.1. It has therefore developed a decentralized 'regional' organizational structure to help develop responsiveness to local market needs and regulations.

The demand for sugar in wealthy Western economies is slowing down, due to health concerns and the arrival of sugar substitutes in the form of artificial sweeteners and starches. This has encouraged Tate & Lyle to broaden its market to Asia and the emerging economies of Eastern Europe, as well as to diversify into associated product areas, such as sweeteners, where it markets sucralose. In the 1980s it made numerous acquisitions in the United States, such as Staley (now Western Sugar). As a result it now has 20 per cent of the North American sugar market. Indeed, Tate and Lyle is now so multinational that only 16 per cent of its total sales come from its

---

[5] Michael V. Gestrin, Rory F. Knight and Alan M. Rugman (1998). The Templeton Global Performance Index, Templeton College, University of Oxford. Kingfisher, Annual Report and Accounts, 1997, 1998; 'Corporate Profile: Kingfisher', The Times, London, February 1 1999, p. 44; Financial Times, May 18 1988, December 12 1989; and Bernard M. Wolf, 'The Role of Strategic Alliances in the European Automotive Industry', in Alan M. Rugman and Alain Verbeke (eds.) Research in Global Management, vol. III, (1992), pp. 143-163. Greenwich, Conn: JAI Press.

British home-base; 36 per cent are from the United States; 23 per cent from the rest of Europe and 24 per cent from the rest of the world. Truly a transnational firm.[6]

Rhône-Poulenc

Rhône-Poulenc is a French-based chemicals firm that has sought, through mergers and acquisitions, to become a global top ten player. The chemicals industry is highly competitive and in both bulk and speciality chemicals is usually a Quadrant 1 of Figure 10.1. strategy. Major producers include US firms such as DuPont and Dow Chemicals and European firms such as Hoechst, BASF, Ciba Geigy and ICI. In 1985 Rhône-Poulenc was the twelfth largest chemical company in the world, but 80 per cent of its sales were in Europe.

The chemicals industry is increasingly structured on a 'triad' basis and so Rhône-Poulenc decided to consolidate on its successful European base and move into the US market in the 1980s. By 1996 21 per cent of its total sales were in the United States. Between 1986 and 1989 it made 18 acquisitions in the United States, the major ones being Union Carbide Agrochemical Products in 1986 and Stauffer Basic Chemicals in 1987. By 1990, Rhône-Poulenc was at number seven.

Managing the US operation was not easy. The takeover of Union Carbide worked well, as its pesticide products were complementary to Rhône-Poulenc's herbicides and fungicides and the corporate cultures were similar. The Stauffer one was more difficult as there were overlapping product lines and the US managers in Stauffer had little international experience.

In order to make a go of its diverse US operations, Rhône-Poulenc adopted a decentralized organizational structure, consolidating its US business into a strong US country group with headquarters at Princeton, New Jersey. The language of business was English, not the French of the parent firm. This was a Quadrant 4 strategy. As an intermediate step on the path towards integration, the US regional headquarters served Rhône-Poulenc well as it helped to create a US presence in the face of strong triad-based rivalry, with efficient production and effective staffing. In the future a

---

[6] Tate & Lyle Annual Report, 1995; Tate & Lyle Annual Report, 1996; Tate & Lyle Annual Report, 1997; www.hoovers.com/capsules/42402.html 'Hoover's Company Capsule – Tate & Lyle Plc'

more 'transnational' structure (in Quadrant 3), will be required for this company.[7]

Nokia and Ericsson

The world's largest producer of mobile phones is Nokia, based in one of the smallest countries, Finland. Nokia is the leader in Europe and is second only to Motorola in the United States. Motorola is the leader in analogue technology but Nokia and Ericsson are fighting it out in digital mobile phones.

Nokia was founded in 1865 and was a major manufacturer of paper products before it transformed itself into a high-technology producer of electronics products, especially cellular phones, starting in the 1970s. By 1997, Nokia was the largest company in Finland with sales of nearly US$10 billion. It had sales in 130 countries and employed 36,000 people in production in 45 countries.

From early on Nokia has pursued foreign sales; today only five per cent of its sales are in its home base. This internationalization strategy was necessary because Finland only has three million people. First Nokia became the mobile phone leader in Scandinavia, despite competition from Ericsson of Sweden. Next it became the leader in Britain, then the rest of Europe, and it formed strategic alliances with US distributors such as Radio Shack and also with US telecom companies like AT&T. Nokia has developed special phones for Chinese and Japanese users.

Nokia spends a large amount on R&D and is attempting to provide mobile phones which can use 'global roaming', i.e. work across different telecom systems around the world. This requires that the company work closely with different political regimes in order to try to develop an industry standard, ie be in Quadrant 1 of Figure 10.1. In this venture it joins with its

---

[7] Rhône-Poulenc (1996). Annual Report 1995: Rhône-Poulenc, Courbvoie, Cedex, France. Rhône-Poulenc (1997). Annual Report 1996: Rhône-Poulenc, Courbvoie, Cedex, France. Rhône-Poulenc (1998). 'News: Rhône-Poulenc Rorer Announces Measures to Improve Productivity'. Internet: Rhône-Poulenc Home Page, 4 June, p.1.

Banks, H. (1996), 'The road from serfdom: after almost being strangled by nationalization, France's Rhône-Poulenc is back on its feet as one of the world's great chemical companies', Forbes, Vol. 158, No.10, 21 October, p.156(4).

Hunter, D. (1995), 'Reshaping Rhône-Poulenc', Chemical Week, Vol. 156, No. 23, p.30(4).

Owen, D. and Green, D. (1997), 'MCC 27 June 1997 / Financial Times: Front Page – First Section: Rhône-Poulenc to Focus on Pharmaceuticals Business'. Internet: FT McCarthy.

great rival, Ericsson. The two companies are attempting to establish GSM as the standard for mobile phones across Europe, and as one of the global standards. The next generation of mobile phones may build on a system like GSM.

LM Ericsson has over 100,000 employees and sales of US $20 billion in the 130 countries in which it operates. In 1997, Ericsson was the world's largest producer of digital mobile phones. Only 6 per cent of its sales occur in Sweden, with nearly 40 per cent of its sales in Europe, 27 per cent to Asia and 16 per cent to North America. Unlike Nokia (which started as a paper and rubber producer) Ericsson has always been in telecommunications, starting in 1876 as a telephone manufacturer. It has always been innovative and, today, one fifth of all employees work in R&D. In other areas of business it has developed telephone switches in which it competes with firms such as Canada's Nortel and France's Alcatel. Ericsson was well positioned to benefit from the telecom deregulation of the 1980s and 1990s. This has created new demand, especially for new equipment like mobile phones where there were few local monopoly producers.

Ericsson has formed alliances with Compaq, Intel, Hewlett Packard and Texas Instruments. These firms act as key suppliers of components and products that Ericsson uses for voice and data transmission. Ericsson's relative weakness is a poor brand name, compared to Nokia and Motorola. It has the production technology but needs to improve on its marketing side.

Firms like Ericsson and Nokia will benefit from the alliance between AT&T and British Telecom, and that between Sprint, France Telecom and Deutsche Telekom. These big alliances help set standardized services (in Quadrant 1 of Figure 10.1.) to which mobile phone producers can respond efficiently. In the future mobile phones will become even smaller, but the two producers from small countries, Nokia of Finland and Ericsson of Sweden, will become even bigger.[8]

Thames Water

Thames Water plc is the largest British water company, established in 1989 after Prime Minister Margaret Thatcher privatized the water industry. It supplies the water and sewage services to over 11 million people in the Thames Valley, from the ancient university city of Oxford to one of the world's largest urban areas in London.

---

[8] Annual Reports.

The activities of Thames Water's core water utility division are still subject to regulation by OFWAT, the UK water regulator, which sets price controls and regulatory standards over water and sewage services every five years. OFWAT's policy is to force the British regional water monopolies to make price cuts to the water bills of their customers, a commodity type strategy in Quadrant 1 of Figure 10.1. The managerial paradox is that any increases in operating efficiency in the water utility are essentially taxed away every five years. In the intervening period there is some incentive for the overall company to use economic efficiency improvements in the utility division to help fund development of its non-regulated commercially-based business.

Thames Water is no exception to this policy. Whereas some water utilities have moved into other sectors (such as electricity and gas, which are also in Quadrant 1 of Figure 10.1), Thames Water has decided against the multi-utilities approach adopted by other British water companies such as United Utilities and Hyder. Instead its strategy is twofold. First it has expanded into commercial aspects of the water business. Half of its 11,000 employees now work in water-related businesses, such as the design, engineering and maintenance of water membrane systems and related water treatment products, or in the servicing and marketing of water-related businesses.

Second, it has engaged in international diversification. Thames Water has major projects in Australia, Turkey, Indonesia, Ukraine, Malaysia, the Philippines and Thailand. In November 1999 it bought a large US water utility in New Jersey and is now well positioned to expand its operations in the United States. This is a geographic extension of its firm-specific advantage in water production and supply. The international market for water is worth several billion dollars a year and potential profit abroad is much greater than in Britain. Water is the oil of the twenty-first century. The major global rivals are the two giant French water companies, Vivendi, formerly CGE (Génerále des Eaux) with annual sales of over US$30 billion, and Suez-Lyonnaise des Eaux with annual sales of US$20 billion. There are few North American commercial water companies due to the fragmented and regulated nature of the US municipal and Canadian provincial markets.

In Indonesia, Thames Water has a 25 year contract to supply fresh water to half of the population of the capital city, Jakarta. In March 1998 this contract was temporarily rescinded by the new President as he alleged that it was signed with the son of the former President Suharto. Despite being the first Western business to be disrupted by this type of political risk, within a month Thames Water had signed up with the new Government of Indonesia.

In the Australian project in Adelaide, Thames Water supplied the technical expertise in collaboration with a French partner. The French did the political lobbying, and their skill in this is reflected by winning the contract shortly after the French government conducted a series of nuclear tests in the Pacific which were strongly opposed by the Australian and New Zealand governments. The political image of Thames Water in Asia was not affected by this association and the British company tends to have a 'neutral' political risk exposure.

Thames Water has already learnt some harsh lessons in international business. Former CEO, Mike Hoffman, made a big mistake by acquiring an East German design and contracting business (UTAG) in 1992. This lost money as the expected demand for water market infrastructure post-reunification did not expand in Germany as much as anticipated. Thames Water also did not research the local politics where there remained strong local municipal regulations. So Thames Water sold off its German venture and under new CEO, Bill Alexander, has developed a new portfolio of international operations which build on its core skills. The board and new CEO also decided to integrate closely all the international operations with its basic British utility business. Over the next OFWAT regulatory period (2000-2005) Thames Water will need to build its international operations up further to contribute to its profits and continue moving from a regulated utility to an international business.[9] Its long-term strategy is to reposition itself from the commodity type utility of Quadrant 1 or 2 to a Quadrant 3 transnational company.

P&O

Few people know that the 'Princess' cruise ships, which were the 'love boats' of TV fame, are owned by a British company, P&O. This is a US$ 10 billion transportation and service business that is one of Britain's most international companies.

The Peninsular and Orient Steam Navigation Company, known as P&O, was the sea transportation backbone of the old British Empire. In the

---

[9] Sources: Annual Reports of Thames Water PLC.

Note: The above analysis of Thames Water reflects the private opinion of Professor Alan M. Rugman. Officers at Thames Water have not been involved in the preparation of this material in any way.

nineteenth century it won British government contracts to deliver mail to the Spanish peninsula and (via Africa and the Indian subcontinent) to Australia and the Far East. In the past P&O's ships have been commandeered by the British government in wartime to serve as transport vessels. As recently as the Falklands War of 1982 its large flagship, Canberra, played a central role in the British war effort.

Today P&O is using this familiar brand name as a base for its British Commonwealth cruise ships, for cross channel ferries, container ships, and for pan-European trucking. In North America, it operates the 'Princess' cruise ships separately, following a nationally responsive Quadrant 4 of Figure 10.1 strategy. These cruise ships include Sun Princess, Dawn Princess, Grand Princess and the giant, Ocean Princess. These are 'regional', not global brands. With an older population of North America 'baby boomers' the growth in cruises has been striking. Occupancy on P&O is usually at 100% of capacity. P&O is the leading cruise tour operator along the North American West Coast to Alaska. Cruises are sold through 28,000 travel agents. The British and European cruise market is quite different from the North American one and was served by Canberra (until its withdrawal in 1997 after 36 years service), Oriana and Arcadia (formerly Star Princess).

P&O containers ranked in 1996 as the seventh largest carrier in the world. It then merged with Nedlloyd Lines to form P&O Nedlloyd which is in the world's top three. This is a truly global operation with routes across all the world's oceans; moving the goods of the triad. These container ships are linked up with P&O European Trucks, which is the largest integrated distribution and transport source in Europe. P&O Ferries (which merged with Stena Line in 1996) is the largest operation between Britain and the continent of Europe and it continues to do well despite the opening of the cross-channel Eurotunnel in 1995. In the past P&O also owned and managed the Earl's Court Olympia exhibition halls in London, but is selling off this non-core business. In addition, it has sold Bovis Homes, a leading British house builder, and the Bovis Construction Group.

P&O has an interesting strategic challenge of integrating diverse businesses, from trucks to boat shows. In particular it needs to link its very capital intensive cargo ships, which require good information technology and operational efficiency, with its cruise ships which are in the leisure and entertainment business. The long-term strategy falls into Quadrant 3 of Figure 10.1, a transnational company. The moulding of an engineering and technical culture with the marketing, sales, and service activities of the cruise ships is an interesting managerial challenge. P&O has tackled this by extensive programmes of management training. For example, it has developed a series of senior management programmes at Templeton College, Oxford University over the last ten years. These have helped to improve business efficiency and also moved managers into new areas of customer service, such as environmental and regulatory issues. As a result, P&O is a successful and growing business with managers attuned to the needs of international business.[10]

Philips and Matsushita

In terms of triad-based competition, the 1980s saw the emergence of Japanese winners in the consumer electronics industry. One of the most successful Japanese MNEs is Matsushita. Initially successful with colour televisions (it makes Panasonic TVs), its best known product was the video cassette recorder (VCR), a field which it dominates by using the VHS system instead of Sony's betamax format and others produced by European and American rivals. Paradoxically the VCR was originally developed in California in 1956 by a US firm, Ampex, but development and distribution of the product was captured by Matsushita's clever strategy. In order to dominate world business in VCRs, Matsushita made the VHS format the industry standard. It achieved this, not just by its own massive production and worldwide sales, but by licensing the VHS format to other MNEs such as Hitachi, Sharp, Mitsubishi and even its great European-based rival, Philips. Other companies like GE, RCA and Zenith (who sold VCRs under their own brand name) were tied into the VHS format because of the production and process technology retained by Matsushita in its strong Japanese home base. Massive global economies of scale enabled it to cut VCR prices by a half over its first five years. It operates in Quadrant 1 of Figure 10.1.

In contrast to Matsushita, Philips was in desperate trouble by the 1980s. Built up in the inter-war period of protectionism and strong government regulations it had developed a very decentralized organizational structure. Individual national country managers held the power in Philips and they were slow to respond to the Japanese threat in the post-war period. As a result Philips lacked economies of scale and its radios, TVs and VCRs were all too expensive, compared with similar Japanese products. Philips had over 600 manufacturing plants across the world, all developing products for local markets. The challenge facing Philips was how to restructure its entire

---

[10] Annual Reports of P&O.

business away from Quadrant 4 of Figure 10.1 (a locally responsive national organization), towards becoming a more integrated and leaner manufacturer capable of reaping the necessary economies of scale through standard production in the triad markets. This required a move to Quadrant 3 or even to Qadrant 1, to compete with its Japanese rival.

In essence, the Japanese had changed the rules of the game in the consumer electronics business. Matsushita, as a centralized, high quality, low price and innovative company was beating the decentralized and nationally responsive European firm. One response by European firms was to lobby their governments for protection in the form of anti-dumping actions and tougher customs inspection of Japanese products. But such 'shelter' only buys some breathing room before MNEs like Philips need to restructure and fit their organizational capability to the required industry strategy.

Finally, the response of Matsushita to more protection has been to switch overseas sales from the export mode to one of foreign direct investment. This means that the Japanese firm can evade European trade barriers such as anti-dumping actions, since it actually manufactures in European countries, such as the United Kingdom, where it has a major plant in Cardiff, Wales. But this also means that Matsushita needs to make its foreign subsidiaries as useful as possible by encouraging local initiatives, (moving from Quadrant 1 to Quadrant 3), even where these conflict with its international, centralized Japanese-based management culture. The same government regulations which made Philips too decentralized are now being reapplied half a century later to make Matsushita less global and more local.[11]

Fuji Xerox and Xerox

Fuji Xerox was established in 1962 as a joint venture between Xerox and Fuji Photo Film. It is regarded as the most successful partnership between US and Japanese firms. Fuji Xerox developed from a sales operation for Xerox products in Japan into a fully integrated organisation with its own R&D and manufacturing. By 1990, its sales of US$ 4 billion were a quarter of Xerox's worldwide revenues.

By then Fuji Xerox had a world product mandate to supply the entire Xerox Group with the low-to-mid-range copiers that were the core of its

---

[11] Chris Bartlett and Sumantra Ghoshal, *Managing Across Borders*, second editions, 1989. Boston, Mass: *Harvard Business School Press*.

business. Indeed, as the Xerox monopoly on large copiers began to dwindle in the 1970s it was its Japanese partner, Fuji Xerox, which rode to the rescue with its new and high quality smaller copiers. If it had not been for Fuji Xerox developing new copier technology, Xerox would have died.

In 1975 Xerox was forced by the US Federal Trade Commission to license its original core copier technology to rivals such as IBM, Kodak, Ricoh and Canon. Thereafter Xerox's early monopoly in the world copier business was eroded sharply by intense rivalry, mainly from Japanese competitors such as Canon and Ricoh but also from Kodak and IBM. These rivals produced higher quality, lower price, more technologically advanced and more reliable copiers than Xerox, which only had an old brand name.

Fuji Xerox recognised the threat and its managers, acting autonomously, started R&D into new small copiers. The US head office was very slow to take on board the technology and products of its Japanese partner. Loss of market share, especially to Canon, eventually led to ever closer degrees of co-operation between Xerox and Fuji Xerox. In particular, the high quality standards of Fuji Xerox were spread throughout the Xerox Group. The total quality management (TQM) techniques of Fuji Xerox helped Xerox regain market share once these new production processes were accepted by Xerox top management. In this context Xerox was helped by having its partner, Fuji Xerox, based in Japan, which was the hotbed of TQM and copier innovation in the 1970s and 1980s.

One of the reasons for success in this collaboration between Xerox and Fuji Photo Films was that the latter acted as a silent partner in the 50/50 joint venture and allowed Fuji Xerox to develop its own management cadre, who became skilled in R&D and copier technology, and in the manufacturing and marketing of small copiers. Fuji Xerox transformed itself from a marketing subsidiary into a full line business which ended up more innovative and responsive to the market than Xerox itself.[12] The strong brand name is a classic Quadrant 1 strategy. The small copiers were also developed in Quadrant 1, using the Japanese home base diamond determinants of competitiveness (Porter, 1990).

---

[12] Benjamin Gomes-Casseres and Krista McQuade, 'Xerox and Fuji Xerox', Harvard Business School Case 9-391-156; David T. Kearns and David A. Nadler (1992). *Prophets in the Dark: How Xerox Reinvented Itself and Beat Back the Japanese*. New York: Macmillan; and Benjamin Gomes-Casseres, 'Group Versus Group: How Alliance Networks Compete,, *Harvard Business Review*, July-August, 1994, 62-74.

HSBC

What is the world's largest bank? Prior to the merger of Citicorp and Travellers in 1998, it was the Hong Kong and Shanghai Banking Corporation (HSBC). Formed in 1865 by a Scotsman in the former British Colony of Hong Kong, HSBC grew to have over 5,000 bank offices in 78 countries by 1997. In the process it became the world's first truly global bank, offering a full range of financial services from retail to corporate banking to insurance and financial management. HSBC built this global business on its strong Hong Kong base. The bank owns Hong Kong Bank and most of Hang Seng Bank, giving it over 40 per cent of the market in the now Hong Kong Special Administrative Region of China created on 1 July 1997. It also has a large presence in Britain, owning what was previously the Midland Bank chain.

It is less well known that HSBC is also the owner of the Marine Midland banks in the United States, and the Hong Kong Bank of Canada. It has also acquired large banks in Latin America including Banco Bamerindus in Brazil and Grupo Financiero Serfin in Mexico. In all these cases HSBC greatly improved the efficiency of the under-performing local banks through better systems and processes. All of this is consistent with Quadrant 1 strategy.

HSBC is now well developed across the triad regions of Asia, Europe and the Americas. Its diversification strategy helped to insulate it from the Asian financial crisis of 1997/98. And its first mover advantage as a truly global bank will prove hard to match by banks in the still regulated markets of North America and Europe. There is constant pressure in banking to reduce costs through greater scale economies and improved information technology, and HSBC is well positioned to continue as an industry leader because of its successful globalization strategy.

In retrospect, the world's largest bank came from one of the world's smallest economies. And it did this despite the regulatory barriers to entry for foreign-owned firms in Europe and North America. As a result the HSBC is an example of a bank using modern management systems and market forces to win over old-fashioned protectionism in a highly regulated worldwide industry.[13]

---

[13] 'An Empire at Risk: HSBC', *The Economist*, September 7, 1996.

Kahn, S. 'The Future of Global Banks', *Global Finance*, 12:5, May 1998, p.28.

Green, W. 'Bland – and Proud of it', *Forbes*, 159:14, July 7, 1997, p.94.

Procter and Gamble

Procter and Gamble is Unilever's major competitor. It too, largely operates on a local basis. In its latest organizational restructuring, called Project 2005, Procter and Gamble has grouped its 200 plus brand products into seven major business units. Each of these are co-ordinated globally, from different locations, although several are still run from the US head office in Cincinnati. But other business units are directed from Japan, Venezuela and Austria. While the seven product divisions are called 'global' business units, in practice they operate in a decentralized manner with strategies being developed locally and/or regionally. The product delivery and marketing are local, as befits a customer-based products business. The 'back office' of payroll, financing, human resource management and other general services and processes is co-ordinated on a more global basis, to achieve internal economies of scale and speed to market. The best practice of each subsidiary is to become the benchmark for all subsidiaries. In more formal terms, Procter and Gamble is trying to deliver an organizational structure in Quadrant 3 of Figure 10.1, in which it attempts to meet the twin goals of economic efficiency and localization.

Procter and Gamble's board no longer resembles an old-fashioned US midwest family business; the members are from different countries and include a South American, a Canadian, Europeans and Asians. But these members bring regional/triad viewpoints to the board, rather than a single homogenous global view. This is an MNE that straddles the triad; it is not a driver of globalization but a result of local markets and triad-based food, safety and consumer legislation.

Hewlett Packard

Today, as never before, multinational enterprises have to be concerned about their public image. Consumers, employees and shareholders all expect corporations to behave responsibly and ethically towards the communities in which they operate. Some companies have learned the hard way that they are accountable. For instance, Royal Dutch/Shell had to apologize to its shareholders when its environmental and human rights report card did not measure up to their expectations. Today's MNEs are trying to meet the expectations of the stakeholders, and some companies, like 3M, Kodak and Hewlett Packard, are outdoing themselves.

Hewlett Packard Environmental Management Policy (EMP) oversees the environmental quality of its products through their life cycle. The company's EMP is complemented with an Environmental Management System (EMS). Through its EMS, Hewlett Packard audits its operations regularly. Business managers are accountable to the CEO on their environmental standing. The system is based on the principles of total quality management (TQM). The quality of the products is thereby linked to their effect on the environment, through the production process. As Hewlett Packard then expands into developing countries, it helps to raise their environmental standards because the US standards are embedded in its production process.

Environmental issues are an integral part of the planning and decision process. Hewlett Packard designs and constructs its facilities to minimize waste generation promoting energy efficiency and ecosystem protection. It pursues a strategy of pollution prevention to reduce the generation of chemical and solid waste and actively addresses contamination resulting from its operations. It also encourages suppliers to adopt similar environmental principles.

In 1992, the company began a product stewardship programme. This maintains the following guidelines: to design products and packaging to minimize the energy they consume, use fewer raw materials and more recycled materials; to develop products that are easier to reuse or recycle and to reduce waste and emissions from the manufacturing process. The first priority is to source hazardous waste. Hewlett Packard then finds ways of recycling, treating and disposing of these wastes. It is important to note that its EMS and EMP were found to be consistent with international standards set in the ISO 1400. [14]

These are Quadrant 3 of Figure 10.1 strategies – i.e. responsive to environmental regulations by an efficient MNE whose production processes are efficient. Some strategies help to raise the environmental standards of poorer countries, as was confirmed in the NAFTA–based research reviewed earlier in Chapters 4 and 6.

---

[14] Alan M Rugman and Alain Verbeke, 'Multinational Enterprises and Green Capabilities: Coping with Environmental Regulations', (revised) Templeton College, University of Oxford; Alan M Rugman and Alain Verbeke, 'Corporate Strategies and Environmental Regulations: An Organizing Framework,' *Strategic Management Journal*, 19(4), April 1995, pp. 363-376. http://www.hp.com/abouthp/envrnmnt/; 'Shellman says sorry (Cor Herkstroter),' The Economist, May 10, 1997, p. 95.

3 M

The 3M Company is a large US MNE based in Minnesota, which makes over 50,000 products in everything from office supplies, to construction and building maintenance to chemicals. It employs over 73,000 people and has operations in 60 countries. How does the firm manage such large international operations? One way is by matching its international strategies with the needs of the local market. Some goods such as home videocassettes are standardized and are sold on the basis of price and quality. Culture and local usage are not important considerations. Other products are greatly influenced by local preferences or regulations; telecommunications is an example. Each country or region of the world has its own modifications for local application. 3M operates in Quadrant 3 of Figure 10.1.

The 3M Company balances its global strategies and national responses on a region-by-region basis. For example, in Europe it has set up a series of business centres to address local differences. It also uses European management action teams (EMATs) to balance the needs of subsidiaries in responding to local expectations with the corporation's need for global direction. EMAT meetings, which usually occur quarterly, are designed to create action plans for the European subsidiaries. When the meetings are over, the members then return to their respective subsidiaries and begin executing the plans. In Asia the company uses a different approach, relying heavily on its Japanese operation to provide much of the needed direction to the subsidiaries. There are also regional centres in Singapore and South Korea that help subsidiaries to address their local markets. In Latin America, meanwhile, 3M uses a macro approach, conducting business on a national rather than regional basis.

The company also carefully identifies those products that it will sell in each geographic area while following two basic strategies: to be the first in the market with a new offering, because this puts the competition at a disadvantage, and to grow new markets gradually by picking out those products that address the country's most pressing needs and focusing exclusively on them. According to its annual report:

'We don't believe in formulating a single global strategy for selling videocassettes in India and laser imagers in France and post-it brand notes in Brazil. For each of 3M's 23 strategic business centres in each region the company's strategy is a blend of global, regional, and local companies and that will continue.'[15]

---

[15] Harry Mammerly, 'Matching Global Strategies with National Responses,' *Journal of Business Strategy*, March/April 1992, pp. 8-13; Kevin Kelly, '3M Run Scared? Forget About it,' *Business Week*, September 16, 1991, pp. 59, 62; James Braham, 'Engineering Your Way to

Enron

Working for Enron, a US utility company producing and trading natural gas, was once not seen as an exciting career move for top quality MBAs. Indeed, in 1990 new CEO Kenneth Lang found that Enron did not even recruit from top US business schools such as Harvard, Stanford and Chicago. Instead, Enron went to second and third tier schools, as its experience was that these MBAs were more stable and committed to careers in the gas utility business. Lang's response was to fire the HR director who was failing to recruit top class people. As CEO he has injected enthusiasm and vision into working for Enron. He spends a large amount of his time in recruitment, stating that being a world class company means recruiting world class people. Now the company competes with consulting firm McKinsey for MBAs from Harvard and others of the world's top business schools.

When Enron was formed in 1985 by a merger of two US gas companies, it became the largest natural gas utility in the United States, with the largest gas pipeline system and more gas-fired independent power plants than any other company in the world. This is a classic Quadrant 1 position in Figure 10.1.

A British equivalent is BOC Group, which in 1999 was subject to a US$7.4 billion take-over by Air Liquide of France and Air Products of the United States. The merger regulators of the EC may require that some of BOC's cylinder gas may need to be disposed of, as will some of its tonnage gas (sold to industrial customers by pipeline). In addition, as much as a quarter of BOC's bulk gases (oxygen, nitrogen and argon) may need to be sold off, as may some of its helium.

In 1997 Enron's revenues were over US$10 billion. The company, with its head office in Houston, owned and operated energy plants in 15 countries and had new projects in another 15. This represented 15 per cent of total sales. One of Lang's strategies was to build up the international side of Enron's business, providing exciting opportunities and responsibilities for fast track MBA recruits.

In 1992 Enron Development Corporation (EDC) signed a contract for US$2.8 billion to develop the Dabhol Project for a gas-fired power plant in the Indian state of Maharashtra. In 1995 this contract was cancelled by the new BJP Socialist government of Maharashtra. The project was one-third

the Top,' *Machine Design*, August 22, 1991, pp. 65-68, and http://www.3m.com.; 3M, *Annual Report*, 1997.

complete at the time of cancellation and employed 2,600 people. The head of EDC, Rebecca Mark, renegotiated it and Enron eventually offset this political risk.

Subsequent to this experience, Ms Mark has been involved in running Wessex Water, a privatized UK utility which was bought by Enron in 1998. Ms Mark set up a global water services company, Azurix, to bid for international contracts as water companies were privatized especially in Europe and in North and South America. In early 2000, Azurix was not doing well as it had not won any significant contracts. It lost a potential contract to Vivendi for Berlin's water service. Its stock price had fallen to US$7 from a high of US$23.88 in July 1999. In contrast to Azurix, Thames Water (discussed above) has been much more successful in its new international operations. By late August, Azurix's stock was at US$5 and Ms Mark had resigned.

Enron has developed a new core competence (firm-specific advantage) in organizational learning and managing political risk. This has strengthened its position in Quadrant 1 and given it the option of moving into Quadrant 3, should it wish to do so. It has been one of the first firms in a stable and traditional energy-related sector to develop a knowledge-based business, staffed by skilled and well-trained people who are managers rather than engineers. This gives Enron a competitive advantage compared to the average energy business. Even commodity-type utilities can become effective international businesses by developing such dynamic organizational capabilities.[16]

Nortel Networks

Northern Telecom, now called Nortel Networks, had transformed itself from a Canadian-based multinational enterprise in 1977 to a North American-based MNE by 1987 to a quadrant 3 transnational corporation by 1997. Between 1985 and 1998, its revenue increased from US$4.2 billion to US$18.7 billion and total employees from 46,500 to 80,000.

In 1985, over 90 per cent of its sales were within North America. Today Nortel has 92 per cent of its sales outside Canada, and 40 per cent of all sales

---

[16] Adapted from Sumantra Ghoshal and Christopher A. Bartlett, 'Play the Right Cards to Fit the Aces in the Pack', *Financial Times*, 28 July 1998; and Sumantra Ghoshal and Christopher A. Bartlett (1997), *The Individualized Corporation*. New York: Harper Business. Andrew Inkpen 'Enron Development Corporation', in Paul W. Beamish, Allen Morrison and Philip M. Rosenzwig, *International Management: Text and Cases* (1997). (Chicago: Irwin). Enron Annual Reports.

outside of North America. It has a very large ratio of R&D to sales of over 20 per cent (R&D spending in 1995 was US$1.6 billion on revenues of US$10.7 billion). One in four of Nortel's employees focuses on R&D, working in 42 R&D facilities in 17 countries, along with numerous joint ventures and strategic alliances. Overall, the number of knowledge workers has increased from 42 per cent in 1985 to 66 per cent in 1995, rising to 75 per cent by 1998.

While Nortel competes globally in the telecommunications sector, it is not operating as if borders do not exist. Despite the apparent globalization of this sector, there remains a very high degree of government regulation and a set of regionally-separated national markets. Even with the WTO's International Technology Agreement of 1995, there is no single world market for telecommunications. Nortel must be flexible enough to respond to differences in national regulations and consumer tastes, so it has adopted a policy of national responsiveness. Other companies which are nationally responsive include Unilever and Asea-Brown Boveri (ABB). With a national responsiveness strategy, a firm like Nortel can be 'close to the customer' and responsive to the local regulator. Such decentralized firms are called 'transnational corporations' (TNCs). Nortel qualifies as a TNC on three grounds.

First, Nortel has decentralized decision-making, to reflect the regional nature of the telecommunications market for products and services. A large degree of autonomy is given to product-sector and country managers.

Second, Nortel has an internal managerial resource strategy which decentralizes major decision making to some 200 top executives in more than a dozen markets around the world. In 1987, Northern Telecom was run by five to ten people out of head office in Mississauga, Ontario. The 200 top managers making vital decisions today operate with the large degree of autonomy typical of the TNC.

Third, Nortel's decentralized top management structure is held together by heavy use of the Internet for inter-office communication. Nortel has its own internal electronic voice mail, and data network which is heavily used by senior managers, as well as all other employees. The senior managers are members of the President's Council, which conducts its business through the corporate intranet.

The key managerial challenge for Nortel today is how to organize effective 'networks' with allies and strategic partners across the segmented regional markets characteristic of the telecommunications sector. Nortel's objective is to be the global resource for digital network solutions and services. It aims to deliver a total network solution of technical assistance, training, customer service and documentation in partnership with its clients. By building and integrating both wireline and wireless digital networks on a global basis and operating as a TNC Nortel has moved towards achieving this objective.[17]

In 1998 Nortel purchased Bay Networks, a Silicon Valley internet firm for Cdn$11.2 billion. It did this to refocus the firm as an internet-based provider of digital networking solutions. It also did this nearly 2 years before the world's biggest ever merger, of internet leader AOL and entertainment/magazine leader Time Warner, in January 2000.

Conclusions

It has been found in this chapter on the strategies of 20 large MNEs that multinational firms do not succeed with global strategies, they need regional/triad strategies. These were some of the key results of the case studies:

- Unilever has been moving to consolidate its many national and regional brands into a manageable number and it is operating on a regional basis. In contrast, Procter and Gamble is attempting to set up seven worldwide product groups, the top management of which is spread around the triad. Both companies are nationally responsive.
- Hewlett Packard is widely recognized for its leadership in adopting environmentally-sensitive production processes, which may give it a 'first mover' strategic advantage in developing green capabilities (Rugman and Verbeke, 1998).
- 3M has been successful in adopting triad-based regional marketing and distribution strategies, rather than a global marketing strategy. Indeed, none of these 20 firms has developed a pure global strategy.
- Philips has been in trouble as its country managers were too powerful and the firm was too decentralized. The push for a single EU market to provide a 'home-base' to offset the advantages of US and Japanese rivals is a logical response.
- In contrast Matsushita has successfully penetrated the US and European triad markets but is now attempting to get more value out of its subsidiaries and be a little nationally responsive.
- Rhône-Poulenc had to review its US acquisitions (like Stauffer) and

---

[17] Annual Reports of Northern Telecom/Nortel.

how these had to be managed locally, due to the American staff's potentially adverse reaction to French language directives. Its activities in penetrating the US part of the triad base met with only mixed success.

- Thames Water is an example of a privatized utility. It shows water companies are nationally based, due to strong home government regulations and culture. Its international activities have been opportunistic rather than strategic, but are now being more systematically planned and greater strategic skills are observable in its senior managers.

- Nokia and Ericsson. These two mobile phone producers are successful as domestic champions and have been able to enter other triad markets despite strong national regulations.

Conclusions: Firm Strategy and Government Policy

Introduction

In the first half of this concluding chapter I examine the future of the WTO and international trade and investment agreements. I do not find any evidence that multilateral trade and investment liberalization will be resumed. Instead, regionally-based trade agreements will proliferate, reinforcing the barriers to entry to the triad blocs. The power of government and the nation state will remain strong and reinforce the triad at the expense of globalization.

In the remainder of the chapter I explore the broader social and ethical issues related to the activities of multinational firms. I look at the interaction between NGOs and MNEs and conclude that their future is more complex than usually recognized.

Regional trade agreements

Today, the world's economies do not trade freely; they are members of triad-based trade blocks. Table 11.1 lists the membership of the major trade groups in Europe, the Americas and Asia.

As table 11.1 reports, the EU has 15 members. There is also a rather large list of 13 countries in the process of negotiating to join it. These include Hungary, Poland, the Czech Republic, the Baltic States, Romania and Turkey.

The EU may also be extended to include Ukraine and other former parts of the Soviet Union. So the EU 'bloc' is already on track to have 13 countries added to the existing 15 member states (with some of these 13 joining the full EU by 2004). These 28 countries, plus the four EFTA members make up most of Western, Central and Eastern Europe. The four members of EFTA have a linked form of free trade with the EU.

In the Americas, two major trade groups have emerged – the fully integrated three NAFTA members and the rapidly growing four members of

Table 11.1: The World's Trade Agreements, by Triad Group

EUROPE			AMERICAS						ASIA	
EU (15)	Enlargement of the EU	EFTA (4)	NAFTA (3)	CARICOM (14)	CACM (5)	Andean (5)	MERCOSUR (4)	LAIA (11)	ASEAN (7)	APEC (21)
Austria	Talks started March 1998	Iceland	US	Antigua and Barbuda	Costa Rica	Bolivia	Argentina	Argentina	Indonesia	Australia
Belgium	Cyprus	Liechtenstein	Canada	Barbados	Guatemala	Colombia	Brazil	Bolivia	Malaysia	Brunei
Denmark	Czech Rep.	Norway	Mexico	Belize	El Salvador	Ecuador	Paraguay	Brazil	Philippines	Canada
Finland	Estonia	Switzerland		Dominican Republic	Honduras	Peru	Uruguay	Chile	Singapore	Chile
France	Hungary			Grenada	Nicaragua	Venezuela		Colombia	Thailand	China
Germany	Poland			Guyana				Ecuador	Brunei	Hong Kong
Greece	Slovenia			Haiti				Mexico	Vietnam	Indonesia
Ireland	Talks to start in Feb, 2000			Jamaica				Paraguay		Japan
Italy	Bulgaria			Montserrat				Peru		Korea
Luxembourg	Latvia			St Kitts & Nevis				Uruguay		Malaysia
Netherlands	Lithuania			St Lucia				Venezuela		Mexico
Portugal	Malta			St Vincent and the Grenadines						New Zealand
Spain	Romania			Suriname						Papua New Guinea
Sweden	Slovakia			Trinidad and Tobago						Peru
UK	Turkey									Philippines
										Russia
										Singapore
										Taiwan
										Thailand
										United States
										Vietnam

Sources: Adapted from http://europa.eu.int/abc-en.htm; www.efta.int; http://www.caricom.org; http://wellsfargo.com/inatl/wrldalmn/intro/other/; http://www.sice.oas.org/; http://www.aladi.org/; http://www.sadc-usa.net/members/default.html; http://www.imf.org/external/np/sec/decdo/ecowas.htm; http://www.usia.gov/regional/ea/apec/apecfac2.htm

EU – European Union; EFTA – European Free Trade Agreement; NAFTA – North American Free Trade Agreement; CARICOM – Caribbean Community and Common Market; Mercosur–Southern Core Common Market; LAOA – Latin American Integration Association; ASEAN – Association of South-East Asia Nations; APEC – Asian Pacific Economic Community

Mercosur, to which Chile and other Latin American countries are also being linked. The most likely development will be an eventual joining of the NAFTA and Mercosur groups, with affiliate status for the CARICOM and other Latin American countries.

In Asia, the seven members of ASEAN have turned a defence and security grouping into an economic and trade association. And, APEC has the potential to link at least two partners of the triad – Japan and the United States. I examine this possibility further in the next section.

The Future of the WTO

As discussed in Chapter 2, the history of the GATT/WTO means it is largely a legal and technocratic institution. It is a body with a small secretariat (of 200 people) to resolve trade disputes. It is not well equipped to prepare research papers, nor does it have expertise in the new areas of trade policy formulation and corporate strategy. A legally-based appellate body, set up to administer rules negotiated by sovereign governments, it is not experienced in dealing with political issues, nor with NGOs. It was good at fixing tariff cuts, but not at the new agenda of trade in services, intellectual property standards, and so on.

One problem is that the WTO has granted some access to NGOs. But these also lobby country governments, who then prepare platforms and negotiate overall trade and investment treaties. In contrast, business groups are involved only at a country level and have never been allowed to meet with GATT/WTO officials, which means they are not treated as well as NGOs. Due to the victory of environmental and other anti-trade NGOs, business groups are now becoming NGOs and they were in the NGO pack at Seattle. But, basically, all NGOs should be excluded from the WTO. It is a technical body. Lobby groups need to talk to their own governments. Future meetings of the WTO should exclude all NGOs; business and environmental/social groups. Unless this can be accomplished, the future of the WTO looks bleak. It will continue as an appellate body, but will not be able to push on with an agenda of trade and investment liberalization. In that case, APEC may emerge as a useful alternative forum for world trade and investment liberalization.

Asia-Pacific Free Trade: APEC

The Asia-Pacific Economic Community is still an embryonic free trade area. It alone bridges the triad by including both Japan and the three

NAFTA countries as members. China, Taiwan, South Korea, the Philippines, Indonesia, Malaysia and the other South East Asian countries, Australia, New Zealand and Chile are also members. [1]

APEC has evolved into a quasi-institution with an important trade and investment agenda since its founding meeting in Canberra, Australia, in 1989. The membership of APEC is unique in involving the People's Republic of China, Taiwan Province of China and Hong Kong Special Administrative Region of China (hereinafter Hong Kong, China); two of the world's economic super-powers (the United States and Japan); and all the other important economies bordering the Pacific Ocean. APEC has also evolved in political importance, as (starting in 1993 at the Seattle meeting) there have been seven annual meetings of heads of government, in addition to the ongoing meetings of trade and finance ministers. The government leaders also met in 1994 in Bogor (Jakarta), Indonesia; in 1995 in Osaka, Japan; and in 1996 in Subic Bay (Manila), Philippines. In 1997 they met in Vancouver, Canada; in 1998 in Malaysia and in 1999 in New Zealand.

The participation of government leaders has transformed APEC from a largely technical and low-key talk-shop to a quasi-institution in which the member economies are becoming increasingly committed to economic cooperation and free trade. While not a formal international institution like the WTO, APEC has an emerging consultative process that helps to overcome the disadvantages of its very small secretariat and lack of well-developed procedural rules. Such economic substance as exists is being added through the recent development of a trade and investment agenda, carried out by committees reporting to leaders subject to peer group pressure. In particular, there is a growing process of trade-liberalizing measures. This process reflects the consultative style of Asian trade and business negotiations, rather than a Western-type rules-based style. APEC, in short, is an evolving Western-style international institution with an Asian shape.

The main sign of progress in trade liberalization can be traced back to the 1994 declaration in Bogor, Indonesia, whereby APEC's member economies undertook to meet the goals of free and open trade and investment in the region. Investment is mentioned in the declaration, although most of the

---

[1] The 21 members of APEC in 1999 were: Australia; Brunei Darussalam; Canada; Chile; the People's Republic of China; Hong Kong, China; Indonesia; Japan; the Republic of Korea; Malaysia; Mexico; New Zealand; Papua New Guinea; Peru; the Republic of the Philippines; Russia; Singapore; Taiwan Province of China; Thailand; The United States of America; Vietnam.

subsequent action has been focused on trade liberalization. More specifically, members agreed to eliminate tariffs in developed countries by 2010 and in all developing countries by 2020. While these two categories were not defined, the declaration set all members on the same path towards trade liberalization. In the 1995 meetings at Osaka, all members agreed to an 'action agenda' in which their internal trade barriers would be identified and a voluntary commitment made to reduce them.

There are two key principles behind the common framework of the Osaka action plan of each economy. First, it is comprehensive, as all members in APEC have agreed to eliminate tariffs and foster investment across all sectors. Second, it is flexible, to reflect the economic reality of different stages of development and divergent conditions. However, this flexibility is confined to timing (i.e. 2010 or 2020 to eliminate trade barriers) rather than to systemic sector exclusions; the only sector with special treatment is agriculture.

To implement these free trade measures, APEC members have agreed to trade liberalization measures parallel to the main principle of the GATT/WTO. In particular, they have agreed to most-favoured-nation treatment (non-discrimination) and transparency. The tariff reductions organized through APEC will be fully consistent with the WTO membership of most of these 21 countries (although neither the People's Republic of China nor Taiwan Province of China belong to the WTO). In this sense, APEC is a forum of 'open regionalism', as trade-reduction benefits help members, and no new external tariffs are introduced against non-members.

At the 1996 meetings in the Philippines, each of the members filed Individual Action Plans (IAPs). The individual IAPs are now on record as a collective initiative called the Manila Action Plan for APEC (MAPA), and there is a commitment to implement this beginning in 1997. The MAPA is a process leading towards the comprehensive trade and investment liberalization of 2010 or 2020 agreed to in the Bogor declaration of 1994. APEC members have agreed to build on MAPA, to deepen the IAPs and to improve their comparability and comprehensiveness (APEC Leaders' Declaration, 1996). In Vancouver, the IAPs were reviewed and amended to take account of private sector views. This was facilitated by the formal acceptance (at the Philippines summit of 1996) of advice from the APEC Business Advisory Council (ABAC). The agenda of ABAC is to make recommendations to the leaders of APEC concerning the movement of business people; the enhancement of FDI; alignment of professional standards; advice on infrastructure planning; policies for small and medium-size enterprises; and greater business participation in economic and technical cooperation.

In the IAPs, each member filed a formula revealing its own barriers to trade across 13 areas, including tariffs, non-tariff barriers, obstacles to trade in services and intellectual property. The identification of such trade (and investment) barriers provides a necessary benchmark against which future measures to liberalize trade and investment can be negotiated. The filing of IAPs is similar to the GATT/WTO process of individual country trade-policy review mechanisms, which have also been useful in benchmarking trade barriers and providing an agenda for future reductions in such barriers. Further progress on reducing trade barriers within APEC is highly likely, but the untold story is how investment barriers are to be liberalized.

To summarize, in the Bogor Declaration at the conclusion of the Indonesian summit of 1994, the members agreed to lower all tariffs by 2010 for advanced countries and 2020 for less developed countries. They also agreed to the national treatment principle for FDI, although little has been done to implement this yet. Indeed, APEC has only a very small chance of succeeding. These are its problems:

- It has no permanent secretariat and relies on the trade bureaucracy of each year's host nation to advance its agenda. In the 1997 Canadian Summit and in the 1999 New Zealand Summit, considerable progress towards trade liberalization was achieved. In contrast, the 1998 summit in Malaysia saw little progress, due to the philosophical difficulty its leader has with free trade.
- APEC was the only organization to include China, Hong Kong, Taiwan and Singapore as member economies. China has now taken back Hong Kong, but tensions remain with Taiwan. There are also political tensions between China and Japan and between China and the Philippines. These make economic progress difficult.
- The inclusion of the NAFTA countries and Chile helps to offset the US-Japan power struggle to some extent, but the domestic protectionist influences on the US Congress do not bode well for serious future trade and investment liberalization with the Asian countries, especially Japan, China and Korea. The Congress is unlikely to back China's entry to the WTO.

On the other hand, APEC's potential benefits are enormous. With the WTO in disarray after Seattle, APEC is the best remaining forum for multilateralism. Even slow progress towards tariff cuts and the extension of preferential treatment for developing countries by the newer members will keep multilateralism moving. It is also a working group which brings together potential triad rivals, offers China a place in the trade councils of the world and provides potential economic development bridges to less developed countries.

Atlantic Free Trade: TAFTA

In contrast to APEC, the EU has no formal linkages with Asian countries. It does have a series of bilateral trade agreements with, for example, Chile and potentially, Canada. It also has linkages with Caribbean countries in the Lomé convention and its subsequent extensions. But the EU has its hands full in accommodating the emerging economies of Central and Eastern Europe. As discussed earlier, of the dozen or more European economies keen to join the EU, some will probably gain admission within a few years. These include:

- Hungary
- Poland
- Czech Republic

The future status of the Baltic countries, Turkey, the former Soviet republics of Eastern Europe, including Ukraine, other European countries like Romania, and so on, is less certain. Probably a form of economic association will be worked out, with the basis as a free trade agreement, but no common market, common economic or social policy.

Proposals to develop a Transatlantic Free Trade Area (TAFTA) have been floated for the last few years, but to little effect. The view in Brussels is one of distrust, and even dismay, at the lack of leadership in the United States, with a weak President and strongly protectionist Congress. Until the US political situation changes, there will be few bridges built between the European and North American triads. Indeed, trade wars are more likely, as discussed in Chapter 2.

The EU has concluded a series of bilateral trade agreements across the triad. One of these is with Mexico, due to start in July 2000. As Mexico is one of the three members of NAFTA, this will give European firms better access to US and Canadian markets. Mexican products will gain greater access to the EU. (Mexico also has trade agreements with six Latin American countries and may expand this to include three more.)

As a result, the car industry in North America may well change, with more production by Europeans in Mexico in order to access the richer markets to the North. Renault is investing with its Japanese-owned partner, Nissan, in a new joint venture in Mexico. Volkswagen, already in Mexico, is spending one third of its world budget over the next five years on expanding its Mexican production. Hyundai of Korea is also investing in the country.

It is clear that in a few years (when the tariff cuts are fully effective) Mexico will be well positioned to be a bridge between the two major triad blocks of Europe and North America. Its success may, in turn, lead to a bigger merger of trade blocks, namely a form of association between NAFTA and Mercosur. This will probably occur within five years.

Another agent of change is Chile, which has concluded a set of separate bilateral trade agreements with Canada, Mexico and the EU. This proliferation of bilaterals by key trade partners will force the United States into a reviewed list of regional issues, if not open multilateralism.

The end of NGOs?

One reason for the end of globalization is the new emphasis on corporate social responsibility brought forward by NGOs. Paradoxically, their agendas are consistent with the triad-based capitalism that exists today. The NGOs are opposed to US-driven global capitalism in which US values and products are imposed on the world. In practice, business does not operate this way and this image of global capitalism is simplistic and not supported by the facts.

Instead, today, we have a system of triad-based global competition. The European, North American and Asian firms compete viciously for market shares, lobbying their regional governments for shelter and subsidies, and for alliances with NGOs to devalue the reputations of their rivals. The interests of quasi-protectionist corporations and NGOs are often aligned. For example, environmentalists were a godsend to the US forestry industry, challenged by Canadian and European competitors. Environmental issues, health standards, safety standards, can all be twisted by triad-based home firms to keep out more efficient foreign competitors. This was demonstrated, in a NAFTA context, in Rugman, Kirton and Soloway (1999).

Apart from the alliances between domestic business and NGOs, there will be an effective corporate response to the accusations of NGOs. The business sector is well equipped to counter NGO's propaganda. It can do this in several ways. Advocates for business will come from the large army of MBAs graduating annually. In North America, over 350,000 students either graduate in business administration or earn MBAs each year. In Britain, over 100 universities offer MBA programmes and these are also expanding across Europe. In Asia, a similar boom is underway. All these graduates want jobs, indeed highly paid jobs, in consulting, merchant banking, corporate management, and so on. They need to repay their student loans and make progress through their organizations. As the ethical value of businesses are called into question the legions of MBAs will be articulate defenders of their own self interest. They are more than capable of seeing off even the most dedicated environmentalist NGOs.

Corporations will increase their spending on their corporate affairs and public relations departments. Every MNE, and each subsidiary, now has articulate and well trained media spokespeople. They are increasingly effective in presenting the company's viewpoint and in providing the industry background that overworked journalists turn to for briefings and information. Most senior executives of MNEs now receive media training and key members of the senior management team, of both head office and in subsidiaries, are capable of arguing their corner.

In addition, there are specialist intermediaries. Consulting firms and public relations firms can provide briefs, new images and the personnel to take companies through a suitable change process when they need to be more stakeholder friendly. Finally, academics will provide the rationale for big businesses to operate efficiently by making studies of their activities, which will show that the MNEs provide social benefits. This team of MBAs, corporate leaders, specialist advisers and academics is more than a match for the NGOs.

The NGOs themselves face a problem of legitimacy. Most NGOs are set up by dedicated enthusiasts who need an organization, even a small one, to push forward their agendas. The dedication and passion of these founding members should never be underestimated. Yet most NGOs fail to develop systems to make themselves publicly accessible. They fail to hold elections for office and tend to become vehicles for the careers of the inside group. Their passion for the issue, and the use of the Internet to disseminate their viewpoints, lead to a false sense of relevance and importance.

Seattle may well have been the high water mark for the hundreds of NGOs with a self-appointed agenda on the WTO. The bad publicity generated by the more extreme groups has undermined the legitimacy of the more moderate groups. In future, expect the NGO movement to split. Groups like Oxfam and WWF have long track records of success in their principal areas, they have earned public respect for their good work and dedication, so their views on the WTO will have an impact. Yet the dozens of small NGOs, run by a few activists, will find it difficult to capture a mainstream audience. Unless a coalition can be built (as the unions did in the past) most of the small NGOs will fade into insignificance. Their proposals will still be on the Internet, but no one will read them.

Increasingly, search engines will be targetted to sites which offer 'credentialized' research, rather than nonsense. Users will turn to the Oxfam site and a university research centre site, as these are reorganized as authoritative, accountable and accurate. Information overload is a problem of excess supply. The system to fix it will be one where legitimacy counts, and as users become more sophisticated they will turn to the sites of the better known NGOs, universities and research organizations and companies.

Management training, leadership and ethics

A big mistake NGOs make is to assume that they have a monopoly on ethics and social awareness. The simplification of NGOs as 'goodies' and MNEs as 'baddies' is not only naive, it is now being actively rejected by MNEs.

Virtually every senior manager in an MNE will have attended, at the company's expense, a rather large set of executive training programmes for middle managers in MNEs. These provide skills for managers to organize others, to produce more efficiently, to raise standards of quality control and to broaden and deepen sales to domestic and international markets. For managers in service organizations the focus will be on methods of improving customer satisfaction and service quality. So far, so good. Management training is about improving the functional ability of managers in the traditional areas of finance, production, human resource management and marketing.

However, in the 1990s, a new service industry has emerged in the world's élite executive training centres, such as Harvard Business School, IMD in Switzerland and Templeton College, University of Oxford. These now arrange leadership programmes for the most senior managers in MNEs and other organizations, including those in the public sector, and even NGOs.

In a leadership programme, the focus is no longer on the improvement of 'hard' functional skills but on the development of the 'soft' skills of people management and individual competencies. There has been an explosion of popular fads, backed by a more substantial academic literature on leadership. In one of the more influential contributions, Peter Senge (1990) has advocated the need for the creation of the 'learning organization', in which managers address the process by which products and services are created and their relevance to society and the environment. Such an organization respects the individuals who work for it and interact with it. In turn, the organization is in harmony with the individual's soul.

Senior managers are not well versed in getting in touch with their feelings. So facilitators are required to find their souls. These may well not be the usual business school professors, or even the popular gurus, but poets. One very successful poet who relates to organizational development and the individuals working within the organization is David Whyte.

In David Whyte (1994) he argues that individuals must discover their role in a complex organization by regaining their soul. People can unlock their creativity for leadership by self awareness, self realization and self confidence. The soul is difficult to find, but poetry, by cutting to the heart of one's emotions, can help in this personal journey toward self discovery.

Poets like David Whyte can now command large daily fees to work with corporate leadership groups around the world. They are merely the latest servants of the corporate agenda, developing a robust learning organization in which all board members and senior managers have been sensitised to moral, ethical and social issues through a process of self awareness. You can now expect these highly skilled and self confident managers to fight even the most committed NGO advocate to a draw.

As a final example of corporate values, most of these senior managers will have extensive media training. Today, the CEO and corporate affairs vice presidents are not alone in articulating the company's vision, performance and social awareness to the media. Most senior managers are being equipped to join in the public relations fight for image, recognition and public support. The lessons of Exxon Valdez, Nestlé baby formula in Africa, and related PR disasters have been learnt. Now managers are trained to be honest and direct, admitting problems and failure where they have occurred, but moving on to the solutions they will provide. Centres of corporate social responsibility and academic journals on business ethics have multiplied at leading universities like flowers in May. Today, MNEs are poised to become better corporate citizens than NGOs.

As an example, Thames Water, the largest British water company (but still only one tenth the size of its two French rivals, Vivendi and Suez Lyonnaise des Eaux) was the first Western business to be kicked out of Indonesia in 1998 and then reinstated by the new government. It is engaged in a project to supply half the population of Jakarta with fresh water, a moral imperative on its own.

In the Turkish earthquake of 1999, Thames Water mobilized its earthquake-resistant dams and pipelines to resupply the devastated areas quickly, flying in technical personnel to help the local municipalities whose pipes had burst. It also provided plane loads of engineering equipment, tablets to clean the water and many related water treatment and supply services at the time of crisis. This is a typical corporate response to a natural disaster. MNEs are specialised in their businesses and they are the best equipped to fix things when they break. Rarely will NGOs have the resources or know-how to respond to emergencies alone. Instead, they now work with MNEs in making common cause to relieve world poverty and foster economic development, especially in times of natural disaster and crisis. The agendas of MNEs and NGOs are congruent, not disparate.

In conclusion, I see a balance emerging between the corporate agenda and the NGO agenda. Both sides have clear, articulate and passionate participants. There will be no knock out points in the debate about the future of the WTO and globalization. If there is such a thing as global capitalism, it will not be defeated by NGO activity. The activities of triad-based MNEs will continue to grow, but their corporate responsibility will increase due to the successful monitoring of NGOs and the existence of an internal group defending the ethics of MNEs. The world will continue to develop in this complex manner. We have seen the end of globalization but not the beginning of the end of business.

NGOs as political insiders

The end of NGOs will present some of the more intelligent activists in NGOs with an interesting dilemma. If they are unable to manage the system from without, is it worth joining a company or mainstream media organization, to change it from within? This is the age old problem for the young idealist, and the usual observation is that the organization proves to be more robust than the individual's early radicalism.

The environmental movement, like other NGOs, is now at a crossroads. In most of the triad based economies its members are now actively connected with government. In Germany, the Green Party actually is the government, with its leaders being members of the government team in a coalition with the Social Democrats. In the United States, within the Beltway, the NGOs are actively involved with the key staffers of Senate and House Committee Chairs and are also influential with the EPA and in activities at NAFTA's CEC. There are personal stories which are becoming more than anecdotal.

In Canada, the leading environmentalist of the 1980s was Elizabeth May.

During 1986-88 she took a staff position as Special Policy Adviser to the Federal Environment Minister, Tom McMillan, of the Progressive Conservative government of Prime Minister Brian Mulroney. After two years of speech writing and behind the scenes activities to advance the environmentalists' agenda she resigned and is now with the Sierra Club of Canada.

In Britain, Tom Burke, Director of the Green Alliance, in 1991 accepted a similar post as special advisor to the Environment Minister, Michael Heseltine. Unlike Elizabeth May, Tom Burke stayed on as an influential green lobbyist with successive British environment ministers Michael Howard and John Gummer. As a result, the British environmental lobby has been absorbed into the mainstream of British politics and government. This makes it possible for ENGOs to help influence, indeed determine, government policy. It also makes them more responsible and publicly accountable. This somewhat reduces their freedom to campaign for change using passion rather than facts. Environmental protest is becoming politically institutionalized.

The Internet is global but users are local

One of the most misleading aspects of the debate about globalization is the two-faced role of communications technology. The Internet truly is a global service; once a certain wealth level is reached to access it by computer and either phone or network then everyone can participate. The power of the Internet was confirmed when AOL merged with Time Warner in January 2000, linking the world's largest Internet service provider (ISP) with the leading media group in the United States. Time Warner owns CNN, Fortune magazine, Sports Illustrated, People and other internationally known brand names. This merger will probably lead to other linkages between ISPs and media/entertainment groups, e.g. between Yahoo and Disney.

Yet, while the AOL/Time Warner group will expand its market in North America and possibly in Europe and Asia, this is still not a global business. The Internet is a service vehicle, which is used for communication and, perhaps in the future, for entertainment services. It is not able to bring people and goods physically together – it can only transmit messages and orders for business goods and services which still need to be delivered locally. Only in the case of media/entertainment will the AOL/Time Warner group be able to co-ordinate worldwide distribution of its news, magazines and videos. While these products are valuable, they cannot match the aggregate value of the triad-based automobile and other manufacturing sectors. So global entertainment is a possibility but global business is not.

We are deceived by the publicity generated by pop stars, media events, the growth of US-based pop culture and related entertainment activities. But these are largely peripheral. We are doubly deceived by the Internet. It is not a medium for exchange, nor a product in itself. It is a tool for communication. It does the same job as the telephone and satellite. It provides a global service for local users.

Globalization and its false critics

In his first BBC Reith Lecture for 1999, Anthony Giddens painted a vivid portrait of all that is wrong with globalization. As shown earlier, especially in Chapters 1, 3 and 4, his views are representative of those of other recent critics of globalization such as Susan Strange (1998), John Gray (1998), Murray Dobbin (1998) and others.

The pace of science, technology and electronic interchange has increased risk and given people the feeling that they are not in control of their lives – there is a runaway world (Giddens, 1999). Globalization is stated by Giddens to be led by the West as it 'bears the strong imprint of American political and economic power' (Giddens, 1999 p.4). With this statement, Giddens is today still making the mistakes of writers in the 1970s such as Barnet and Mueller (1974). They argued that the power of the nation state was being eroded by the MNEs. Giddens states that he agrees with the radical statement that nations have lost most of the sovereignty they once had.

These simplistic and misinformed views can be contrasted with the research output of probably the best known and most widely respected scholar of the MNE, Raymond Vernon, who died in 1999 after a long career at Harvard University as the world expert on MNEs and public policy. In his book *Sovereignty at Bay*, published in 1971, Ray found that (despite the book's title) the power of the nation state was not being eroded by MNEs, but that there was a seesaw of balance between governments and firms, determined by the particular circumstances of the times. In his final book, Vernon (1998) reconfirmed this analysis; indeed he predicts a strengthening of the regulatory framework facing MNEs.

I have attended a number of academic conferences over the years, drawing together scholars from business schools, political science departments, area studies and economics. In all of these, the balance of discussion, based on the evidence, is that the nation state remains robust as a regulator of MNEs. No evidence has been advanced to demonstrate that governments are fading away in the face of the power of triad-based MNEs. Indeed, these findings hold across the triad.

In Eden (1994) it was found that MNEs in North America and their governments were both dealing with changing institutions, but were also agents of change. Dunning (1997) shows that the deepening structural interdependence of the world economy has not led to a fall in sovereignty, and that governments respond in different ways to the complexity of MNE activity. In Prakash and Hart (2000) the governance structure of countries and international institutions are examined and found to be adequate in coping with globalization. Again, the contributors analyze both firms and governments and explore changes in their balance of power.

Hirst and Thompson (1999) are what Giddens would call 'sceptics' of globalization. They find that the economic facts indicate that globalization is not new. The world economy has been just as integrated in the past, such as in Victorian times when the British Empire was a hegemony. As noted in Chapter 1, Moore and Lewis (1999) have demonstrated that 'global' economic activity existed in the ancient world; that MNEs are over two thousand years old. Sceptics also argue, and this is confirmed by the data in this book, that most economic exchange is regionally-based, rather than being global. However, I have found that the extent of internal triad-based trade and investment is not widely understood, and is frequently confused with evidence of globalization.

The logic of this book is quite relentless. No credible evidence can be found to support the viewpoint that a system of global capitalism exists. There is no evidence for globalization, that is, of a system of free trade with fully integrated world markets. Instead, the evidence on the performance and activities of multinational enterprises demonstrates that international business is triad based and triad related. Virtually all of the world's largest 500 multinational enterprises are operating in a strong triad home base, with some access to another triad. Almost none of them have true global strategies. Multinational enterprises actually organize production, marketing and other business activities by triad.

The future for international business is more of the same. There is no trend towards globalization, but strong evidence of the hardening of triad blocs. Political pressures and NGO activities are reinforcing the triad, not creating a global system. Global governance issues, as at the WTO, are now largely irrelevant to regional/triad issues of accountability and transparency. The latter are particular problems for both the EU and Japan, and one not totally resolved in North America.

We have reached the end of globalization. The debate has been misfocused on the power of multinational enterprises. These operate subject to strong government constraints rather than in a free market. We have reached the end of the beginning of a new debate about multinationals and triad power.

Conclusions: key themes

- Globalization is misunderstood – it does not, and has never, existed in terms of a single world market with free trade.
- Triad-based production and distribution is the past, current and future reality.
- Multinational enterprises operate within triad markets and access other triad markets; they have regional, not global, strategies.
- National governments strongly regulate most of the service sectors, thereby limiting free market forces; the extent of regulation is not decreasing.
- NGOs are currently influential; however, in the future their lack of accountability and lack of legitimacy will reduce, or at least limit, their influence.
- In the future, neither MNEs nor NGOs will dominate; rather there will be a complex situation where both continue to exert influence, with minor variations in impact.

References

Adams, David, 'America's complex links with banana republics,' *The Times*, March 15, 1999.

Barlett, Donald L. and Steele, James B. 'Special Report: Corporate Welfare,' Time.com, November 16, 1998

Barlow, Maude (1990). *Parcel of Rogues: How Free Trade is Failing Canada.* Toronto: Key Porter Books.

Barnet, Richard J. and Mueller, Ronald E. (1974). *Global Reach: The Power of the Multinational Corporation.* New York: Simon and Schuster.

Bartlett, Christopher A. and Ghoshal, Sumantra (1989). *Managing Across Borders: The Transnational Solution.* Boston: Harvard Business School Press. Second edition (1998) London: Random House Business Books.

Bartlett, Christopher and Ghoshal, Sumantra (1995). *Transnational Management: Text, Cases and Readings in Cross-Border Management*, Second Edition, New York: McGraw-Hill.

Birkinshaw, Julian M. (1997). 'Entrepreneurship in Multinational Corporations: The Characteristics of Subsidiary Initiatives, *Strategic Management Journal* 18(3): 207-229.

Birkinshaw, Julian M. and Hood, Neil (1998). *Multinational Corporate Evolution and Subsidiary Development.* London: Macmillan.

Brewer, Thomas L. and Young, Stephen (1995). 'The Multilateral Agenda for Foreign Direct Investment: Problems, Principles and Priorities for Negotiation at the OECD and WTO', *World Competition* 18(4), 67-83.

Brewer, Thomas L. and Young, Stephen (1998). *Multilateral Investment Rules and Multinational Enterprises.* Oxford: Oxford University Press.

Cecchini, P. et al (1988). *The European Challenge: 1992 – The Benefits of a Single Market.* Aldershot, Hants: Wildwood House.

Clarke, Tony and Barlow, Maude (1997). *MAI: The Multilateral Agreement on Investment and the Threat to Canadian Sovereignty.* Toronto: Stoddart.

D'Aveni, Richard A. (1994). *Hypercompetition: Managing the Dynamics of Strategic Manoeuvering.* New York: Free Press, Macmillan.

Dobbin, Murray (1998). *The Myth of the Good Corporate Citizen: Democracy Under the Rule of Big Business.* Toronto: Stoddart.

Doern, G. Bruce and Tomlin, Brian W. (1991). *The Free Trade Story: Faith and Fear*. Toronto: Stoddart.

Dufey, Gunter and Giddy, Ian H. (1978). *The International Money Market*. Englewood Cliffs, N.J.: Prentice-Hall.

Dunning, John H. (1997) (ed.). *Governments, Globalization and International Business*. Oxford: Oxford University Press.

Economist, 'Pharmaceuticals: Carving up Europe's drugs industry', August 26, 1995.

Economist, 'Pharmaceutical takeovers: stocks, drugs and Roche's role,' May 31, 1997.

Economist, 'The Eastern Caribbean banana row', May 31, 1997.

Economist, 'Expelled from Eden', December 20, 1997.

Economist, 'Drug mergers. Popping the question', January 24, 1998.

Economist, 'Beyond the behemoths,', February 1, 1998.

Economist, 'The mother of all mergers', February 7, 1998.

Economist, 'All fall down', February 28, 1998.

Economist, 'Biotechnology: hardy hybrids', June 6, 1998.

Economist, 'Deutschland über alles?' July 4, 1998.

Economist, 'Monkey business', Nov 14, 1998.

Economist, 'Mobile telephones. Wireless war', January 9, 1999.

Economist, 'Telecommunications. Look, no wires', January 23, 1999.

Economist, 'The risks for free trade', January 30, 1999.

Economist, 'Going bananas', March 6, 1999.

Economist, 'The beef over bananas', March 6, 1999.

Economist, 'Renault and Nissan, Renissant?' March 20, 1999.

Economist, 'Europe's ailing drug makers', April 10, 1999.

Economist, 'Mergers and alliances. Hold my hand', May 15, 1999.

Economist, 'Mobile telephones' light touch', September 25, 1999.

Economist, 'A mobile merry-go-round,' October 23, 1999.

Economist, 'Drug mergers. Courting trouble,' November 6, 1999.

Economist, 'Drug induced seizures', November 13, 1999.

Eden, Lorraine (1994) (ed.). *Multinationals in North America*. Calgary: University of Calgary Press.

Edwards, Michael (1999). *Future Positive: International Co-operation in the 21st Century*. London: Earthscan.

European Union, 'EU and US Held WTO Consultations on FSC Export Subsidies', *Press Releases*, December 17, 1997.

European Union, 'WTO Panel Condemns US Export Subsidies', *Press Releases*, September 20, 1999.

Feketekuty, Gaza and Stokes, Bruce (1998) (eds.) *Trade Strategies for a New*

Era: Ensuring US Leadership in a Global Economy. New York: Council on Foreign Relations.

Fina, Erminio and Rugman, Alan M. (1995). 'A Test of Internalization Theory and Internationalization Theory: The Upjohn Company', *Management International Review* 36(3): 199-213.

Financial Express, 'Glaxo plans world's biggest pharmaceutical merger with US firm', March 31, 1999.

Fitzgerald, E.V.K. (1998). 'The Development Implications of the Multilateral Agreement on Investment'. An independent study for the Department for International Development of the United Kingdom. Oxford: Queen Elizabeth House.

Fukuyama, Francis (1992). *The End of History and the Last Man*. New York: Free Press.

Gestrin, Michael and Rugman, Alan M. (1996). 'The NAFTA Investment provisions: Prototype for Multinational Investment Rules' pp. 63-78 in P. Sauvé and A.B. Zampetti (eds.), *Market Access after the Uruguay Round: Investment, Competition and Technology Perspectives*. Paris: OECD.

Gestrin, Michael, Knight, Rory F. and Rugman, Alan M. (1998). *The Templeton Global Performance Index*. The Oxford Executive Research Briefings: Templeton College.

Gestrin, Michael, Knight, Rory F. and Rugman, Alan M. (2000). *The Templeton Global Performance Index 2000*. The Oxford Executive Research Briefings: Templeton College.

Giddens, Anthony (1999). *Runaway World: How Globalization is Reshaping our Lives*. London: Profile Books.

Graham, Edward M. (1996). 'Investment and the New Multilateral Trade Context', in pp. 35-62 in P. Sauvé and A.B. Zampetti (eds.), *Market Access after the Uruguay Round: Investment, Competition and Technology Perspectives*. Paris: OECD.

Gray, John (1998). *False Dawn: The Delusions of Global Capitalism*. London: Granta Books.

Hart, Michael (1994). *Decision at Midnight: Inside the Canada-US Free Trade Negotiations*. Vancouver, B.C.: UBC Press.

Hettne, Björn, Inotai, András and Sunkel, Osvaldo (1999) (ed.) *Globalization and the New Regionalism*. London: Macmillan.

Hirst, Paul and Thompson, Graham (1999). *Globalization in Question: The International Economy and the Possibilities of Governance*, second edition. Cambridge: Policy Press.

http://www.vodafone-airtouch-plc.com/media

http://www.mannesmann.com/

Hurtig, Mel (1991). *The Betrayal of Canada*. Toronto: Stoddart.

Jordan, Grant and Maloney, William (1997). *Protest Businesses: Mobilising Campaign Groups*. Manchester: Manchester University Press.

Kanter, Rosabeth Moss (1995). *World Class: Thriving Locally in the Global Economy*. New York: Simon and Schuster.

Khan, Shahrukh Rafi (1999). *Do World Bank and IMF policies work?* London: Macmillan.

Kindleberger, Charles P. (1970). *Power and Money*. New York: Basic Books.

Kogut, Bruce (1985). 'Designing Global Strategies: Comparative Value-Added Chains'. *Sloan Management Review*, Summer: 15-27.

Lawrence, Robert Z. (1996). 'Towards Globally Contestable Markets', pp. 25-34 in P. Sauvé and A.B. Zampetti (eds)., *Market Access after the Uruguay Round: Investment, Competition and Technology Perspectives*. Paris: OECD.

Lee, Kelley (1998). 'Globalization and Health Policy: A Review of the Literature and Proposed Research and Policy Agenda'. Draft.

Lee, Kelley (1999). 'The Global Dimensions of Health' paper for Nuffield Foundation Seminar, February 1999.

Lipsey, R., Schwanen, D. and Wonnecott, R. (1994). *The NAFTA: What's In, What's Out, What's Next?* Toronto, Ontario: C.D. Howe Institute.

Moore, Karl and Lewis, David (1999). *Birth of the Multinationals: 2000 Years of Ancient Business History – From Ashur to Augustus*. Copenhagen: Copenhagen Business School press.

Ohmae, Kenichi (1990). *The Borderless World*. New York: Harper Collins.

Ohmae, Kenichi (1996). *The End of the Nation State: The Rise of Regional Economies*. New York: Free Press/Simon and Schuster.

Ostry, Sylvia (1997). *The Post-Cold War Trading System: Who's on First?* Chicago and London: University of Chicago Press.

Pendlebury, Maurice and Groves, Roger (1994). *Company Accounts: Analysis, Interpretation and Understanding*, third edition. London and New York: Routledge.

Porter, Michael E. (1990). *The Competitive Advantage of Nations*. New York: Free Press.

Prakash, Aseem and Hart, Jeffrey A. (eds.) (2000). *Coping with Globalization*. London: Routledge.

Rawcliffe, Peter (1998). *Environmental Pressure Groups in Transition*. Manchester: Manchester University Press.

Reich, Robert B. (1991). *The Work of Nations*. New York: Alfred A. Knopf.

Rugman, Alan M. (1980). *Multinationals in Canada: Theory, Performance and Economic Impact*. Boston: Martinus Nijhoff/Kluwer.

Rugman, Alan M. (1981). *Inside the Multinationals: The Economics of*

Internal Markets. New York: Columbia University Press.

Rugman, Alan M. (1994) (ed.). *Foreign Investment and NAFTA.* Columbia, S.C.: University of South Carolina Press.

Rugman, Alan M. (1996a). Selected Papers. Volume 1: *The Theory of Multinational Enterprises.* Cheltenham: Edward Elgar.

Rugman, Alan M. (1996b). Volume 2: *Multinational Enterprises and Trade Policy.* Cheltenham: Edward Elgar.

Rugman, Alan M. (1997). 'New Rules for Multinational Investment', *The International Executive* 39(1): 21-33.

Rugman, Alan M. (1999). 'Negotiating Multilateral Rules for Investment' pp. 143-158 in Michael Hodges, John Kirton and Joseph Daniels (eds.) *G8's Role in the New Millennium.* Aldershot: Ashgate.

Rugman, Alan M. and Anderson, Andrew D. M. (1987). *Administered Protection in America.* London and New York: Routledge.

Rugman, Alan M. and Anderson, Andrew D. M. (1997). 'NAFTA and the Dispute Settlement Mechanisms'. *The World Economy*, December: 935-950.

Rugman, Alan M. and D'Cruz, Joseph (1997a). 'Strategies of Multinational Enterprises and Governments. The Theory of The Flagship Firm', pp. 37-68 in Gavin Boyd and Alan M. Rugman (eds.) *Euro-Pacific Investment and Trade: Strategies and Structural Interdependencies.* Cheltenham: Edward Elgar.

Rugman, Alan M. and D'Cruz, Joseph R. (1997b). 'The Theory of the Flagship Firm', *European Management Review* 15(4), August: 403-411.

Rugman, Alan M. and D'Cruz, Joseph R. (2000). *Multinationals as Flagships: Regional Business Networks.* Oxford: Oxford University Press.

Rugman, Alan M. and Gestrin, Michael (1991). 'EC Anti-Dumping Laws as a Barrier to Trade'. *European Management Journal* 9(4): 475-482.

Rugman, Alan M. and Gestrin, Michael (1996). 'A Conceptual Framework for a Multilateral Agreement in Investment: Learning from the NAFTA', pp. 147-175 in P. Sauvé and D. Schwanen (eds.), *Investment Rules for the Global Economy.* Toronto: C. D. Howe Institute.

Rugman, Alan M. and Hodgetts, Richard (1995). *International Business: A Strategic Management Approach.* New York and London: McGraw-Hill.

Rugman, Alan M. and Hodgetts, Richard (2000). *International Business: A Strategic Management Approach*, second edition. London: Financial Times/Prentice Hall – Pearson Education.

Rugman, Alan M., Kirton, John and Soloway, Julie A. (1999). *Environmental Regulations and Corporate Strategy: The NAFTA Experience.* Oxford: Oxford University Press.

Rugman, Alan. M., Lecraw, Donald and Booth, Laurence (1985). *International Business: Firm and Environment*. New York: McGraw-Hill.

Rugman, Alan M. and Verbeke, Alain (1990). *Global Corporate Strategy and Trade Policy*. London: Routledge.

Rugman, Alan M. and Verbeke, Alain (1998). 'Corporate Strategy and International Environmental Policy', *Journal of International Business Studies* 29(4): 819-833.

Safarian, A. Ed. (1993). *Multinational Enterprises and Public Policy*. Cheltenham: Edward Elgar.

Schwanen, Daniel (1998). 'Chilling Out: The MAI is on Ice but Global Investment is Hot', C.D. Howe *Commentary* No. 109 (June 1998). Toronto: C.D. Howe Institute.

Senge, Peter (1990). *The Fifth Discipline*. New York: Doubleday/Currency Books.

Sjoblom, Leif (1998). 'Success lies One Step Ahead of the Consumer', *FT Mastering Global Business*, part two, 2-3.

Smith, Alistair (1995). 'The Development of a Multilateral Agreement on Investment at the OECD: A Preview', pp. 101-112 in C. J. Green and T. L. Brewer (eds) *Investment Issues in Asia and the Pacific Rim*. Dobbs Ferry, New York: Oceana.

SmithKline Beecham, 'SmithKline Beecham Plc Termination of Merger Discussions', *PR News*, February 23, 1999.

Soloway, Julie, A. (1999). 'Environmental Trade Barriers under NAFTA: The MMT Fuel Additives Controversy', *Minnesota Journal of Global Trade* 8:1 (Winter 1999) pp. 55-95.

Stickney, Clyde P. and Weil, Roman L. (1997). *Financial Accounting: An Introduction to Concepts, Methods and Uses*, eighth edition. Fort Worth: The Dryden Press.

Stopford, John M. and Dunning, John H. (1980). *The World Directory of Multinational Enterprises*. London: Macmillan.

Strange, Susan (1986). *Casino Capitalism*. Oxford: Basil Blackwell.

Strange, Susan (1988). *States and Markets: An Introduction to International Political Economy*. London: Pinter.

Strange, Susan (1996). *The Retreat of the State*. Cambridge: Cambridge University Press.

Strange, Susan (1998). *Mad Money*. Manchester: Manchester University Press.

Tolchin, Martin and Tolchin, Susan (1988). *Buying Into America: How Foreign Money is Changing the Face of our Nation*. New York: Times Books.

Tomlinson, John (1999). *Globalization and Culture*. Cambridge: Polity Press.

Turpin, Daniel V. (1998). 'Challenge of the Overseas Chinese', *FT Mastering Global Business*, part two, 8.

United Nations Conference on Trade and Development (UNCTAD) (1997). *World Investment Report*. New York and Geneva: United Nations, annual.

United Nations Conference on Trade and Development (UNCTAD) (1999). *World Investment Report*. UNCTAD: Geneva.

United Nations (1998). *World Investment Report 1998*. (UNCTAD: Geneva).

Vause, Bob (1997). *Guide to Analysing Companies*. London: Profile Books.

Vernon, Raymond (1971). *Sovereignty at Bay*. New York: Basic Books.

Vernon, Raymond (1977). *Storm Over the Multinationals*. London: Macmillan.

Vernon, Raymond (1998). *In the Hurricane's Eye: The Troubled Prospects of Multinational Enterprises*. Cambridge, MA: Harvard University Press.

Vodafone-Airtouch, 'Announcement of Intended Offer to Mannesmann Shareholders', Press Release, November 19, 1999.

Ward, Halina and Brack, Duncan (eds.) (2000). *Trade, Investment and the Environment*. London: Earthscan.

Wells, Louis T. (1983). *Third World Multinationals: The Rise of Foreign Investment from Developing Countries*. London: MIT Press.

Whyte, David (1994). *The Heart Aroused: Poetry and the Preservation of the Soul at Work*. New York: Doubleday-Bantam/Doubleday Dell.

Winham, Gil and Grant, Heather A. (1997). 'Designing Institutions for Global Economic Co-operation: Investment and the WTO', Paper for Halifax Pre-G7 Summit Conference, May 1995, pp. 248-272 in G. Boyd and A. M. Rugman (eds) *Euro-Pacific Investment and Trade: Strategies and Structural Interdependencies*. Brookfield, VT: Edward Elgar.

World Trade Organization, European Communities – Regime for the Importation, Sale and Distribution of Bananas-Complaint by Ecuador, Report of the Panel, WT/DS27/R/ECU, 22 May 1997.

World Trade Organization, *Focus*, October 1998.

World Trade Organization, *Focus*, November 1998.

World Trade Organization (1998). 'Health and Social Services: Background Note by the Secretariat'. Geneva: Council for Trade in Services, World Trade Organization.

World Trade Organization, European Communities – Regime for the Importation, Sale and Distribution of Bananas – Recourse to Article 21.5 by Ecuador, WT/DS27/RW/ECU, 12 April 1999.

Index